AF560459

HISTORICAL ROLE OF ISLAM

HISTORICAL ROLE OF ISLAM

Zikr-ur-Rahman

ANMOL PUBLICATIONS PVT. LTD.
NEW DELHI - 110 002 (INDIA)

ANMOL PUBLICATIONS PVT. LTD.
4374/4B, Ansari Road, Daryaganj
New Delhi - 110 002
Ph.: 23261597, 23278000
Visit us at: www.anmolpublications.com

Historical Role of Islam

First Published, 2004
ISBN 81-261-1900-4

PRINTED IN INDIA

Published by J.L. Kumar for Anmol Publications Pvt. Ltd., New Delhi - 110 002 and Printed at Mehra Offset Press, Delhi.

Contents

Preface

Islam is not only a religion or faith. It's a philosophy, culture and above the rest, a complete code of conduct, for this life and the life, hereafter. Islam came on the scene as a strong force, a stream and a light, which impacted the whole contemporary world.

Under the banner of Islam, emerged a new disciplined nation, enriched with a new culture and civilization, which swept the millennia old civilizations and centuries old dynasties, like those of Rome, Egypt and Persia. The first few generations of the followers of Islam, conquered almost half of the known world and became the most powerful political and military force on earth.

Contrary to common belief, Islam not only conquered lands and capitals, it also won over the hearts of people and helped the nations change their course of life and action for ever. A large portion of Asia, Africa and a sizable chunk of Europe came under the sphere of Islam. In fact, the early medieval Europe was a dark continent. It received light from Islam only. Today's Western Europe owes a lot to Islam and Muslims for promotion of science, philosophy and even their sophisticated culture.

Truly speaking, Islam has made a great contribution to the evolution and growth of intellect, education and the civilization at large. For centuries together Muslim philosophers and scientists led the intellectual world, before the renaissance.

This book deals with the historic role, Islam played in the evolution, development and growth of various sciences, philosophy, logic, literature, art, architecture and other areas, like social justice and human rights. This modest work covers all the dimensions of Islam's influence on the world and discusses the ever-lasting impact, this religion has left on the civilised society and rule of law.

The undersigned is contented and full of pride that he has been able to present this research-based work in a purely academic and empirical manner.

Editor

ONE

Introduction

The modern period has surpassed every other period in the matter of material progress and scientific explorations. But with all that, the experts in the field of sociology, psychology and medicine are amazed at the alarming increase in the number of neurotics and those suffering from other nervous disorders. An atmosphere of fear and distraction pervades the whole world, in which the future of humanity appears dark, particularly the architects of this new civilization find themselves ill-at-ease and bereft of all pleasure even in the super-abundance of social amenities and a life of ease and luxury. The utopia or at least the golden period that the learned men and thinkers of the nineteenth century had been contemplating on the basis of the scientific inventions and explorations, had soon become a confused dream.

It appears that the greater the progress of the means at man's disposal, the more his restlessness and anxiety. The countries with a very high standard of living, have a greater percentage of psychological affections than in other countries not so privileged. This is borne out by the statistics published by the government of the United States of America. This distraction is not the creation of the two world wars or the dread of a third holocaust, but the outcome of the psychological atmosphere provided by the modern civilization for its sons ("the brave sons of the brave new world" Tr.). Although the colonial powers are constantly creating conditions which keep the nations under their sway, the restlessness we are speaking about here, pervades even those nations that have apparently escaped becoming the target of imperialism. And it has taken into its grip even those nations that have been benefited immensely through exploitations of the colonial people. We find this anxiety and disquietitude even in societies that have come up under the new social theories and principles. The same restlessness is realized in the entire East and West, even the Socialist order in the Soviet Russia reflects this uneasiness.

The proof of the agitated state of minds is provided by the large number of suicides so common among the civilized and highly cultured nations of the world. The most amazing among these are the incidents occurring in the Scandinavian countries, when we know they are among the highest developed countries of the world both economically and culturally. More amazing is the fact that some of the people of those countries commit suicide getting "sick at heart" of their luxurious pattern of living. This explains that the distractions and their moral perversion which have raised a cry of protest and grief from their parents who are really sick at heart, are the creation of the modern civilization and culture, and are the outcome of the ideology at work behind them.

The modern western civilization, as we know, came into existence from contact of the west with the Islamic culture and other Muslim countries. The Scholastics and philosophers of the Islamic world were very much interested in the Greek philosophy. They rendered their books into their own language, and notwithstanding the strong opposition of the church, set out to study and propagate them. And when the western people had acquired breadth of vision and they inferred these facts which were diametrically opposed to the knowledge and teachings of the church, a long drawn struggle ensued between the church and science. At long last the philosophers and the thinkers succeeded in this struggle after they had been through an exasperating course of imprisonment, inquisitions, verdicts of heresy and ex-communications and all sorts of troubles and calamities. When this renaissance movement of the west could stand on its feet it had the clear stamp of two things: love of the Greek philosophy, formed with purely materialistic and idolatorous concepts, and disgust of religion and animosity of the religious people and rebellion against them. So we find that the opinions of the western thinkers were formed and developed under these two factors, and it was under the shadow of these powerful elements that all the philosophical and moral schools of the west have developed which pervade the western mind and heart to this day.

So the bases on which the western civilization rests are purely materialistic and far removed from the spirituality of religion and its intrinsic effects. And the result is that religion is losing its sway and authority in the western countries day by day, and the man in the west finding himself drifting towards the deepest abyss of degradation, is confronted with the severest distraction and apprehension. Their thinkers and others endued with insight want to review and bring into action the spiritual values of religion, but from where are they to come upon them. The evil tree of atheism and materialism is bearing its bitter fruit and is deeply rooted now.

Whichever of the revealed religions you may take, one of its characteristics is that it develops justice and equity, confers satisfaction on the heart and the soul, and reducing the pain of miseries and troubles, lightens the burden of life which otherwise hangs heavy upon man. And along with that it makes short shrift of carnal urges and ignoble passions. Islam in its heyday had accomplished this feat. But when this Divine Mission ceased to work in our collective life and the effective weapons awakening the aspirations in the individual and the party, rousing their resolutions and their passions of sacrifice and affection, became blunt, we amply tasted the bitterness of the misery which the western civilization has provided for its sons.

Plight of Faith

It is not our aim here to sit in judgement on the dispute between the western civilization and the religion with which it has waged a war in its early days and has finally got rid of it. It is enough for us at the moment to point out the causes of the poverty of this civilization and culture due to which it has proved miserably inadequate and helpless in conferring tranquility of mind and soul on man. The reason lies in the fact that when this civilization parted ways with religion and chalked out a path for itself, deviating far from that of religion since it had been engaged in a life and death struggle against it, it took the hypothetical stand that it could continue its journey, all alone, without having recourse to any other faith which may be helpful in keeping its soul fresh and its conscience alive. But this was an erroneous notion. And we are once again witnessing today, that a sincere passion for mutual co-operation between the various governments of the western countries and the churches, is emerging to lessen the bitterness and devastation of the western civilization. I have observed that several methods and various means are being put into practice to achieve this end in view.

A person who has toured Switzerland recently must certainly have observed a procession accompanied by a musical band moving about parks and other places of recreation. These religious processions are arranged by the church, and comprise young men, old people, boys and very young girls, who invite the attention of people to themselves by chanting religious songs to musical accompaniment. A crowd thus gathers round them and whoever likes listens to the speakers in the procession.

Any person visiting Hyde Park in London can see for himself that there too, particularly on Sundays, speeches are delivered and it is a free for all. Among the speakers there are preachers of the church, whose endeavour is to invite the attention of the greater part of the crowd in the park, to themselves through their eloquence and effective style of speaking. Similarly, in areas that are particularly well known for their cinema halls, it is often noticed in the din and noise of the crowd, that a person is ascending an iron stage, held in position by his companions. The person on the stage harangues people on the theme of religion. One night, I saw a person standing in the doorway of a cinema hall and loudly warning people against the evil effects of cinema on their morality. All this was going on in the presence of the police and it did not in the least object to it or obstruct their path. Some people listened to him attentively but I did not see any one person mending himself and abstaining from cinema.

It is a common practice in Europe and America that a society or a recreation club is associated with the church where young boys and girls dance and sing and enjoy themselves chatting, joking and having fun. They travel together and hold meetings. I happened to attend such a meet, and noticed that they had on their programme singing, playing musical instruments, eating, drinking and keeping awake during the nights and nothing else. I asked their manager, "Do you also present to the participants in your meetings, religious teachings and preaching?" The answer was in the negative. I asked him, "Why then does the church arrange and put up with all the expenses of these societies and their meetings when they are very much like the societies in their make-up with which the church has nothing to do". He said in reply, "Is it not enough for the benefit of the church that boys and girls traverse the enclosure of the church to participate in the meetings of the society, and in this way they have the existence of the church also in their minds. A traveller in Europe cannot fail to notice in some hotels a copy of Bible on a table by his bedside, supplied by the "Association of the lovers of the Holy Bible". The aim underlying this practice is obviously to induce the traveller to look through it before going to bed or on awakening in the morning, thus reviewing his faith and belief. In most universities of Europe there are organizations under the name of "Christian Students' Union" whose weekly meets are addressed by the priest of the church who present the principles and basic tenets of the Christian religion, and some students also participate in the discussion.

The government of West Germany imposes contributions and collects a national fund in the name of the church, so that it may help in the propagation of Christianity. I saw, once, in the hospital attached to the Cologne University in West Germany, a huge Cross of bronze set in a wall of my ward in front of my bed. Later, I discovered that such crosses were set in every room. I enquired about the wisdom underlying these fixtures, and was told that it was the phenomenon of the activities of the church which reminds people of their religion. And all that was there in spite of the fact that the hospital was run by the university and had no direct link with the church. In this connection, I can never forget the religious films produced in Hollywood on a vast scale which has held people spell-bound. Many of us must have heard of the Moral Re-armament organizations which abound in most European countries. Their representatives have toured the Middle East and the Far East, for example Cairo. I have seen their centre in Switzerland situated near Suzan. These organizations apparently lay stress only on moral excellence and mercy and justice.

This is a brief account of the activities that continue in the western countries for the revival of religion and morality, and very explicitly elucidate the point that the western nations, to lessen the evils of their civilization and culture, have come to realize the need of enlisting the aid of religion and morals. But in spite of all those efforts, we can assert with great conviction that the reins of control are no more in the hands of the religious leaders, moral teachers and social experts. They have lost the opportunity they had, the calamities and afflictions are on the increase, and this civilization must come to its destined end.

This also is a fact that the trend of return to religion and elevating the spiritual level of the common people, has also at its back the dread of the propagation and domination of Socialism. But religion in Europe, due to its "poor condition" and the sceptical attitude created by the western philosophies, is totally incapable of confrontation with the flood of Socialism. Therefore social and economic measures have become inevitable to barricade the onslaught of the Red Menace. Materialistic intellect such as the western intellect is, cannot perceive anything other than material. Nor can it agree to anything else, whereas Socialism too is a branch of the same evil tree and a fruit of its bitter fruits. This is the fact which has multiplied its abomination manifold, and made its detriments so common.

The Socialist philosophy of Marx and Engels appeared on the political horizon in the nineteenth century. One of them (Marx) was a German Jew and the other was also a German national. The conditions became all the worse because of this philosophy, since it created a wide gulf between man and his spiritual solace; the creed of belief in God and the Hereafter departed from the hearts, and the moral bases on which human societies have been leaning for the collective peace and tranquility from the early dawn of history to this day, had collapsed. The first ever dominion claiming to uphold the principles of communism had come into existence, and tried to improve the lot of its people. But it miserably failed in this attempt, and could never succeed in its objective of removing every form of anxiety and restlessness from the individual and collective life of its people, and rid them of all apprehension and terror, due to its materialistic philosophy of life. Rather, all against it, the communist state has clamped some additional dreads on its citizens, included in which is the apprehension that in case of criticising the state and its policies they must come by an unhappy end. Again, the mental perturbation and fear that haunts the members of the communist parties is much greater than that pervading the minds of the common citizens of the communist state. It is binding on every member of the communist party to loudly support every suggestion, every opinion of their leaders and defend and follow them blindly or else be resigned to the fate reserved for dissenters.

So communism, in rejecting God and His faith, has deprived itself of that last bulwork in which man found strength against fear, calamity, deprivation and oppression. Communist state, whereever established, has on the strength of despotism, fear and terror and cruelty, turned men into flocks of timid sheep and goats and a herd of dumb-driven cattle, that have been deprived of all intention and a free will. And they have been deprived of those high ideals that are the goal of every dignified human society.

In short, both the offshoots of the western civilization, capitalism and Socialism have destroyed the peace and tranquility of man and trampled upon his highest aims and objectives. The reason lies in the fact that this civilization made material prosperity its real target. And then things came to such a pass that whoever failed to attain this goal became "wretched". But even those who achieved this aim, got nothing out of it save grief and dejection. And this dejection and weariness culminated in suicide.

Truth Confessed

Anyway, the west has now started realizing its moral and spiritual bankruptcy and most of the people are turning their eyes towards the East with the hope that they might possibly come upon something in the religions and beliefs rife here that may successfully fill their spiritual void, and they may once again be the recipients of human dignity that they have lost. If you notice in these countries and particularly in America that certain people there, are embracing Buddhism, Bahaism or Islam, there is no cause for amazement. Among them there are two groups that embrace Islam. One is that agreeing with Islam at the intellectual and ideological level, and the other is that satisfied with it at the intuitional and spiritual level.

Once a fresh convert to Islam, Mr. Abu Bakr, an orientalist of British extraction, told me the story of his embracing Islam. He had been professor of English language in Fuad University, and it was there that he embraced the religion of peace. He is at present the secretary of the Eastern section of the National Library, London. Explaining the reason behind his opting for Islam, he said that the western civilization has trampled under the feet both the human dignity and beauty of man's life. I said to him, "Where the loss of human dignity is concerned, I won't question your opinion about it, but how did you come to have that opinion about beauty, whereas the western people have a very high opinion of the western civilization as regards beauty of natural scenery, the beauty of dress, the beauty of the mode of living and that of the habitation, beauty of the female sex-in short, there is consideration of every type of aesthetic taste in it." He said in reply, "This civilization has destroyed the beauty of the soul and intuition and morals".

During the summer of 1956 I had delivered a harangue in the congregation mosque of Paris. In keeping with the occasion of the birth of the Prophet, I had talked of the Islamic mission based on equity and justice and affection, and had brought out the point that this attribute of Islam has been prominent even during the period of conquests and rule. I had also hinted at the greatest massacre of history in Algiers. After this harangue, among the persons who were introduced to me was a certain gentleman of Italian extraction (born in Rome) freshly converted to Islam, Mustafa Wilson by name. He was the Italian Consul in Paris. On embracing Islam he took leave of the diplomatic office held by him. He is now at the head of a party of French young men who have sincerely taken to Islam, although at present his organization is little known-almost obscure. All these people gather once a week at the residence of their leader. All of them dress in a purely oriental fashion and some of them, notwithstanding their youth, have grown a neat beard. In this weekly meeting of theirs, some portion of the Quran is recited and the Islamic faith is studied. 'Mr. Mustafa Wilson (on being introduced) said to me; "The stress laid by you on the aspect of mercy and tenderness in the Islamic conquests, I have noted very carefully. Most probably you were refuting the totally false charge of the western writers that the Muslims in their warfare had justified for themselves cruelty and hard-heartedness. You should not be worried on that score. Every nation has a distinctive feature of its own on the moral plane which becomes its hallmark. The most outstanding feature of the morality of the western nations is that they are absolutely hypocratic in all their assertions of mercy and affection."

An Arab Muslim was talking to these French young men on the theme of the greatness of Islam and its progressiveness. He went so far in this vein that it appeared he was speaking in some Arab country on the subject of attainment of power and glory. So he stressed the point that Islam invites them to procure strength, to manufacture tanks, aeroplanes and what not. One of the converts to Islam said to him, "My brother, we have come from western civilization to Islam for the reason that this civilization has crippled our nerves through wars and armaments. Annihilating our souls and making our lusts abiding through materialism have put an end to our humanity. So mention to us only the spiritualism of Islam in which we have sought human dignity and spiritual satisfaction." Similarly, a Swiss girl, who is stationed in Paris and is trying to obtain a degree in Psychiatry stated to me, "I am a poor girl and my parents are not in position to undertake my total support in this habitation of "traders" and "libertines and fornicators". You must have observed that in this city man becomes a hungry beast of an evil nature. I thought of getting employment with some family to supplement my subsistence while working for my degree. And in this quest I looked for an oriental family in whose spiritual atmosphere my nobility and humanity may be safe. So I got a part-time job with a Hindu family in Paris. But I am constrained to state with regret that there too I could find no trace of our lost assets (human dignity and humanity). I discovered much to my grief that their souls too were lacking in nobility!".

These are some examples in which the story of the man in the west in quest of the spiritual life has been recounted - spiritual life in which he may get rid of the evils of his materialistic civilization, distraction and helplessness and anxiety and restlessness, whose springs have welled up in their own interiors prompted by this civilization. You will realize this fact whenever talking to any person from the west with balanced thought and moral and spiritual consciousness.

In as much as materialistic life is concerned, the western civilization has reached its zenith. But as you have already noticed material prosperity alone cannot take man to peace and prosperity. Rather, need is felt of a civilization and culture in which along with the material progress there may be a drive for balanced spiritual growth. And neither of these two aspects of human life may overstep its due limits creating an unpleasant effect on the other. Is such a culture possible and can it be brought into existence? And does there exist a nation that can come forward to meet this challenge? It is not possible for the western world to occupy this lofty position. For the present it is at the highest point of its material power and its role of troublemaker. But in days to come when its might gives way and decline sets in, it will be found sadly lacking in the capacity and capability to provide and keep intact the world leadership needed for the maintenance of peace and tranquility and dignity and honour. As for the socialist world it is all the more difficult for it to discharge this duty since it is thoroughly steeped in materialism and has declared a war against the spiritual, religious and moral values. The Socialistic civilization too along with the western civilization must add to the wretchedness and restlessness of the world, so much so that the entire castle of this civilization along with its western and Eastern architects and citizens shall one day crumble to dust.

Where the heathenic and idolatrous religions of the East are concerned, they too cannot take upon themselves this responsibility, since civilization and culture can stand on the strength of knowledge and healthy ideology which is absolutely free from superstition and nonsensical whims. And idolatory in itself is the very opposite of all these things. Moreover, the civilization that the world demands and the spiritualism for which it is thirsting, is such a positive and constructive spiritualism which may be helpful in the progress and advancement of mankind. As against this the duality (and multiplicity) of the East is a negative approach which prompts man to escapism, impedes the path of fulfilling the rights and obligations, and regards the material progress of man an abomination, abstention from and fighting against which is obligatory. In the present age the Muslim Ummah and no other is capable of playing this cultural role and becoming the standard-bearer of the civilization of future. Following are the reasons for this proposition:

Firstly we are the bearers of a creed which is the most advanced in the matter of bringing into existence a civilization. This is the creed of extremely clean, lucid, exalted, most sublime and perfect unity of God. This creed respects intellect and gives it such strength that little known or less important facts get included in the category of information or knowledge. This is a moderate creed of highly dignified human morality which keeps man away form excess in mercy and affection and from deficiency in equity and justice. And similarly it establishes and maintains a balance between love and duty-consciousness. This is the source of such laws which aim at liberality and easiness and not difficulty and hardship, and which are based on wisdom and expediency. In it the expediency of the individual is a guarantee for the collective expediencies, and it is not sacrificed to those of the collection or society. Human expediency in general is what is always kept in view, without abrogating or destroying the national and regional characteristics and local preferences.

Secondly, we are heir to a positive and constructive spirituality. This is a divine spirituality which accompanies a soldier in the battlefield, the craftsman in the factory, a learned person in his study, the philosopher in his discussion and debate, and the ruler in his state. This accompanies every person, in a serious mood or in jest, in motion or stationary, during the day or the night, in prosperity or adversity, in sound health or in sickness. But never once it creates any difficulties in his way, but takes him from one excellence to another. This spirituality reminds him of God Who created him, of the earth which he moves about, of the mankind with whom he lives, of the unity of the universe of which he is a part and of that God, the cherisher of the worlds, whose servant and slave he is.

Thirdly, we have also proved in the past that we have the power of giving birth to such civilizations. Whatever might have been the adverse remarks of our antagonists and rejectors, no one dare deny the fact that our civilization had proved much more a mercy and good fortune for mankind. Our civilization proved the best ideal in the matter of superiority of morals, the rule of justice and equity, the freshness of the spirit, and in the various modes and periods of humanity. When in a period of much less enlightenment and backwardness in knowledge and thought, we have been in a position to establish such a wonderful human civilization, we are much better equipped and better placed today with the advancements in knowledge and inventions and explorations of the modern age, to establish such a civilization.

When we take the reins of this much awaited civilization in our hands, we shall not make our flight into space an argument for the denial of God. We shall not make our inter-continental rockets and missiles an instrument of threatening the nations of the world and bringing them compulsively into our sphere of influence. We shall not make radio a means of misleading mankind and cinema a means of defrauding (and demoralizing) people. We shall not make woman the means of the satisfaction of our lust. We shall not exploit and plunder the various nations of the world on the strength of the advancement of civilization, nor ruin their honour and wealth. These are the reasons or only some of them, that have made us a unique Ummah, which duly deserves to hold aloft the banner of a new civilization, which puts an end to the wretchedness of man and confers on him peace, tranquility and solace and quietitude generously, after the western civilization has failed humanity.

When we contemplate the foundation of our creed, we find that our heavenly revelation is clearly pointing to the fact that we stand out among the nations of the world as a unique Ummah that can play the cultural role for mankind. This distinction is not based on the race or sex, since Islam did not approve of these nonsensical notions even for a moment. Rather, it is based on the first two reasons presented in the preceding lines:

The Quran tells us:

> You are the best of peoples, evolved for mankind, enjoining what is right, forbidding what is wrong and believing in God. (AI Quran III: 110)

This Quranic verse points to our creed and morals which has made us the best Ummah.

In another verse it has been said:

> (They are) those who, if We establish them in the land, establish regular prayer and pay regular zakat, enjoin the right and forbid wrong. (Al Quran XXII: 41)

At another place it has been said in the Quran:

Thus have We made of you an Ummah justly balanced, that ye might be witnesses over the nations, and the Apostle a witness over yourselves. (AI Quran II: 143)

This Quranic verse has made us the standard-bearers of a Mission. And that Mission is to lead mankind and always keep guiding them to the path of the truth and goodness. This obligation is not limited to any particular period or to a certain race.

When we responded positively to the message of nature and held aloft the banner of this Mission, we led humanity to the goal of peace, guidance and light. Then relinquishing the charge of this onerous duty we sought refuge in escape. This noble verse of the Quran is exhorting us to take up this banner once again and hold aloft that torch through which,the nations now groping in the darkness of distraction, selfishness, oppression and fatal despair, and seeing no other way out of their misery save suicide, may get rid of their troubles. The individuals are putting an end to their lives with ordinary lethal weapons or poisoning themselves. And the nations are piling stocks of atomic and hydrogen bombs for mass annihilation.

What Sort of Future?

The view of playing the new cultural role by us that I have presented here will be derided by two groups. The first of these is that enslaved by the western civilization and it has lost faith in its own nation that it can ever come up to be the adversary of the western people, not to say of occupying the exalted position of leadership of the world. These are the people due to whom our ummah is confronted with countless troubles and perversions of thought. We are thankful to God that this class of our nation is constantly dwindling numerically. The reason lies partly in the follies of the modern civilization and its crimes perpetrated against its followers and other weaker nations, and partly it is due to the ideological and political awakening of our ummah which augurs well. The period of the political slavery of the western imperialism has come to an end. And along with that the period of our political leaders is also coming to a close who regarded the end of imperialism something impossible. In the same way the period of the cultural bondage of the "civilized" west will shortly come to an end, and we shall also get rid of the conservative "enlightened and liberal" leaders, who were really nothing more than the abominable phenomenon of ignorance, slavish mentality and stupidity.

The other group is that which admits that the western civilization must come to its ruination due to its excessive mischief and trouble making. But like us they do not recognize the possibility of our laying the foundation of a movement of a modern civilization, when there is such a vast difference between us and the civilized nations. So all talk of cultural leadership appears to them a flight of fancy, an impossibility, even mid-summer madness.

But when we talk on this subject we do not assert that the end of the western civilization and change of hands in the cultural leadership is a matter of ten, twenty or even fifty years. There are some natural laws governing the establishment and demolition of civilizations which are inevitable. When the foundations of a strong fort are damaged, to the casual observers it appears for a sufficiently long time that it is strong and impregnable, whereas in spite of its grim appearance it is in a state of degradation and decay, and it is not long before it is in ruins.

From the beginning of our renaissance we have been through various stages, every- later stage of which was the natural outcome of the preceding one. When we awakened we found ourselves badly entangled in the meshes of colonialism. From most countries we have turned out colonialists, and God-willing will be able to extern them from the rest in the near future. Now we have started learning those manners and practices, and organizing our lives according to them, which are the inevitable demands of the modern civilization. And this is the same civilization which had, the day before, become the master of our destiny, and which had conquered our countries and dominated them. Then we went a step further on the way of attaining power. We exploited our natural resources and did our best to become independent of the west in the matter of manufactures. Now all our efforts are directed towards becoming members of the comity of the civilized nations and their partners in political power and economy. At this stage it is essential for us to establish a norm of civilization in which both the cultural difficulties of the modern age and our own peculiar circumstances and needs have been considered. Similarly, it is also necessary- for us before the conclusion of this stage to prepare a plan of action for the coming stage. Shall we go on existing under this very civilization and running after these people who are centuries in advance of us, so that helplessness and misery surround us on all sides and our aspirations are reduced to a merger with our predecessors on this path and become like them. Or shall we chalk out a new path of action for ourselves which may serve to spur us on to further advances and also safeguard us against the difficulties, calamities, and degradation and depression that have overtaken these civilized nations?

Factually we cannot catch up with the western nations in material strength a few years hence. It is not so easy for us to have satellites or inter-continental rockets. And supposing we do acquire all these things in a few years time from now, even then the west during this interval must have advanced much ahead of us. So the right course to adopt would be to make all possible endeavours to attain power and along with that we should design a new cultural norm for ourselves and for the entire humanity. The fact is that in the choice of the pattern of civilization we can have full freedom, and we have ample time at our disposal to consider the difficulties and hazards of the present day civilization. The reason for adopting such a course is not only that in the present stage we cannot get rid of the hold of this civilization on us since there is no way of doing that, but our real aim is to get free of this evil and become immune against its contagion at some future stage. The way of achieving this goal is clear for us provided we have a staunch belief in our principles and tenets of faith, and have certainty about those values whose accuracy and truth have been proved by experience also, and which go into the making of the caravan of our civilization. The spark of temerity and exaltation in our great nation has not yet died down. The fires of daring and passion, of laying down the life for a noble cause have not been extinguished yet, and in spite of receiving wounds constantly from the invaders and putting up with the strokes from the internal traitors, it never yielded to the perpetrators of oppression and tyranny.

If we achieve this end we will find that we have turned the modern period of human history in the most important direction. In this way we shall be able to put the stamp of our spiritual and moral authority over the two continents of Asia and Africa, which will make them more fortunate and deserving of peace and security. At this juncture wearied, helpless and straying, the west must also turn to us and acquire from us that which will lessen its wretchedness and affliction. That will be the day when leadership will change hands and we shall be the leaders of the world, and before some people in their moments of insanity put an end to the human race, we shall have succeeded in turning away humanity to another direction.

But with all that it occurs to me time and again that the trend of historical incidents is not in keeping with the sequence of events thinkers and writers have taken into their minds. Who knows what may happen tomorrow? This world of ours teems with unpredictable events. Something happens, at one end of the globe and has a deep impact on those living at the other end. However, it does not prevent us from pondering over the future. The historical events are moulded by God according to the views of the thinkers and the call of the prophets to the truth and message of the reformers.

Anyway the topic of this book and those talks of mine were broadcast from Radio Damascus between Muharram 20, 1375 A.H. (Sept. 8, 1955) and Rabi II, 23, (December 15, 1955). In these talks I had presented some of the resplendent aspects of our civilization. These are those facets that would fascinate the very fair-minded man of thought and vision. I have not taken up an exhaustive study of these cultural manifestations nor did I try to analyse them academically, since I was addressing people whose intellectual level was different. My aim in delivering these speeches was to make those people listen who would listen to them and adopt the best aspect of what I have said. Particularly in my mind were those young men and thinkers who believe in God and repose faith in their history. But I could not continue this series of talks, since I was preparing for an academic tour of the western countries, which terminated in 1956. Otherwise I had in mind to present many more of such delightful events. These are the patterns of humanity in our cultural history from which positive spirituality radiates. These are the glorious examples of Belief in God, pursuit of truth, chastity of psyche, illumination of soul, beauty of disposition, sympathy for mankind and just and equitable rule. All this was in spite of the fact that they fully participated in all the tumultuous events of the culture and civilization and were all the time very actively busy in the arena of life. And this vast multitude includes rulers, men learned in the religious lore, philosophers and leaders, traders and officials, men and women, young and old and prosperous and the needy alike. And they were not the visionary ideals of the imaginary world of the philosophers and intellectuals, but specimens of human excellence that lived with the people on this earth.

So captivating are these examples of positive spirituality in which our civilization stands out unique among all the old and the new civilizations. True, that history is acquainted with some spiritual persons who were born in various nations, particularly in the Far East. And even today there are people who are dominated by a chaste trend of spirituality. But all such persons had an individualistic and negative approach to civilization. They hated the bustle of life and resorted to escape from culture and civilization. They have existed in temples, mountain tops, caves and in wilderness. But the specimens of our cultural history are those who entered the thick of the struggle in the arena of life and mended and adorned it. And in this striving to reform and making life more pleasant for people, they unflinchingly offered any sacrifice of life and property that was needed for this purpose. And this is the real secret of the unparalleled beauty of our amazing spiritual specimens in the history of civilizations.

The aim of the publication of these radio talks is to divert the gaze of people to these agreeable specimens, whose presence is a strong argument in support of the fact that we have the capability of establishing a civilization that was much superior and much more perfect than the present one, and to remind the younger generation of our nation to establish such an exalted civilization the way it was founded by their ancestors. This is the most opportune time for such a reminder since our nation is stepping into a new portal of history with great enthusiasm and fervour, so that it may build a better and superior future. The Muslim Ummah still retains the habits, disposition and talents of the ancestors. Therefore, when they hear the stories of the excellence and eminence and respectability and exaltation of their ancestors, they are moved to great activity, and with great alacrity jump into the field of action.

> I pray to thee (O God !) to move our young men to sighs and sobs of early dawn (And) once again provide the young eaglets with feathers of flight,
>
> My Lord! It is my earnest prayer and longing,
>
> That Thou make my vision and insight much more common.
>
> Iqbal

In presenting these 'agreeable scenes, it was never my intention to assert that each and every thing in our history was beautiful and resplendent. There is no civilization in history whose standard-bearers were entirely free of equivocations. What is meant is the corroboration of the fact that the facets high-lighting the stable humanity are stronger and better in our civilization. It is also our aim to refute the charges of those critics who cannot but find faults and defects only in our civilization, and who are bent upon expunging ours from the history of lasting and well-established civilizations of the world. Yet another aim is to bring to naught the vicious endeavours of all those who intend to conceal from the view of our younger generation all our historical impressions and traditions so that they may drown our younger generation along with themselves. The civilization in which they want to merge our younger generation is doomed to certain annihilation. If the one page of its history comprises some excellence, thousands of pages have been blackened with faults and lowness and evil deeds. The real target of colonialism is this, for which it has been endeavouring. And the favourite pursuit of their hangers-on, their adorers and devoted servants too is to sing the praises of the western civilization.

I have presented only a few specimens of the agreeable portion of our civilization ! I hope that those making a historical study of our civilization shall take it to completion in great detail and full elucidation, so that it may appear before our younger generation in its real attractive form and perfect grace and beauty, from which radiations emanated in the past and which had infused the spirit of life in the middle ages. The nation that remains ignorant and unaware of its history in spite of having a glorious past, has no "present" either. And the nation that remains alienated from its peculiar characteristics and excellence has no future, since every ummah and civilization has a national relationship with its past and it is its fundamental characteristics that bring a civilization into existence.

Those passing sarcastic remarks like "It is the favourite pastime of the idle and the good-for nothing to get acquainted with the past and to go on mourning over it", forget the fact, in spite of the past being a fountain-head of goodness and blessings, that to ignore and deride the past is the way of the ignorant and malicious persons. Our prosperity lies in our benefiting from our treasure-houses of the past in the building up of our present, so that our growth and ascent may have a happy end, our future may be prosperous and the means of the survival of the ummah may be the part and parcel of all endeavours in this direction. In this way our past honour and excellences derived from our ancestors together with the future greatness may become uniform. In this way our caravan shall retain its continuity on the path of history, the links of the past and those of the future shall be joined and become continuous and the edifice shall be advancing towards perfection. And the fact is that the completion of institutions depends on the Will of God, and He it is Whose graciousness and help are needed in everything we do.

TWO

Historical Background

Islam, the Religion of Peace, was not the creation of Mohammad (PBUH) any more than other religions were of those to whom their origins are respectively attributed. No religion is the creation of any single individual, nor does it appear all of a sudden, revealed to this or that Seer as it is always claimed. Islam, like any other religion, was the product of the conditions of the time, and of the surroundings in which it flourished.

Before the Advent of Islam

Though living on the side of the fateful road on which the conquering armies of the Assyrians, Persians, Macedonians and Romans had marched back and forth, the inhabitants of the vast Arabian Peninsula maintained their freedom by virtue of the natural aspects of their country and the mode of life moulded by these aspects. But the fierce love of freedom, together with the exigencies of a nomadic existence, had split the inhabitants of the Arabian desert into a number of tribes perpetually engaged in feuds and warfare.

Separated from the rest of the mankind, the Arabs took the stranger for an enemy. The poverty of his country had added to the growth of that spirit. These two factors went into the making of the codes of law and morality of the Arabs. They believed that, as descendants of the outlawed Ismael, they were doomed to live in a dreary desert while rich and fertile lands were assigned to the other branches of the human family. Consequently, they felt justified in recovering by force a portion of the heritage, they believed, they had been deprived of.

The Roman historian Pliny, six hundred years before the appearance of Mohammad, found the Arabs occupied with two lucrative professions, robbery and trade, in addition to their native calling of sheep-raising and horse-breeding. In the earlier stages of social evolution, these two professions of robbery and trade are usually distinguished by a thin and elastic line of demarcation. The trader makes his profit by purchasing things at the cheapest price and selling them at the highest. The cheaper the price he pays, the greater is his profit. Robbery or theft places him in possession of things at the lowest price. Therefore, once the morality of the fundamental principle of trading is admitted, the right of the trader to act so as to make the greatest possible profit becomes legitimate. Then, competition keeps the price of his wares down. The most convenient way of eliminating competition is to rob the rival. By that stratagem, not only is the competitor kept away from the market, but his goods go there as the property of the more efficient party. Further, robbery is an effective weapon to establish monopoly on trade-routes and markets. In its earlier stages of development, trade is everywhere conducted with these practical policies which must shock a modern merchant. Still, robbery was the weapon with which his less orthodox predecessors established the noble profession which he now carries on so righteously with the laudable maxim: Honesty is the best policy.

Besides, robbery imperceptibly ripens into the manly political virtue of war likeness, so much glorified in the savage adolescence of mankind. Given to robbery by the physical aspects of their homeland, the Arabs were naturally destined to develop unusual talent in trade as well as in war. Their bravery and war likeness were almost legendary. The famous historical work, "Ayam al Arab", composed in the most flourishing days of the Saracen Empire, records no less than seventeen hundred memorable battles fought by the Arabs before the rise of the Prophet. So, if the Saracens distinguished themselves as warriors, they did not derive that virtue from their Islamic faith. They had been warriors before they were called to wield the sword in the service of God. The military achievements of Islam should be credited not so much to the religious teachings of the Arabic Prophet as to the social conditions of the country in which it was born.

The wars conducted by the Arabs before the appearance of the Prophet were mostly internecine feuds fought with savage fierceness, but strictly according to the quaint codes of honour, chivalry and nobility. The profuse spilling of blood did not fertilise the sands of Arabia, but it did, eventually, become prejudicial to the profitable economic consequences of robbery, the legitimate profession of trade conducted by the primitive Arabs. Economic necessity demanded termination of the proud but ruinous virtue of internecine wars, and diversion of the traditional Saracen valour in more profitable channels. The, ideas, born out of that necessity, eventually crystallised into the " Religion of Mohammad ".

Itself a vast stretch of sandy wilderness, Arabia, however, is surrounded in three sides by populous countries — homes of ancient civilisations, where industry and agriculture thrived from time immemorial. On the south is the ocean on which navigated vessels carry the trade of India. Thanks to her geographical position, Arabia was intersected by the routes of Caravan trade and maritime commerce, interchanged among India, Persia, Assyria, Syria, Palestine, Egypt and Abyssinia. In earlier days, the trade-routes connecting Africa and Asia lay through the south and north of the Peninsula, avoiding the unknown interior of the sandy wilderness. But the exorbitant taxation of Byzantine despotism, supplemented by the endless extortion of its local officials, drove the traders to hazard the encounter of the fierce but hospitable Beduin in the heart of his home.

In the beginning, the Arab collected his tribute according to his peculiar code of law and morality. But in course of time, he discovered that trade would be more profitable than robbery. Of all the Arabian tribes, the Koreish were the first to exchange the turbulent for a peaceful but more profitable profession. They inhabited the coast-line of the Red Sea and commanded the Abyssinian trade long before the Asiatic traffic also came their way. In the earlier centuries of the Christian era, the capital of the Koreish tribe, Mecca, had become the point where the important trade-routes from south to north and east to west intersected. At Yemen, on the Arabian Sea, the Koreish caravans took over the commodities from India; at a point near modern Aden, their precious burden was increased by the African riches from Abyssinia. The journey northwards terminated at the busy marts of Damascus, where corn and manufactured articles were bought with the exchange of aromatics, pearls, precious stones, tusks, etc. The lucrative exchange diffused plenty of riches in the streets of Mecca. When, later, the east-west trade-route also passed through Mecca, the prosperity of the Koreish became unbounded, and their ambition proportionately grew.

But other Arabian tribes, jealous of their freedom, and envious of the prosperity of the Koreish, stood faithfully by their traditional codes of law and morality, whose profane origin was no longer admitted. They were raised to the nobility of offensive and defensive warfare, on the authority of tribal gods. The old national pastime of robbery which had previously been played at the expense of unwary strangers, turned out ruinous to the new national occupation of trade. Termination of the tribal feuds became an essential condition for further political progress. The task of establishing unity, by the logic of historical events, devolved upon those who controlled the economic forces making for the historically necessary goal. The Koreish appeared as the chosen people of history.

In the midst of their ceaseless feuds, all the Arabian tribes worshipped and sacrificed at the temple of Caaba near Mecca. The Koreish head seized the control of the seat of national worship, and the sacerdotal office of great power and extensive privilege had been captured by the Hashemites -the most important family of the tribe. The Hashemites, therefore, commanded national respect and veneration, in addition to the opulence derived from trade. Eventually, a scion of the Hashemite family issued the call for unity in the form of a new religion which denied all gods but one.

The severe monotheism of Mohammad not only echoed the yearning for unity on the part of a people torn asunder by internecine feuds; it was also destined to find a ready response from the neighbouring nations, tormented by the intolerance of the Catholic Church. The religious life of the people of Persia, Mesopotamia, Syria, Palestine and Egypt had been hopelessly confused by the conflicts of Magian Mysticism, Jewish conservatism and Christian bigotry. Rigid rites and rituals had taken the place of religion; hypocritical ceremonies had driven away devotion; dogmatic theology had prosecuted faith; and God had disappeared in a confusing crowd of angels, saints and apostles. The stringent cry of the new religion" There is but One God "softened by great toleration, subject to this fundamental creed, was enthusiastically hailed by the distressed multitudes searching for the secure anchor of a simple faith in the stormy sea of social disintegration, intellectual bankruptcy and spiritual chaos. The historic cry was raised by the caravan traders of Arabia who had stood outside the ruinous conflict of arms and beliefs, had prospered economically, and progressed in spirit, while their older and more civilised neighbours had stagnated, decayed and disintegrated. The propagation of the stern belief in the Oneness of God prepared the ground for the rise of a military State which unified all the social functions — religious, civil, judicial and administrative. The unitarianism of the Saracens laid the foundation of a new social order which rose magnificently out of the ruins of the antique civilisation. Such a creed was sure to attract the attention of the multitudes barbarously persecuted for religious heterodoxy. The new faith allowed freedom of conscience to all who placed themselves under its protection. Islam rose as a protection against religious persecution and refuge for the oppressed.

The accommodating nature, cosmopolitan spirit, democratic policy and the monotheistic creed of Islam were the creation of the geographical position of the land of its birth. Surrounded with countries oppressed by native despotism or devastated by foreign invasions, Arabia maintained her freedom. The persecuted sects from Egypt and Persia as well as from Christendom fled to the free and hospitable desert where they could profess what they thought, and practise what they professed. When the Empire of the Assyrians was conquered by the Persians, and the altars of Babylon subverted by the Magis, the Sabian priests retired to the neighbouring desert with their ancient faith and the precious knowledge of astronomy. Previously, Assyrian invasion had driven many a devout son of Israel in the same hospitable wilderness. All the Hebrew prophets, down to John the Baptist, lived, meditated and preached in the depth of the Arabian desert. The invasion of Alexander having avenged the wrong done to the Assyrians, the more orthodox disciples of Zoroaster, who did not wish to desecrate the purity of their faith by the toleration of Greek idolatry, migrated to the free atmosphere of the Arabian desert to join hands with their Babylonian adversaries.

Gnosticism and Manichxanism-those hybrids of oriental mystic cults-Greek metaphysics and Christian Gospel, all thrived luxuriantly on the sandy soil of free Arabia. Finally, Catholic orthodoxy drove to the same smelting pot of Arabian hospitality the Nestorian Jacobite and Eutychian heretics who preferred the simplicity of the Gospel to the idolatry of the orthodox Church. The freedom of exile brought the representatives of those diverse faiths into closer contact enabling them to see what was common to them all. In the calm atmosphere of toleration, their heterodoxy disappeared, the fire of proselytism died out, and the common essence of the teachings of the learned guests was imparted to the hospitable Beduin. In short, the Barbarians of the desert inherited the best the religions of antiquity had to offer, namely, the faith in the existence of one supreme God who is exalted above all the powers of heaven and earth, but who had revealed himself to mankind from time to time through his Prophets. Here is the essence of Islam crystallised in the spiritual consciousness of the Arabian people before Mohammad appeared with the mission of building a new religion on its basis. The spirit of Islam was not invented by the genius of Mohammad; nor was it revealed to mankind. It was a heritage of history conferred on the Arabian nation. The greatness of Mohammad was his ability to recognise the value of the heritage and make his countrymen conscious of it.

The Arabs had acquired the notion of one supreme God; but out of habit and for tribal interests, they still practised their old polytheistic worship. To be benefited by the positive outcome of earlier religions, delivered to them as a heritage of history, they must change their traditional mode of worship. A supreme effort must be made with the purpose; and Mecca was the most strategic point to lead the attack from.

The particularist freedom and internecine feuds of the Arabian tribes were mutually compromised and composed at Mecca. All routes of trade led there. The unity of the economic interest of the decentralised nation had created at Mecca a symbol of precarious spiritual unity. All the tribes from distant parts of the vast desert, while visiting the market of Mecca, worshipped in the temple of Caaba. Each had introduced there its own emblem of devotion. The temple had been adorned with no less than three hundred and sixty idols of men, eagles, lions, etc. But the prosperous tribe of Koreish dominated the trade of Mecca, and the powerful family of Hashim had seized control of the temple. It was natural that the new spirit of a rising faith, which would further economic interest through national unity, should be first felt consciously at the heart of the nation. So, it happened that a member of the Hashemite family began to preach the new religion.

Once the family of Hashim and the tribe of Koreish were converted to the new faith, the whole nation would follow soon. All the tribes must visit Mecca for the purposes of trade. Those who controlled the trade of Mecca could easily dictate the faith and conscience of the entire nation. But prejudice and habit induced the Koreish to persecute the innovating zeal of their kinsmen. They were afraid that trade would be driven away from Mecca, should the Pantheon of Caaba be disturbed. But there were others ready to assume the leadership of the revolution, when the most eligible candidate failed. Medina espoused the cause of the Prophet, and the call of unity found enthusiastic response in other quarters. The supremacy of Mecca was menaced. One family after another defected from the Koreish conservatism, and joined the revolutionary Hashemites. Before long the Koreish capitulated before their exiled kinsmen, but only to capture the sceptre of the "Commander of the Faithful".

As soon as the followers of the Prophet captured Mecca, a perpetual law was passed that no unbeliever should be allowed to set foot on the territory of the Holy City. The new religion was imposed upon the entire nation with the potent weapon of economic boycott. Caaba was cleared of its idols and became the shrine of " Mohammad's God ". Once the standard of the new religion was raised, the whole nation flocked under it. The ground had been prepared. The faith had unconsciously taken hold of the mind of the nation before it was preached. Economic interest demanded its establishment.

Spread of Islam

The apparently sudden rise and the dramatic expansion of Mohammedanism constitutes a most fascinating chapter in the history of mankind. A dispassionate study of .this chapter is of great importance in the present fateful period of the history of India. The scientific value of the study by itself is great, and the meritorious quest for knowledge is sure to be handsomely rewarded. But with us, to-day in India, particularly with the Hindus, a proper understanding of the historical role of Islam and the contribution it has made to human culture has acquired a supreme political importance.

This country has become the home of a very considerable number of the followers of the Arabian Prophet. One seldom realises that many more Mohammedans live in India than in any single purely Islamic country. Still, after the lapse of many centuries, this numerous section of the Indian population is generally considered to be an extraneous element. This curious but extremely regrettable cleft in the loose national structure of India has its historical cause. The Mohammedans originally came to India as invaders. They conquered the country and its rulers for several hundred years. That relation of the conqueror and the subjugated has left its mark on the history of our nation which today embraces both. But the unpleasant memory of the past relation has been progressively eclipsed by the present companionship in slavery. The effect of British Imperialism is no less painful and ruinous for the bulk of the Muslim population than for the masses professing Hinduism. So completely have the Mohammedans become an integral part of the Indian nation that the annals of the Muslim rule are justly recorded as chapters of the history of India. Indeed, nationalism has gone farther in effacing the painful memory of the past.

The practice of seeking consolation for the shame of the present in the real or legendary glory of the past has dressed the Muslim rulers of India in brilliant national colours.

Yet, an Indian, who prides in the prosperity of the reign of an Akbar, or boasts of the architectural accomplishments of a Shahjahan, is even today separated most curiously by an unbridgeable gulf from his next door neighbour belonging to the race, or professing the faith, of those illustrious monarchs who are believed to have glorified the history of India. For the orthodox Hindus who constitute the great majority of the Indian population, the Mussulman, even of noble birth or high education or admirable cultural attainments, is a 'mlechha'-impure barbarian-who does not deserve a social treatment any better than accorded to the lowest of the Hindus.

The cause of this singular situation is to be traced in the prejudice born, in the past, of the hatred a conquered and oppressed people naturally entertained for the foreign invader. The political relation out of which it sprang is a thing of the past. But the prejudice still persists not only as an effective obstacle to national cohesion, but also as a hindrance for a dispassionate view of history. Indeed, there is no other example of two communities living together in the same country for so many hundred years, and yet having so little appreciation of each other's culture. No civilised people in the world are so ignorant of Islamic history and contemptuous of the Mohammedan religion as the Hindus. Spiritual imperialism is an outstanding feature of our nationalist ideology. But this nasty spirit is the most pronounced in relation to Mohammedanism. The current notion of the teachings of the Arabian Prophet is extremely ill-informed. The average educated Hindu has little knowledge of, and no appreciation for, the immense revolutionary significance of Islam, and the great cultural consequences of that revolution. The prevailing notions could be laughed at as ridiculous, were they not so pregnant with harmful consequences. These notions should be combatted for the sake of the Indian people as well as in the interest of science and historical truth. A proper appreciation of the cultural significance of Islam is of supreme importance in this crucial period of the history of India.

The great historian Gibbon describes the rise and expansion of Islam as "one of the most memorable revolutions which has impressed a new and lasting character on the nations of the globe". One is simply amazed to contemplate the incredible rapidity with which the two mightiest empires of the ancient time were subverted by the comparatively small bands of nomads issuing from the Arabian desert, fired with the zeal of a new faith. Hardly fifty years had passed since Mohammad assumed the role of the singular Prophet spreading his Message of Peace at the point of the sword, when his followers victoriously planted the banner of Islam on the confines of India on the one side, and on the shores of the Atlantic on the other. The first Khalifs of Damascus reigned over an Empire which could not be crossed in less than five months on the fleetest camel. At the end of the first century of the Hegira, the " Commanders of the Faithful " were the most powerful rulers of the world.

Every Prophet establishes his pretension by the performance of miracles. On that token, Mohammad must be recognised as by far the greatest of all Prophets, before or after him. The expansion of Islam is the most miraculous of all miracles. The Roman Empire of Augustus, as later enlarged by the valiant Trajan, was the result of great and glorious victories won over a period of seven hundred years. Still, it had not attained the proportions of the Arabian Empire established in less than a century. The Empire of Alexander represented but a fraction of the vast domain of the Khalifs. For nearly a thousand years, the Persian Empire resisted the arms of Rome, only to be subdued by the "Sword of Gud" in less than a decade. Let a modern historian describe the miracle of the rise of Islam.

"Nowhere was there a vestige of an Arabian state, of a regular army, or of a common political ambition. The Arabs were poets, dreamers, fighters, traders; they were not politicians. Nor had they found in religion a stabilising or unifying power. They practised a low form of polytheism ..... A hundred years later, these obscure savages had achieved for themselves a great world power. They had conquered Syria and Egypt, they had overwhelmed and converted Persia, mastered Western Turkestan and part of the Punjab. They had wrested Africa from the Byzantines and the Berbers, Spain from the Visigoths. In the West they threatened France, in the East Constantinople. Their fleets, built in Alexandria or the Syrian ports, rode the waters of the Mediterranean, pillaged the Greek islands and challenged the naval power of the Byzantine Empire. Their success had been won so easily, the Persians and Berbers of the Atlas Mountains alone offering a serious resistance, that at the beginning of the eighth century it, must have seemed an open question whether any final obstacle could be opposed to their victorious course. The Mediterranean had ceased to be a Roman lake. From one end of Europe to the other, the Christian states found themselves confronted with the challenge of a new Oriental civilisation founded on a new Oriental faith."

How did that stupendous miracle happen ? That has been one of the baffling questions for historians. Today the educated world has rejected the vulgar theory that the rise of Islam was a triumph of fanaticism over sober and tolerant peoples. The phenomenal success of Islam was primarily due to its revolutionary significance and its ability to lead the masses out of the hopeless situation created by the decay of the antique civilisations not only of Greece and Rome but of Persia and China- and of India.

Islam's Message

Vulgar interpreters of the Islamic history lay stress upon its military achievements either to praise or to deprecate its farreaching revolutionary significance. If the undoubtedly brilliant military conquests of the Saracens were the only measure of the historic role of Islam, then it would not be a unique historical phenomenon. The depredations of the barbarians of Tartary and Scythia (Goths, Huns, Vandals, Avars, Mongols etc.) approximated, if not equalled or excelled, their military accomplishments. But there is a vast difference between the tidal waves that occasionally rolled over West, South and East, from the border land of Europe and Asia, and the Arabic eruption of religious frenzy: Like tidal waves the former rolled on in their cataclysmic greatness, only to subside, sooner or later, having distributed death and destruction far and wide. The latter, on the contrary, was an abiding historical phenomenon, which ushered in a brilliant chapter of the cultural annals of mankind. Destruction was only a subsidiary part of its mission. It pulled down the played-out old, to construct a necessary new. It demolished the holy edifices of the Caesars and the Chosroes, only to rescue from their impending ruin the accumulated treasures of human knowledge, to preserve and multiply them for the benefit of posterity.

The prodigious feats of the Saracen horsemen are not the only distinctive features of Islam. They simply captivate our attention which must marvel at them, and impel us to search out and admire the causes of such a tremendously dynamic historical phenomenon. The miraculous performance of the "Army of God " usually dazzles the vision and the more magnificent achievements of the Islamic revolution are seldom known to the average student of history, even if he be a follower of Mohammad. Yet, the martial victories of the followers of the Arabian Prophet were but the prelude to a more magnificent and lasting performance in the social and cultural fields. They only created the conditions for political unity which opened up an era of economic prosperity and spiritual progress. The stupendous ruins of the Roman and Persian Empires had to be cleared away so that a new social order could rise with new ideas and new ideals. The dark superstition of the Magian mysticism, and the corrupt atmosphere of the Greek Church vitiated the spiritual life of the subjects of the decrepit Persian and Byzantine Empires rendering all moral and intellectual progress impossible. The severe monotheism of Mohammad wielded the formidable scimitar of the Saracen not only to destroy the profane idolatry of the Arabian tribes; it also proved to be the invincible instrument of history for freeing a considerable section of mankind from the evil spirit of Zoroaster as well as from degenerate Christianity given to the superstition of miracle-mongering, to the deadly disease of monasticism and to the idolatrous worship of Saints. The amazing achievements of Saracen arms only prove that they were wielded in the service of history-for the progress of humanity.

The rich spiritual legacy of the glorious civilisation of ancient Greece was almost buried under the dreary ruins of the Roman Empire, and lost in the darkness of Christian superstition. The grand mission of rescuing the invaluable patrimony, which eventually enabled the peoples of Europe to emerge from the depressing gloom of the holy middle-ages and build the marvellous monument of modern civilisation, belonged to the Saracen arms, and to the socio-political structure erected on the basis of Islamic Monotheism. The sword of Islam, wielded ostensibly in the service of God, actually contributed to the victory of a new social force - the blossoming of a new intellectual life - which eventually dug the grave of all religions and faiths.

Islam rose rather as a political movement than a religion in the strictest sense of the word. In the initial stages of its history, it was essentially a call for the unity of the nomadic tribes inhabiting the Arabian desert. Upon its speedy realisation, the politico-religious unitarian doctrine became the flag under which the Asiatic and African provinces of the Roman Empire survived the dissolution of the antique social order. The previous revolt had miscarried itself. Christianity had lost its original revolutionary fervour becoming, on the one hand, the ideology of social dissolution (Monasticism), and a prop for the decaying Empire, on the other. But the social crisis continued, aggravated by the degeneration of Christianity. The message of hope and salvation came from the Caravan traders of .Arabia who had stood outside the corrupting atmosphere of the decomposed Roman world, and prospered by their advantageous position. The "Revolt of Islam" saved humanity.

A famous authority on Islamic history writes the following about the mission of Mohammad: "He found a whole nation -in the full tide of rapid improvement, eagerly in search of knowledge and power. The excitement in the public mind of Arabia, which produced the mission of Mahamet, induced many other Prophets to make their appearance during his life time."

The people, for whom Islamic history is summarised in the exploits of fanatical hordes, dramatically offering the dismayed world the choice between the Koran and the sword, with the blood-curdling cry of "Allah Akbar", do not know, or conveniently overlook, that only the immediate successors of Mohammad occupied themselves solely with temporal and religious conquest-, and even they were distinguished from the barbarian ravishers of humanity like Alaric, Attila, Genseric, Chengis or Tamerlane, by the nobility of character, purity of purpose and piety of spirit. Their devoutness might have been fortified by superstition, but was not stained by hypocrisy. Their fanaticism was softened by generosity and sound common-sense. Their ambition was remarkably free from selfishness- Godliness, for them, was not a veil for greediness.

There are few figures in history more romantic, more devout, more sincere and more modest than the first "Commander of the Faithful" Abu Bakr. His memorable injunction to the "Army of God " ran: "Be just; the unjust never prosper. Be valiant; die rather than yield. Be merciful; slay neither old men, nor women, nor children. Destroy neither fruit trees, nor grains, nor cattle. Keep your word even to your enemy. Molest not those men who live retired from the world." The irresistible march of the "Army of God" bears testimony to that this remarkable injunction was uttered sincerely by the venerable chief, and obeyed strictly by the devout followers.

Everywhere the Saracen invaders were welcome as deliverers by peoples oppressed, tyrannised and tormented by Byzantine corruption, Persian despotism and Christian superstition. Fanatically faithful to the revolutionary teachings of the Prophet, and obediently acting according to the noble, wise and eminently practical injunctions of the Khalif, the Saracen invaders easily enlisted the sympathy and support of the peoples they conquered. No invader can establish an abiding domination over conquered peoples, except with their active support or tacit toleration.

The second Khalif, Omar, whose impetuous horsemen had pushed their victorious march through the Persian Empire, to the distant banks of the Oxus, on the one side, and were masters of the second metropolis of the Roman world Alexandria-on the other, made his triumphal entry into Jerusalem on a camel which also carried the entire royal provision and equipage—a small tent of coarse hair, a bag of corn, a bag of dates, a wooden bowl, and a leathern flask of water. Gibbon offers the following account of the simplicity, devoutness, equity, and righteousness of the conquerors of Persia, Mesopotamia, Syria, Palestine and Egypt "Wherever he halted, the company without distinction was invited to partake of his homely fare, and the repast was consecrated by the prayer and exhortation of the Commander of the Faithful. But in expedition or pilgrimage, his power was exercised in the administration of justice; he reformed the licentious polygamy of the Arabs; relieved the tributaries from extortion and cruelty; and chastised the luxury of the Saracens by despoiling them of their rich silk, and dragging them on their face in dirt."

Khaled, whom the Prophet called the " Sword of God", whose almost legendary valour had united Arabia, Mesopotamia and Syria under the banner of Islam, died in the possession only of his horse, his arms, and a single slave. The great hero is credited to have declared in his youth, "it is not the delicacies of Syria, or the fading delights of this world, that have prompted me to devote my life in the cause of religion, I only seek the favour of God, and his apostle".

The valiant conqueror of Egypt, Omrou, was distinguished by poetic genius in addition to martial valour. The following remarkable passage occurs in his report to Khalif Omar : "The crowds of husband men who blacken the land may be compared to a swarm of industrious ants; and their native indolence is quickened by the lash of the taskmaster. But the riches they extract are unequally shared between those who labour and those who possess." That was a view far in advance of time. The idea of social equity was unknown in all the lands of ancient civilisation. The toilers, either as waves or as Sudras, were object of contempt and exploitation. They were hardly considered as human beings. The economic principle; primitively formulated in the memorable injunction of the first Khalif, evolved out of the interest of the Arab traders, revolutionised the old social idea. A part of the wealth produced by the toiling masses, when left with themselves, becomes a powerful impetus to trade. In his administration of the conquered kingdom of the Pharaos and the Ptolemies, the Arab warrior sought with success to mend the glaring inequities that had offended his poetic vision. Egypt, robbed and despoiled for centuries -by the' Greeks and the Romans, prospered under the Saracens.

There is no end of testimonies to prove that even in the predominantly martial period of their history, the Saracens were far from being barbaric bands of fanatical marauders, spreading pillage and raping, death and destruction in the name of religion. Then, the period of conquest was short, as compared to the long era of, learning and culture that flourished subsequently under the patronage of the Khalifs as well as of the tributary and independent Empire. The military period terminated with the establishment of the Abbassides at Baghdad-the "City of Peace" - just about a hundred years after the ascendancy of the Prophet at Medina. Since then, the military activities of the Arabs were essentially of the nature of current defensive and offensive operations of a far-flung Empire.

The stern enthusiasm of the Saracen warriors was softened by time and prosperity. They began to seek riches no longer in war, but in trade and industry; fame, not on the field of battle, but in the pursuit of science and literature; and happiness, no longer in the fanatical worship of one God and his only Prophet, but in the harmless enjoyment of social and domestic life. War was no longer the passion anal proud profession of the Saracens, because they had found interest and delight in a peaceful world created by the prowess of their forefathers. The progeny of the intrepid heroes, who had flocked to the belligerent standard of Abu Bakr and Omar, with the hope of paradise and incidentally earthly spoils, found the modest occupation of trade and industry more profitable, and science and philosophy more gratifying.

Three hundred years of peace, prosperity and progress elapsed before the martial valour of the Saracens was rekindled by Christian aggression in the deceptive form of the crusades. Pillage and plunder, tyranny and oppression came to be associated with Muslim conquests only after the power of the Saracens had been overwhelmed by the Mongol barbarians from Central Asia; Arab learning and culture had been corrupted by the degenerating luxury of the court; and the proud standard of Islam, having lost its original revolutionary lustre, had been prostituted in the rapacious hands of the Turks and the Tartars.

It is a gross misreading of history to confound Islam with militarism. Mohammad was the Prophet not of the Saracen warriors, but of the Arab merchants. The very name with which he baptised his creed contradicts the current notion about its aim. Etymologically, Islam means to make peace, or the making of peace : to make peace with God by doing homage to his Oneness, repudiating the fraudulent divinity of idols which had usurped His sole claim to the devotion of man; and to make peace on earth through the union of the Arabian tribes. Peace on earth was of immediate importance, and greater consequence. The temporal interest of the Arabian merchants required it; for, trade thrives better under peaceful conditions. Since decayed states and degenerated religions bred the germs of continued wars and perennial revolts, their destruction was a condition for peace. The creed of Mohammad made peace at home, and the martial valour of the Saracens conferred the same blessing on the peoples inhabiting the vast territories from Samarkand to Spain.

As soon as a country came under the domination of the Arabs, its economic life was quickened by the encouragement of industry and agriculture. The spirit and interest of the Arab traders determined and directed the policy of the Islamic State. In the Roman world as well as in all the other lands of antique civilisation, the ruling classes detested all productive labour, looked down upon trade and industry. War and worship were their noble professions. With the Arabs it was different. Nomadic life in a desert had taught them to appreciate labour as the source of freedom. With them trade was an honourable as well as a lucrative occupation of the free man. Thus, the Islamic State was based upon social relations entirely different from those of the old. Religion extolled industry, and encouraged a normal indulgence of nature. Trade was free, and as noble a profession as statecraft, war, letters and science. The Khalifs of Baghdad were not only great traders; the earlier ones learned, and actually practised some craft to purchase their personal necessities with the proceeds of manual labour. Most of the great Arab philosophers and scholars came from opulent trading families. The culture and refinement of the courts of Bokhara and Samarkand, the munificence of the Fatemite rulers of Africa and the splendour of the Sultans of Andalusia were equally produced rather by the profits of prosperous trade than by taxes extorted by despotic measures.

Under certain conditions, trade is a potent instrument of spiritual revolution. The aspiration of the Arab merchant produced the monotheism of Mohammad. This, in its turn, inspired the nomads of a desert to establish one of the vastest and most flourishing empires of history. The laws of the Koran revolutionised social relations. Increased production, the result of this revolution, quickened trade which ushered in an era of cosmopolitanism and spiritual uplift. Trade broadens the vision of man. Visiting distant lands, getting used to the sight of strange customs, mixing with peoples of diverse races, the trader frees himself from the prejudices and limitations born of the local conditions of his native land. He develops the capacities of toleration, sympathy and understanding for the habits, views and faiths of others. Observation and inquisitiveness, which guide his voyage on the unknown sea, or direct his steps in strange lands, kill in him the comfort of credulity. The growth of critical faculty places him at the gate of knowledge. The essence of his occupation teaches the trader to think in abstraction. He is not interested in his merchandise as such. His mind is occupied with the idea of profit. It is all the same to him, whether his camels or ships are laden with wool or corn or spices. He is concerned with something which is neither these nor other concrete things he handles. These are simply the means to attain his end—to make profit, which is a category abstracted from the concrete commodity he buys or sells. He appreciates things, not in their intrinsic value, but according to their capacity to produce profit.

Toleration for strange things, the attempt to understand them, freedom from prejudice, faculty of observation, ability to think in abstract—all these qualities acquired by the trader, thanks to the nature of his occupation, go into the making of a philosophical outlook. Having seen different Peoples cherish diverse forms of superstitions as divine, practise equally absurd rites and rituals or expressing devotion, extol prejudices to the dignity of eternal truth. The cosmopolitan mind of the travelled trader indulgently smiles upon the credulity of all, deplores their depravity equally, and respects the common element of faith beneath the superficial diversities of theological dogmas and forms of worship.

The main arteries of international trade of the mediaeval world ran through the countries which embraced Islam and were united in the Saracen Empire. The northern routes of trade with China, which passed through Constantinople to Italy and other countries of Western Europe, had become extremely risky owing to the Scythian inroads and the ruinous fiscal policy of the Byzantine Empire. After their conquest of Syria, Mesopotamia, Persia and the territories across the Oxus, the Arabs captured the Chinese trade and diverted it to pass through their domain of North-Africa and Spain, ultimately to reach the markets of Western Europe. During the eighth to the eleventh centuries, practically the entire trade between India and China, on the one hand, and Europe, on the other, was done by the Arabs. Thousands of traders travelled with their Caravans, loaded with precious cargoes, from the remote frontiers of China and India all the way to Morocco and Spain. They were not persecuted or detested as their kind had been in all the countries of antique civilisation with the honourable exception of Greece. In the Empire of the Saracens, they belonged to the ruling class. Consequently, the learning and culture that thrived so luxuriantly owing to the prosperity of the Saracen Empire bore the stamp of their native broad-mindedness, cosmopolitanism and incredulity. Under the leadership of a martial aristocracy and jealous priesthood, human ideology takes the form of dogmatic faith or misty mysticism. Philosophy -the search for a rational explanation of the Universe-originates in a society ruled by an aristocracy engaged in trade. The city states of the Ionian Greeks were therefore the birth-place of philosophy.

Islam was a necessary product of history-an instrument of human progress. It rose as the ideology of a new social relation which, in its turn, revolutionised the mind of man. But just as it had subverted and replaced older cultures, decayed in course of time, Islam, in its turn, was also overstepped by further social developments, and consequently had to hand over its spiritual leadership to other agencies born out of newer conditions. But it contributed to the forging of new ideological instruments which brought about the subsequent social revolution. The instruments were experimental science and rationalist philosophy. It stands to the credit of Islamic culture to have been instrumental in the promotion of the ideology of a new social revolution.

Capitalist mode of production rescued Europe from the chaos of mediaeval barbarism. It fought and in the long run vanquished Christian theology and the spiritual monopoly of the Catholic Church with the potent weapon of rationalist philosophy. This weapon, invented by the ancient sages of Greece, came to the possession of the founders of modern civilisation through the Arab scholars who had not only preserved the precious patrimony, but added to it handsomely. The historic battle, begun by the nomads of the Arabian desert under the religious flag of Islam, was fought step by step through a thousand years on fields scattered over the three continents, to be won finally in Europe under the profane standard of the eighteenth century enlightenment and bourgeois revolution.

Holy Prophet's Influence

The founder of Islam has been characterised as "the man who, of all men, has exercised the greatest influence upon the human race". There was, however, nothing very extraordinary about the man until he claimed the credit of divine revelation. The foundation of that dubious claim was no more or no less fictitious than in the case of the prophets, apostles and saints of all other religions. Christian arrogance called the Arabian Prophet an "Impostor". But it has been forgotten that he was given that name together with Moses and Jesus. The authorship of the famous book, anonymously published *Three Impostors* which created sensation in Europe towards the close of the middle-ages, was attributed to the Christian King Frederic Barbarossa as well as to the Muslim philosopher Averroes.

If Mohammad (PBUH) was an " impostor ", he did not take up that role any more consciously than others who appeared as instruments through which the fiction of divine revelation became a reality and carried conviction with the ignorant and superstitious masses. Having conceived the ideal of national unity, Mohammad realised that it could not be made acceptable to the warring Arabian tribes unless it were backed up with a supernatural sanction. People enjoying the bliss of ignorance and thinking in terms of preconceived notions, could not be convinced with any other argument. The will of minor gods could be overwhelmed by the will of a greater and all-powerful God. The protection against the wrath of the former could be found in the mercy of the latter. The belief in the absolute sway of one supreme God can alone encourage people to revolt against the tyranny of a whole host of tribal deities. If the supreme God was not there he had to be invented. That was the chain of Mohammad's thoughts. There was no imposture in it. Did not the rationalist Voltaire put forward the same argument more than a thousand years after it had found favour with the Arabian Prophet? But in the latter case, the argument was put forward in defence of reaction; Voltaire advocated the necessity of inventing a God because that would be the only guarantee for the preservation of the decayed system of feudal monarchistic society. At the time of Mohammad, and under the circumstances it was advanced, the argument served a positively revolutionary purpose. When man's mind is dominated by the belief in the supernatural, every progressive idea should be formulated in the terms of those beliefs if it were to secure popular support. Besides, the idea of One God was not the invention of Mohammad. The idea had grown out of social conditions described in the last chapter. Mohammad's mission was to discover evidence for the existence of One God. And if you wish to convince people you must adduce only that kind of evidence which can carry conviction to them.

But Mohammad's (PBUH) search for God was not inspired by cynicism as in the case of Voltaire. It was an honest effort on the part of an ignorant man inspired by a zeal. In quest of the God who alone could save the Arabian nation, he retired to the desert and gave himself up to meditation, fasting and prayer—those familiar practices adopted by the prejudiced seeking divine inspiration even in these days of the twentieth century. And the result was as usual in all such cases. " He was visited by supernatural appearances, mysterious voices accosted him as the Prophet of God; even the stones and trees joined in the whispering." Such experiences always result from cerebral disorder which takes place whenever the prescribed practices are carried too far. Fixed ideas, however fantastic or imaginary, may appear to take concrete form if the mind is focused on them so as to exclude the consciousness of other sensations. A scientific study of the psychology of seers reveals the fact that " inspiration " or any other " religious experience " is the result of a pathological state brought about either accidentally or purposely through prescribed practices.

Mohammad (PBUH) acted as all those of his kind had done before him, or did after him. But in his case, there was a fact which must go to his credit. He was too shrewd a man to be deluded by those psycho-pathological symptoms which are taken for the evidence of spiritual elevation. He was afraid that he was going mad; and might have abandoned his mission if his sagacious wife had not come to his aid in the nick of time. It was the rich merchant Khadija, mature with worldly wisdom, who was quick to appreciate the spiritual value of the mental aberrations of her husband. She persuaded him that his visions were not signs of insanity, but were messengers of God. Taking advantage of his psycho-pathological state of suggestibility, she could easily make him "see" an angel entering the room to deliver to him the Message of God. Undoubtedly, the drama could be enacted only in the setting of ignorance, superstition and prejudice, main characters being played under delusion. But that is how all religions are born. There is no reason to think that Islam was an exception. It was an exception in the sense that, except for the invention of a divine sanction, it contained less of religious dogmas and metaphysical speculation than sound political sense, progressive social principles and admirable codes of personal behaviour. "He did not engage in vain metaphysics, but applied himself to improving the social condition of his people by regulations respecting personal cleanliness, sobriety, fasting, prayer. Above all other works he esteemed alms giving and charity. With a liberality to which the world had of late become a stranger, he admitted the salvation of men of any form of faith -provided they were virtuous."

The Koran was not the work of an intellectual, and hence contains some dude ideas and phantastic speculations. These obvious defects of the Koran easily overshadow its great merit even as the source of inspiration of a great religion. But Mohammad's religion was rigorously monotheistic; and as monotheism it was uncompromising, which outstanding characteristic won for it the distinction of the highest form of religion. The idea of God is the foundation of religion in the philosophical sense. That idea cannot be free of all fallacies unless it leads to the conception of creation out of nothing. The rationalism of ancient philosophers of Greece as well as of India excluded the fantastic conception. Consequently, religions growing out of the background of that primitive rationalism could not conclusively establish the fundamental idea of God. The result was that all the great religions—Hinduism, Judaisrri and Christianity—eventually ended in one or other form of pantheism which logically liquidates religion as such. For pantheism identifying the phenomenal world with God puts the very idea of God under doubt. It disposes of the idea of creation and, consequently, the idea of God must also go. If the world can exist itself, from eternity, it is not necessary to assume a creator. And, deprived of the function of creation, God becomes an unnecessary postulate.

Mohammad's (PBUH) religion cuts the Gordian knot. It frees the idea of God from the embarrassment of primitive rationalism by boldly asserting the highly irrational idea of creation out of nothing. The God stands out in all his glory. The ability to create not only the whole world but an endless series of worlds is the token of his all-powerfulness. To have thus established the idea of God, albeit in a dogmatic and primitive manner, was the credit of Mohammad. For that credit he has gone down in history as the founder of the purest form of religion. Because Islam as a religion is irrationalism par excellence, it so easily triumphed over all other religions which, with all their metaphysical accomplishments, theological subtleties and philosophical pretensions, were defective as religions being but pseudo-religions.

Monotheism, however, is a highly subversive theory. While being itself the highest form of religion, it strikes at the root of the religious mode of thought. Placing God above and beyond the world, it opens up the possibility of doing without him altogether. Islam as the most rigorous monotheistic religion closed the chapter of human history dominated by the religious mode of thought, and by its very nature was open to unorthodox interpretations which eventually liquidated the religious mode of thought and laid the foundation of modern rationalism." We may compare the working of Monotheism to a mighty lake, which gathers the floods of science together, until they suddenly begin to break through the dam ..... The third of the great monotheistic religions, Mohammadanism, is more favourable to Materialism. This, the youngest of them, was also the first to develop, in connection with the brilliant outburst of Arabian civilisation, a free philosophical spirit, which exercised a powerful influence primarily upon the Jews in the middle ages, and so indirectly upon the Christians of the West." Being the most perfected form of Monotheism, Islam played that role. The crudities of the Koran did not prevent its basic idea from flourishing into all its revolutionary consequences.

His severe Monotheism contradicted Mohammad's claim to the sole Prophecy of God. While the Koran recognised Moses, Jesus and other Hebrew Prophets as apostles of God, Mohammad's claim, if not openly disputed in the beginning, was secretly doubted even among his associates. Divinity of its founder is not the fundamental creed of Islam. And that distinction results from its strict Monotheism. Immediately upon the death of Mohammad , his followers were divided on that crucial question. When the news of the Prophet's death reached the camp of the army setting out for the conquest of Syria, the devout Omar refused to believe that the Prophet could die, and threatened to strike off the head of the messenger whom he suspected to be an infidel. Upon that the venerable Abu Bakr admonished the impetuous younger man with the following words: "Is it Mohammad (PBUH) or his God that you worship? The God of Mohammad liveth for ever; but the apostle was a mortal like ourselves, and according to his own prediction, he has experienced the common fate of mortality."

It should be noted that the immediate successor of Mohammad, at the moment of his disappearance, called him an apostle, instead of the Prophet. With the less ambitious designation of an apostle, Mohammad was placed by his followers on the level of other religious teachers and lawgivers. Denial of the divinity of the Prophet made Islam the purest doctrine of Monotheism. Once divinity is conceded to a Prophet, before long he assumes the attributes supposed to belong only to the Supreme Being. The unity of God or the absoluteness of the First Principle can no longer be maintained logically. Dubious theological devices endeavour to reconcile the contradiction. The original simplicity of faith is lost either in theological dogmatism or mystical self-deception. Without the severity of its theology, Islam could not claim the historic role as creditably as it did. When the Prophet is deprived of divinity, or his claim to it is not generally admitted, the scripture cannot command absolute and infallible authority. Consequently, some latitude is left for the mind of the faithful. The teaching of a mortal cannot have the majesty of eternal truth, and scriptural laws cannot claim immutability.

Until the twelfth century, Islam did not possess a homogeneous body of dogmas. Subject to the belief in one God, the Mussulman had a practically unlimited latitude for his spiritual life. And history shows that the Arabian thinkers made free and full use of that flexibility of the new faith. In order to refute the Christian doctrine of Trinity, which they considered to be a vulgarisation of the sublime idea of the Supreme God, Muslim theologists developed the fundamental idea of religion to the most abstract form ever conceived by human mind. They could perform that unparalleled feat of theological ratio-cination because "the Monotheism of Mohammad was the most absolute, and comparatively the freest from mythical adulterations". The same authority testifies to the fact that the fundamental principles of religion laid down crudely by the founder of Islam were pregnant with the possibility of great development. And 'because of their rigid monotheistic nature, the development inevitably transcended the narrow limits of religious thought and culminated into a spiritual aflorescence which closed the age of faith. "Even before the communication of Greek philosophy to the Arabians, Islam had produced numerous sects and theological schools, some of which entertained so abstract a notion of God that no philosophical speculation could proceed farther in this direction, whilst others believed nothing but what could be understood and demonstrated; ..... In the high school at Basra, there arose, under the protection of the Abbassides, a school of rationalists which sought to reconcile religion and faith."!

During the first five or six hundred years of its history, Islam produced not only scholars who occupied themselves more with heavenly bodies than with heavenly beings, who quietly set aside the Koran and placed greater spiritual value on the study of profane books, but revolutionary thinkers who ruthlessly sacrificed faith on the altar of reason. Not a few "Commanders of the Faithful" themselves-those who reigned at Bagdad, Cairo or Cordova until the eleventh century-attached greater value to positive knowledge than to revealed wisdom. The independent Empire of Bokhara preferred poets to the priests, doctors of medicine to doctors of divinity, and encouraged scientific research rather than the propagation of faith.

When we bear in mind that this line of intellectual development was opened up not only by the socio-political conditions created by the triumph of Islam, but originated in the central dogma of Mohammad's religion, neither the curiosities of the Koran nor the primitiveness of the Islamic faith should permit us to underestimate the historical role of Islam.

Essence of Islam

The age of Arabian learning lasted about five hundred years, and coincided with the darkest period of European history. During the same period, India also was lying prostrate, under the triumphant Brahmanical reaction which had subverted or corrupted Buddhism. Eventually, it was thanks to the inglorious success of having overcome the Buddhist revolution that India fell such an easy prey to Muslim invaders.

Under the enlightened reign of the Abbassides, the Fatmids and the Omminades rulers, learning and culture prospered respectively in Asia, North Africa and Spain. From Samarkand and Bokhara to Fez and Cordova, numerous scholars studied and taught astronomy, mathematics, physics, chemistry, medicine and music. The invaluable treasure of Greek philosophy and learning had been buried under the intolerance and superstition of the Christian Church. Had it not been for the Arabs, it would have been irretrievably lost, and the dire consequence of such a mishap can be easily imagined.

Vain piety and hypocritical holiness induced the Christians to spurn the science of antiquity as profane. In consequence of that vanity of ignorance, the peoples of Europe were plunged into the mediaeval darkness which threatened to be bottomless and interminable. The happy resurrection of the divine light of knowledge, lit by the sages of ancient Greece, at long last dissipated the depressing darkness of ignorance and superstition, prejudice and intolerance, and showed the European peoples the way to material prosperity, intellectual redress and spiritual liberation. It was through the Arabian philosophers and scientists that the rich patrimony of Greek learning reached the fathers of modern rationalism and the pioneer of scientific research, Roger Bacon, was a disciple of the Arabs. In the opinion of Humboldt, the Arabians are to be considered "the proper founders of the physical sciences, in the signification of the term which we are now accustomed to give it". Experiment and measurement are the great instruments with the aid of which they made a path for progress, and raised themselves to a position of the connecting link between the scientific achievements of the Greek and those of the modern time.

Al Kandi, Al Hassan, Al Farabi, Avicena, A1 Gāzali, Abu Bakr, Avempace, Al Phetragius, — the Arabian names are so contracted in historical works written in European languages — these are names memorable in the annals of human culture; and the fame of the great Averroes has been immortalised as that of the man who made the forerunners of modern civilisation acquainted with the genius Aristotle, thereby giving an inestimable impetus to the struggle of European humanity to liberate itself from the paralysing influence of theological bigotry and sterile scholasticism. The epoch making role of the great Arab rationalist, who flourished in the first half of the twelfth century under the enlightened patronage of the Sultan of Andalusia, is eloquently depicted by the well known saying of Roger Bacon: "Nature was interpreted by Averroes."

The standard of spiritual revolt against the authority of the Christian Church and the domination of theology, was hoisted in the thirteenth and fourteenth centuries. The rationalist rebels drew their inspiration from the scientific teachings of the great philosophers of ancient Greece, and these they learned from the Arabian scholars, particularly Averroes.

The bigotry of the pious Justinian, in the beginning of the sixth century finally purged the holy world of Christian superstition of the remaining vestiges of pagan learning. The last Greek scholars were forced to leave the ancient seats of learning. They emigrated from the Roman Empire, and sought refuge in Persia; but there also sacerdotal intolerance proved equally hostile to profane learning. Eventually, the derelict science of Athenian culture found a hospitable home in the court of the Abbassides Khalifs of Baghdad, who were so impressed by the wisdom of those foreign infidels that neither Koran nor sword was offered to them. On the contrary, all the remaining votaries of ancient learning, whose knowledge ridiculed faith and indulgently smiled at all religion, were invited to accept the liberal hospitality of the Commander of the Faithful.

The Khalifs not only took the exiled Greek scholars under their protection. They dispatched competent men to different parts of the Roman Empire with the instruction and the means to collect all the available works of the sages of ancient Greece. The precious works of Aristotle, Hipparchus, Hyppocrates, Galen and other scientists were translated into the Arabian language, and the Khalifs gave every encouragement to the propagation of those irreligious teachings throughout the Muslim world. Schools established at State expense disseminated scientific knowledge to thousands of students belonging to all classes of society,- "from the son of the noble to that of the mechanic" Poor students received education free and teachers were handsomely remunerated for their services which were held in the highest esteem. The Arab historian, Abul Faragius, records the following views of Khalif Al Marion regarding the men of learning : "They are the elect of God, his best and most useful servants, whose lives are devoted to the improvement of their rational faculties ..... The teachers of wisdom are the true luminaries and legislators of a world which without their aid would again sink into ignorance and barbarism."

The current notion of the bigotry and fanaticism of Islam loses all historical authenticity when it is known that the men of learning so highly appreciated by the successors of the Prophet, were mostly devoid of any religious fervour, not a few of them holding views frankly heretical; and the general burden of their teachings was the assertion of the reason of mark as the only standard of truth. History does not provide the critical student with many instances of the head of a religious order encouraging the "improvement of rational faculties", as Khalif Al Manon did. For, the cultivation of rational faculties is entirely incompatible with faith. Yet, Al Manon was but one of the illustrious line of Abbassides Khalifs who not only encouraged the propagation of scientific knowledge, but themselves participated in it. Nor were the enlightened Abbassides an exception.

The Fatemites of Africa and the Omminades of Spain rivalled them in political power, material prosperity as well as in the patronage and propagation of knowledge. The library of Cairo contained over one hundred thousand volumes; whereas Cordova boasted of six times as many. This fact gives the lie to another calumny which depicts the rise of Islam as an eruption of savage fanaticism, namely, the tale of the destruction of the famous library of Alexandria. One must have a pious mind or credulous disposition to believe that those who took delight in founding and supporting such noble seats of learning, would have callously set fire to the library of Alexandria; that those who command the gratitude of mankind for having saved its most , precious patrimony, could have possibly begun by contributing to the destruction of that treasure. When dispassionate and scientific study of history dissipates legends and discredits malicious tales, the rise of Islam stands out not as a scourge but a blessing for mankind.

While books written in the eleventh and twelfth century indignantly detail the shocking tale of the burning of the library of Alexandria, the historians Eustichius and Elmacin, both Egyptian Christians, who wrote soon after the Saracen conquest of their country are significantly silent about the savage act. The former, a patriarch of Alexandria, could be hardly suspected of partiality to the enemies of Christianity. An order of Khalif Omar has been usually cited as evidence of the barbarous act ascribed to his general. It would have been much easier not to record that order than to suppress any historical work composed by Christian prelates who had endless possibilities of concealing their composition. A diligent examination of all relevant evidence enabled Gibbon to arrive at the following opinion on the matter: "The rigid sentence of Omar is repugnant to the sound and orthodox precept of the Mohammadan Casuist; they expressly declare that the religious books of the Jews and Christians, which are acquired by the right of war, should never be committed to the flames, and that the works of profane scientists., historians or poets, physicians or philosophers, may be lawfully applied to the use of the faithful."

Since history began to be written with impartial criticism, the tale of the destruction of the Alexandrian library has either been discredited or subjected to grave doubt. In any case, at the time of the Saracen conquest, the library of Alexandria had ceased to be the repository of the valuable records of Greek learning. Long before that time, Alexandria had enshrined Christian bigotry in the place of scientific knowledge and philosophical wisdom. The character of the contents of the library must have changed accordingly. The pagan scholars, driven by Christian intolerance away from the seat of ancient learning, must have carried away the treasures they valued more than all other things. If the flame was actually lit by the order of Omar, it consumed ponderous tomes of theological controversy which had done immensely more harm than good to mankind. The fire of Islam might have consumed the none too precious records of vain and futile theological disputations; but the admirable ardour of the freethinking Khalifs collected, preserved and improved the valuable records of ancient learning, which had left the Alexandrian library before its useless and pernicious contents were put to the flames.

Byzantine barbarism had undone the meritorious work of the Ptolernies. The real destruction of the Alexandrian seat of learning had been the work of St. Cyril who defiled the Goddess of learning in the famous fair of Hyparia. That was already in the beginning of the fifth century. The Christian Saint would not tolerate that philosophical lectures and mathematical discourses held by a young pagan woman should be patronised by the elite of Alexandrian society, while the pious but incomprehensible sermons of the Archbishop were attended only by the rebels. If he was no match intellectually, he possessed the power to eliminate competition once for all. Under his instigation, the rebels, led by a regiment of monks burning with religious frenzy, attacked the seat of Alexandrian learning and, in the name of religion, perpetrated crimes too painful to be recorded and too shameful to be remembered.

"Thus, in the four hundred and fourteenth year of our era, the position of philosophy in the intellectual metropolis of the world was determined; henceforth, science must sink into obscurity and subordination. Its public existence will no longer be tolerated. Indeed, it may be said that from this period for some centuries it altogether disappeared. The leaden mace of bigotry had struck and shivered the exquisitely tempered steel of Greek philosophy. Cyril's act passed unquestioned. It was now ascertained that throughout the Roman world, there must be no more liberty of thought ..... Such assertions might answer their purposes very well so long as the victors maintained their power in Alexandria, but they manifestly are of inconvenient application after the Saracens had captured the city ..... For the next two dreary and weary centuries, things remained, until oppression and force were ended by foreign invaders. It was well for the world that the Arabian conquerors avowed their true argument, the scimitar, and made no pretensions to superhuman wisdom. They were thus left free to pursue knowledge without involving themselves in theological contradictions, and were able to make Egypt once more illustrious among the nations of the earth, to snatch it from the hideous fanaticism, ignorance and barbarism into which it had been plunged."

The works of the sages of ancient Greece were not only rescued, collected and preserved by the Arabs, they were profusely commented and improved upon. Complete works of Plato, Aristotle, Euclid, Appolonius, Ptolemy, Hyppocrates and Galen were available to the fathers of modern Europe at first only in Arabic versions, accompanied by erudite commentaries. Modern Europe learned from the Arabs not only medicine and mathematics. The science of astronomy, which widens the vision of man and reveals before him the mechanical laws of nature, was zealously cultivated by the Arabs. With the aid of new instruments of observation, Arab philosophers acquired exact knowledge about the circumference of the earth, the position and number of planets. In their hands, astronomy began to outgrow its primitive form, (deviations of astrology), cultivated more or less by the priests of all Oriental countries, and to develop into an exact science. Although algebra had been invented by Diophantus of Alexandria, it did not become an object of common study until the age of Arabic learning. As a matter of fact, the name of the science has given currency to the theory of its Arabian origin. But the Arabs themselves modestly acknowledged their indebtedness to the Greek master. Botany was studied for medical purposes; yet the discovery of two thousand varieties of plants by Dioscorides represented the birth of a new science. Alchemy was a secret, jealously guarded by the priests of ancient Egypt. It was also practised at Babylon. In a much later period, rudiments of chemistry were also known to the physicians of India. But the science of chemistry owes its origin and initial developments to the industry of the Arabs. They first invented and named the alembic for the purposes of distillation analysed the substances of the three kingdoms of nature; tried the distinction and affinities of alkalis and acids; and converted the precious minerals into soft and salutary medicine.

It was in the science of medicine that the Arabs made the greatest progress. Masua and Geber were worthy disciples of Galen, and substantially added to what they had learned from the great master; Avicena, born in distant Bokhara, in the tenth century, reigned in Europe as the undisputed authority of the medical science for five hundred years. The school of Salermo, until the sixteenth century, was the centre of medical learning in Europe. It owed its origin to the Saracens and taught the lessons of Avicena.

The distinctive merit of the Arab scholars was the zeal to acquire knowledge through observation. They discarded the vanity of airy speculation, and stood firmly on the ground known to them. That great merit of Arabian learning is decisively evidenced in the following view of its doyen Averroes: "The religion peculiar to philosophers is the study of that which is; for no sublimer worship can be given to God than the knowledge of his works, which leads to the knowledge of him and his reality. That is the noblest action in his eyes; the vilest is taxing, as error and vain presumption, the efforts of those who practise this worship, and who in this religion have the purest of religions." A religion which permitted the propagation of such irreligious views, though garbed in a pious phraseology, could not have its origin in intolerance and fanaticism. For this heterodox view, the philosopher, of course, incurred the wrath of the priesthood; but much more of the Christian than the Muslim.

After a short banishment, Averroes was restituted in his position in the court of the Sultan of Andalusia, and his books survived proscription in the Islamic world. But from their Latin version, the above and similar passages were expunged. Yet, the heretic movements of Europe, Burin; the twelfth, thirteenth and fourteenth centuries drew their inspiration from the suppressed teachings of the Arab philosopher; and it was the heretic movement that shook the foundation of the Catholic Church which had held Europe in spiritual subordination throughout the middle-ages. From the twelfth century onwards, until the triumph of modern learning, Averroeism was analogous to heresy in the horrified eyes of Christian holiness.

And it was not for nothing that it was so. For, the passage quoted above indicated the surest point of departure for the quest of positive knowledge which eventually cleared away the debris of ignorance, sanctified as faith, and glorified as virtue on the authority of theological dogmas.

In this passage, Averroes stated the basic principle of the inductive method-the surest way to true knowledge. If the preconceived notion of a creator is set aside, and if man is made to know him (as distinct from the blind faith in his existence) in his reality through the empirical knowledge of his works, that is, nature, the divine object recedes farther and farther, until it vanishes into nothingness, — the only demonstrable reality about his existence; and a religion which promoted that singular quest for the knowledge of God certainly represented the greatest advance of human ideology under the garb of religion. The latest of Great Religions, Islam was the greatest and as such destroyed the basis of all religions. That is the essence of its historical significance.

The centre of Islam and Arabic learning was in those very historical regions where the older civilisations of the Egyptians, Assyrians, Jews; Persians and Greeks had arisen, clashed and fallen. The positive outcome of those earlier civilisations went into the making of the Arabian culture, and the remarkable monotheism of Mohammad made its own the cardinal principles of the religion of those ancient peoples. It stands to the credit of the Arabian philosophers that they, for the first time, conceived the sublime idea of a common origin of all religions. Not only did they hold the view, singularly broad for the epoch, that all religions were so many efforts of the human mind to solve the great mysteries of life and nature; they went so much farther as to make the bold suggestion that the effort more reconcilable with reason was the greater, nobler and sublimer. This rationalistic view of religion attained the highest clarity in the mind of Averroes.

Thus, together with the invaluable metaphysical and scientific teachings of the sages of Athens and Alexandria, the Arabs contributed something original to the foundation of modern civilisation. It was scepticism-that powerful solvent of all faith. As soon as criticism challenges credulity, a new light dawns on the perspective of human progress. A curious book, anonymously published with the title *Three Impostors*, occupies a prominent place in the early history of scepticism in Europe. The credit for that scandalous composition was attributed either to the heretical Christian Emperor Frederic Barbarossa, or the Muslim philosopher Averroes. The impostors were Moses, Christ and Mohammad. One of the suspected authors was a Christian and the other was a Mussalman. Religion certainly had fallen in bad days.

There had been scepticism before the thirteenth century, but no real incredulity. This doctrine and that had been disputed or rejected; but the foundation of Christian faith had never been touched. It was this foundation which was allied when the idea was conceived that all religions have a common ground. If all religions are essentially the same, then the doctrine and dogmas peculiar to each should be discarded as pernicious obstacles to the realisation of the spiritual unity of mankind. But freed from doctrines and dogmas, religion has no leg to stand upon. Its rationalisation amounts to its destruction. The revolutionary idea of the common origin of all religions was conceived for the first time by the Arab thinkers.

Although Arabian learning reached its climax in Averroes, he was but the greatest and the latest of a long succession of great thinkers and scholars; who flourished from the ninth to the thirteenth century. A brief reference to the substance of the teachings of the more illustrious of them will give some idea of the revolutionary significance of the learning which owed its origin to the cardinal principle of the Mohammedan religion, and was promoted by the staggering achievements of the "Sword of God".

Having established unity, as the terrestrial reflection of their spiritual unitarianism, and promoted economic prosperity in consequence thereof, the new Islamic nation devoted itself to the culture of the mind. For a hundred years, it modestly learned from others, particularly the ancient Greeks. Thus equipped, it began to produce independent and original thought in every branch of learning.

Al Kandi was the earliest of the great Arabian philosophers. He flourished in the capital of the free thinking Abbassides, and leaped into fame in the beginning of the ninth century for teaching that philosophy must be based on mathematics; that is, it should cease to be idle speculation abstract thought should be guided by precise reasoning, based on concrete facts and established laws, in order to produce positive results. The teacher of this doctrine deserves the great distinction of having anticipated Francis Bacon and Descarters by seven hundred years as a forerunner of modern philosophy. Even today there are many " philosophers " and scholars who could be profited by the wisdom taught by the Saracen sage a thousand years ago.

Next to be mentioned is Al Farabi who lived in the following century, and taught at Damascus as well as Baghdad. His commentary on Aristotle was studied for centuries as an authoritative work on the subject. He also excelled in the medical science. Roger Bacon learned mathematics from him.

In the latter half of the tenth century appeared Avicena. He belonged to a rich landowning family of Bokhara engaged in prosperous trade. He wrote on mathematics and physics, but went down in history for his 'contributions to the medical science. The famous medical school of Salermo was a monument to his memory, and his work was the text book of medicine throughout Europe until the sixteenth century. The great physician's philosophical views were so unorthodox that even the free-thinking Emir of Bokhara could not resist the pressure of the Imams who were scandalised by the profanity of Avicena. He had to leave the court of his patron, and travelled all over the Arabic Empire teaching medicine and preaching his philosophy at different seats of learning.

In the eleventh century lived Al Hassan who deserves a place among the greatest scientists of all ages. Optics was his special subject. Having learned it from the Greeks, he went farther than they, who corrected their mistaken notion that the rays of light issue from the eye. By anatomical and geometrical reasoning, Al Hassan proved that the rays of light came from the object seen, and impinged on the retina. There is ground for belief, held by many historians of science, that Keppler borrowed his optical views from his Arab predecessor.

In the same century also lived A1 Gazali, son of an Andalusian merchant. He anticipated Descartes in reducing the standard of truth to self-consciousness. He stands out as the connecting link between the antique and modern scepticism. His memorable contribution to philosophy is better stated in his own words : " Having failed to get satisfaction from religion, I finally resolved to discard all authority, and detach myself from opinions which have been instilled in me during the unsuspecting years of childhood. My aim is simply to know the truth of things; consequently it is indispensable for me to ascertain what is knowledge. Now, it was evident to me that certain knowledge must be that which explains the object to be known in such a manner that no doubt can remain, so that in future all error and conjecture respecting it must be impossible. Thus, once I have acknowledged ten to be more than three, if any one were to say: 'On the contrary, three is more than ten, and to prove my assertion I will change this stick into a serpent'; and if he actually did the miracle, still my conviction of his error would remain unshaken. His manoeuvre would only produce in me admiration for his ability, but I should not doubt my own knowledge."

The principle of acquiring exact knowledge, stated nearly a thousand years ago, by the Muslim savant, still holds as good as then; and the scientific outlook which makes such knowledge possible, is still comparatively rare among Indians, who even in these days of the twentieth century allow themselves to be imposed by feats of magic and "spiritual" charlatanism, and credit these as serious challenge to the reliability of scientific knowledge.

Al Gazali held that knowledge could not possess such mathematical exactness, unless it were acquired empirically, and governed by irrefrangible laws established by experience. He was of the opinion that incontestable conviction could be acquired only through sense perception, and necessary truth, that is, causality. In reason (self-consciousness) he found the judge of the correctness of the perception of senses. One is amazed to find such unique boldness of thought in the atmosphere of a religion generally believed to be the most intolerant and fanatical. Yet, A1 Gazali's scepticism was avidly studied throughout 'the Muslim world of his time. His place in the history of philosophy can be judged from the opinion of the famous French Orientalist Renan, who thought that the father of modern scepticism, Hume, did not say anything more than what had been said by the Arab philosopher who preceded him by seven hundred years. The immensity of the historical significance of Al Gazali's views is appreciated still more clearly when we remember that it was the scepticism of Hume which gave impetus to Kant's " all shattering critical philosophy " that laid a cruel axe at the root of all speculative thought. But Al Gazali's views were a long way ahead of time. Experimental science, as he visualised, was not yet possible. In the absence or infancy of technology, the nature of objects could not be so mathematically ascertained as the philosophers wished. Therefore, in his later years, A1 Gazali fell into mysticism; but his fall was no more strikingly inglorious than that of Kant. Objective drawback clipped the intrepid wings of the soaring spirit of the Arab thinker; whereas subjective predilection overwhelmed the critical genius of Kant.

Abu Bakr, who lived in the twelfth century, was the first astronomer to reject the Ptolemic notion regarding the position of heavenly bodies. He conceived of a planetary system and celestial motion, which tended towards the epoch-making discoveries of Giordano Bruno, Galileo and Copernicus. It is recorded that " in his systems all movements were verified, and therefore no error resulted". Abu Bakr died before setting forth his theory in a complete treatise. His pupil, Al Phetragius, popularised his teaching that all planetary bodies moved regularly. Throughout the middle-ages, the hypothesis was valued as a great contribution to astronomical knowledge. The teachings of a Muslim philosopher, which upset the biblical view of the Universe, penetrated the Christian monasteries. Not only Roger Bacon, but his illustrious opponent, Albertus Magnus, also acknowledged the indebtedness to the astronomical work of A1 Phetragius in which Abu Bakr's views on planetary movement were expounded.

The basic principle of the philosophy of Averroes, the greatest and the latest of the great Arabian thinkers, have already been outlined. He lived at the turning point of the history of the Islamic culture. By the twelfth century, the pinnacle had been reached, and the forces of reaction had gathered strength to overwhelm those of progress. Islamic culture was already on the decline.

The freedom of thought permitted by the simple faith of a nomadic people had attained such soaring heights of boldness as eventually clashed with .the temporal interests of the "Commanders of the Faithful". When the positive outcome of Islamic thought developed so marvellously during five hundred years, was summarised in the highly revolutionary dictum of Averroes, that reason is the only source of truth, Sultan A1 Masur of Cordova, under the pressure of the priests, issued an edict condemning such heretical views to hellfire, on the authority of religion. The denunciation of the - noblest product of Islam naturally marked the beginning of its degeneration from a powerful lever of human progress to an instrument of reaction, intolerance, ignorance and prejudice. Having played out its historic role-to rescue the precious patrimony of ancient culture out of the engulfing ruins of two Empires and the blinding darkness of two religions-Islam turned traitor to its original self, and became the black banner of Turkish barbarism and of the depredations of the Mongolian hordes.

Islam disowned its own. Averroes was driven away from the court of Cordova—the home of free thought for centuries. His books were condemned to the flames, not actually of fire, but of the more merciless sacerdotal reaction. Rationalism came to be identified with heresy. The very names of Averroes and his master, Aristotle, became anathema. In course of time, reaction triumphed so completely that for an orthodox Mohammedan, philosophy stood for " infidelity, impiety, and immorality". But the standard of spiritual progress, admirably held high, and boldly carried forward by the Arabs during five hundred years, could not be lowered and trampled under the fury of vain religiosity any more successfully by Islamic intolerance than previously by Christian piety and superstition. Averroes was disowned by his own people, only to be enthroned by those to whom belonged the future. The fierce contest between faith and reason, between despotic ignorance and freedom of thought, which rocked Europe and shook the foundation of the Catholic Church from the twelfth century onwards, drew inspiration from the teachings of the Arab philosophers. Averroes and Averroeism dominated the scientific thought of Europe for four hundred years.

THREE

Legacy of Islam

Tradition of Culture

And as against this let us relate an incident of 100 A. H, thirteen hundred years from now. A black girl, Fartoonah, wrote a letter to the caliph 'Umar bin-e-Abd-al-Aziz that the boundary wall of her house was very low and the poachers scaling that wall stole her hens. Umar bin-e-Abd-al-Aziz wrote back to her that the governor of Egypt had been ordered to have the boundary wall of her house raised and to undertake other necessary repairs to the house also. He wrote to the governor of Egypt that immediately on receipt of the letter he must have the needful done under his personal supervision. Ayub bin-eshurahbil was the governor of Egypt at that time and the text of the letter read:

"Fartoonah, the freed slave girl of Dhi-Asbah, has written to me that the boundary wall of her house is so low that thieves enter at night and steal her hens. She wants it to be raised and reinforced. On receipt of this letter go to her house and in your own presence have the wall raised and properly strengthened."

On receipt of the letter from the Caliph, he set out in search of the house of Fartoonah and found that she was a poor black woman (a Negress). The governor complied with the orders of the Amir of the believers and had it done under his personal supervision.

This is just one instance of the treatment meted out to the Negoea by us thirteen hundred years earlier, and speaks volumes of the glorious traditions of our civilization.

The Liberal Religion

This is a new aspect of the humanitarianism of our eternal civilization. This characteristic of the Islamic civilization is something new to the history of creed and ideology also, and equally so (unknown) to the history of ancient civilizations that were the creation of some religions or some peoples. When Islam laid the foundation of our civilization, it did not adopt a narrow minded attitude relating to the religions of the past. Rather, the behaviour of the Islamic civilization was in keeping with the following principle laid down in the Quran:

> So announce the Good News to My Servants, those who listen to the words and follow the best (meaning) in it.
>
> (Al Quran XXXIX: 17-18)

The principles and elements of the religious tolerance of our civilization are the following:

1. The Quran brings home to us the point that all revealed religions have sprung up from the same fountain-head:

> The same religion has he established for you as that which he enjoined on Noah. The which We have sent by inspiration to thee and that which We enjoined on Abraham and Jesus: namely that ye should establish Religion and make no divisions therein. (Al Quran XLIL 13)

2. That the position of all the prophets as messengers of God is equal. And in this behalf no one has any superiority over any one else. It is binding on Muslims to believe in all the prophets of God.

The Quran says:

> Say ye: "We believe in God, and the revelation given to us, and to Abraham, Ismail, Issac, Jacob and the Tribes, and that given to(all) prophets from their Lord: We make no difference between one and another of them: and We bow to God (in Islam)." (Al Quran II: 136)

3. That there is no compulsion in Religion. Rather, it has been left to the inclination and pleasure of people:

> Let there be no compulsion in religion.
>
> (Al Quran II: 256)

Wilt thou then compel mankind, against their will, to believe!

(AI Quran X: 99)

4. That the places of worship of all religions are respectable and their defence and support are just as essential as that of our own place of worship, the mosque:

Did not God check one set of people by means of another, there would surely have been pulled down monasteries, churches, Synagogues, and mosques, in which the name of God is commemorated in abundant measure. (Al Quran XXII: 40)

5. That it is not permitted to men to murder one another or oppress one another only on grounds of the difference of creed. Rather, they ought to co-operate with one another in promoting the cause of good and in eradication of evil. The Quran tells us:

Help ye one another in righteousness and piety, but help ye not one another in sin and transgression: (Al Quran V: 3)

However, the differences that have appeared in religious affairs, God Almighty Himself shall decide on the Day of Reckoning.

The Jews say: "The Christians have naught (to stand) upon. " Yet they (profess to) study the (same) Book. Like unto their word in what those say who know not; But God will judge between them in their quarrel on the Day of Judgment. (A l Quran II: 113)

6. That in the life of this world the norm on which the superiority of one man over another is to be judged as also in the sight of God, the basis of superiority is Taqwa or the fear of God, and his beneficence to fellow men. The Prophet has said:

"The people are as if they were the children of God and He loves those most who are the more beneficent to His children".

And God says:

> Verily, the most honoured of you in the sight of God is (he who is) the most righteous of you. (Al Quran XLIX: 13)

7. That the difference of creed should not stand in the way of doing a good turn, love and good treatment of blood relations and entertaining each other:

> This day are (all) things good and pure made lawful unto you. The food of the People of the Book is lawful unto you, and yours is lawful unto them. (Lawful unto you in marriage) are (not only) chaste women who are believers, but chaste women among the People of the Book, revealed before your time, ... (AI Quran V: 5)

8. That in case of the difference of creeds of peoples, they may hold debates, disputation with one another, but in ways that are best and most gracious, with limits of dignity, serenity and respect, and with proper argument, and with a view to convince and satisfy the other party.

> And dispute ye not with the People of the Book except with means better (than mere disputation).(Al Quran XXIX: 46)

Islam did not permit its votaries to behave rudely with the adversaries, nor allowed to revile them on the ground of their false creed, even if they are idolators.

> Revile not ye those whom they call upon besides God, lest they out of spite revile God in their ignorance.
> (Al Quran VI: 108)

9. However, when the Muslim Ummah is being oppressed because of its creed and ideology, to put an end to the mischief of the opponents and to defend their own ideology, it becomes indispensable to put up a fight against their violence.

> And fight them on until persecution is no more and Religion in its entirety is for Allah (alone). (Al Quran II: 193)

> God only forbids you, with regard to those who fight you for (your) faith, and drive you out of your homes, and

> support (others) in driving you out, from turning to them (for friendship and protection). (Al Quran LX: 9)

10. But once the Muslim Ummah has come to dominate a people that had formerly adopted an attitude of aggression and oppression in the matter of the faith of the Ummah or its freedom, it is not permissible for them to take revenge upon this vanquished people in a manner as to force it to relinquish its religion or perpetrate violence on them or even be harsh to them in treatment because of their adherence to their own agreeable beliefs. Rather, it would suffice that the conquered people submit to the Islamic state and sincerely stick to their covenant so that they may come to have the position:

> "They have the same rights as we have, and (they) have the same obligations that we have."

These are the Islamic bases with regard to the religious tolerance in Islam, on which has been raised the edifice of our civilization. These principles make it obligatory for every believer to believe in all the prophets of God and make any mention of them only with due respect, should not oppress the followers of any of them (prophets), have fair dealings with them, treat them gently and kindly and talk to them with a civil tongue, prove a good neighbour to them and accept their invitation to a feast. A Muslim can marry the women of the People of the Book so that family relations may be created and blood ties may be established. Again Islam has made it incumbent on the Islamic state to protect their places of worship, not to interfere in their creed, commit no excess in decision of cases involving them, and in the matter of human rights keep them on a par with the Muslims, and guarantee protection to their life, honour and future just as the protection of the life, honour and the future of a Muslim are guaranteed.

These are the bases on which the Islamic civilization was founded, and the world witnessed for the first time that religion was creating a civilization, without a shade of prejudice against other religions. And this civilization does not throw out the non-Muslims from the field of collective functions. Nor does it bring them down from their position. Since the Prophet laid the foundation of the Islamic civilization, it has maintained this attitude. But when degeneration and decay overtook Muslims, they relinquished their principles, forgot the injunctions of God and His Prophet and became ignorant of the Islamic faith, they also adopted a negligent attitude in the matter of religious tolerance which is on the increase in keeping with the increasing ignorance of their faith and belief.

Holy Prophet as an Ideal

When the Prophet of God migrated to Madinah, it had a fairly large Jewish Population. So the first thing he did in connection with the land of the Islamic government was to negotiate a covenant between the Muslims and the Jews, by which it became indispensable for the Islamic state to respect the beliefs of the Jews and to protect them from harm of any kind whatsoever. And on the other side the Jews were pledged to stand by the Muslims in case of an attack on Madinah. Through this treaty the Prophet inculcated the principles and elements of religious tolerance in the conscience of the Islamic civilization from the first day of its inception.

Some people of the Book were also the neighbours of the Prophet. He always treated them kindly and benevolently, sending gifts to them and accepted gifts from them. Taking advantage of this attitude of the Prophet, due to her evil Jewish nature, a Jewess intended to give a practical shape to her malice and enmity against Islam and the Muslims. So one day she sent a roasted leg of mutton after it had been injected with a lethal poison. She could go so far since she was sure that the Prophet was on good neighbourly terms with her and would as usual accept her gift. When the Abyssinian Christians came to Madinah the Prophet of God made arrangements, for their stay in the mosque, and took upon himself the responsibilities of hospitality and service. And from what he said that day, the following sentence is worthy of consideration.

"These people had a high position for our companions, so I liked to host them myself with due regard for their respectable treatment."

Once a delegation of the Christians from Najran came to Madinah. They too were brought to the mosque for their stay, and were allowed to conduct their service in the mosque in their own way. So they had their service on one side of the mosque and the Prophet prayed with the companions on the other side.

When these people presented their own faith putting forth arguments in its support the Prophet listened to them attentively and very gently and with due respect and courtesy replied to their religious assertions. The Prophet accepted the gift sent by Maquqas, the ruler of Egypt, and also the slave girl, who had the honour of giving birth to the Prophet's son Ibrahim,, who lived only a few months. And one advice given by the Prophet is also this "You should remain well-wishers of the Copts since you have relatives among them."

The Pious Caliphs

Again, after the Prophet, his caliphs ruled on the same lines and maintained his high-ranking, humanitarian policy of religious tolerance. So we find that when 'Umar, the second rightly guided caliph, entered Bait-al-Maqdis as a conqueror, he accepted the condition laid down by the Christians of Palestine that no Jews will be allowed to settle there. While he was in the great church of Bait-al-Maqdis the time of Asr Prayer approached. But he abstained from praying in the church, lest the Muslims in times to come might claim it as mosque on the plea that 'Umar had prayed there once. A woman from Egypt lodged a complaint with 'Umar that 'Umro-bin-al-'As had annexed her house for the extension of the mosque against her will. 'Umar asked 'Umro bin-al-'As to explain. He explained that the number of the believers coming to the mosque for prayer far exceeded the capacity of the mosque. The house of the complainant was adjacent to the mosque and she was offered the price of her property and far in excess of its real worth (as compensation for being dislodged, Tr.), but she declined the offer. Therefore, (it had to be acquired in public interest, Tr.) and was demolished to form part of the mosque, and the costs (and compensation money Tr.) were deposited with the Bait-al-mal, so that she might take it whenever she was pleased. Apparently the explanation offered by 'Umro-bin-al-'As was reasonable, and our present day law also permits it. But to 'Umar it was not acceptable and he ordered demolition of the portion of the mosque built on the site of the woman's house and construction of her house as of old.

This is the pattern of tolerance which has dominated every society that has been influenced by the principles of our civilization. That is why we come across many evidences of the manifestations of religious tolerance unparalleled in the history of mankind-nor even in any civilization of the present era.

In our immortal civilization, it has been seen time and again that the mosque and the church are standing side by side. The religious leaders of the churches had full powers in the religious affairs of their co-religionists and their churches and the Islamic state never interfered in these matters. Rather, it has happened so often that they themselves oppressed one another due to their religious differences, and the Islamic state came forward to mediate and justly decided their disputes, removing difficulties of the way, if any. For example the 'Malachi' sect of the Greek Christians during the period of the Roman empire, always oppressed the Coptic Christians of Egypt. The people belonging to this sect plundered the churches of the Egyptian copts. When the Muslims conquered Egypt they returned all their properties to the copts and meted out justice to them. Later, the Egyptian copts took revenge of the excesses and tyrannies of Malachi Christians they had been perpetrating before the advent of the Muslim rule there. And now the Malachis lodged a complaint with the Abbasid Caliph, Haroon Rasheed, who had all the properties and churches restored to the Malachis after taking them away from the copts. Haroon Rasheed took this action after sounding the Malachi patriarch.

The Generous King

Under the Islamic rule the Christians had full freedom in the performance of their religious ceremonies, and their religious leaders had full authority over their co-religionists. The government never interfered in their personal affairs. The Christians themselves realized that there was such perfect freedom under the Islamic state, even an infinitesimal part of which was not their share during the period of the Roman Empire. In this connection the name of Sultan Muhammad, the conqueror of Constantinople, shall ever remain fresh in the history of open-heartedness and religious tolerance. When he conquered Constantinople, it was excusively populated by the Christians and was the capital of the patriarch for the Eastern Catholic Christians. The Sultan granted amnesty to the entire Christian population and guaranteed safety of their lives, properties, their creed, their churches and their crosses. They were exempted from military service. Their chieftains were authorized to judge and decide all those cases that came upto them from their co-religionists, and also legislate for this purpose. And in this matter the Islamic government never interfered. The Christians of Constantinople themselves felt that there was a world of difference between the attitude and behaviour of Sultan Muhammad and the Byzantine rulers of the past. The Byzantine rulers interfered in the religious differences of people and meted out preferential treatment to the followers of their own churches. So the Christians liked the new system of government very much, and were pleased with their religious tolerance, which had no parallel in their own governments. The Roman patriarch had been allowed so much authority that his position made it a case of state within the state. For five hundred years they lived in this free atmosphere, and so well-protected was this freedom of theirs that they needed no army for their protection, nor had they to pay any taxes for such security. But how disgraceful that the Christians took undue advantage of the special privileges allowed to them due to religious tolerance and about the close of the nineteenth and the beginning of the twentieth century, they resorted to perfidious and treacherous moves to put an end to the local authority and dominion of these towns and cities where they had lived for centuries.

A manifestation of the religious tolerance of our civilization is this also that when the Muslims conquered the Christian lands, in many of their churches the Muslims and Christians offered prayers under the same roof. The Prophet himself, in his life-time offered the Christian delegation from Najran the facility of praying in one section of the mosque in their own way. Similarly, after the Islamic conquest, in the Cathedral of St. John in Damascus, which later came to be called 'Jami' Umvi the Muslims did not prevent the Christians from praying in their own way. Rather, they very open-heartedly allowed the Christians to pray there. And the Christians willingly surrendered half of it to the Muslims, who prayed there side by side with the Christians. It would certainly have been a treat to watch the Muslims and the Christians praying under the same roof side by side, the former facing their Qiblah and the latter facing East. It was a novel phenomenon which has a unique position in history, and speaks volumes about the Islamic civilization being free from religious prejudice and how it had been replete with religious tolerance.

Just Administration

One proof of the religious tolerance in the extreme of the Islamic state is also this that they made selection of the most capable persons and entrusted important posts to them. And in so doing they did never see what was the religious creed of these men. That is why at the courts of the Umayyids and Abbasids, and by the caliphs themselves they were held in high esteem. At Baghdad and Damascus they held charge of the schools of Medicine. Ibne-Athal, a Christian, was the personal physician of Amir Ma'awiyah, and another Christian, Sergeon, was his scribe. Marwan had appointed Athanaseus with another Christian, Isaac, to-some important posts in Egypt. Later they were promoted to the high post of the Treasury officer. This man was high-placed and also extremely rich. He had four thousand slaves. He came to own several villages and gardens. And there was no count of silver and gold in his possession. He got a church built in Al-Raha, out of the rent of the four hundred shops that he owned. His reputation as a learned person attained such a position that Abd-al-Malik, the Umayyid Wiph entrusted, to his care the education and training of his younger brother, Abd-al-Aziz, who became later on governor of Egypt. He is the person whose son was the renowned caliph, Umar bin-Abdal-Aziz.

Among the Christian physicians that were honoured with high ranking jobs there was also one George, son of Bachtesu. He was in great favour at the court of caliph Mansoor, who held him in great esteem and had provided every thing for his comfort and ease. George had an old wife. Mansoor sent him three slave girls, which offer he declined saying, "My faith does not permit taking other wives in the presence of the one I already have." Mansoor was much pleased to hear it and raised his rank still higher. When George fell ill, Mansoor called him to Dar-ahdhiafah (Guest House) and came to see him in person. George sought permission to return to his native land so that he may be buried by the side of his ancestors. Mansoor asked him to embrace Islam so that he may find a place in heaven. But he said in reply, "I would like to be in the company of my ancestors whether they live in heaven or hell. Mansoor laughed at this joke of his and ordered preparations for his journey home and with a gift of ten thousand gold pieces, he arranged his return home.

Similarly, another Christian Salmavaih, son of Banan was the personal physician of Mu'tasim. When he died, Mu'tasim was very much grieved, wept bitterly over his loss, and ordered that he should be buried in the royal fashion according to the ceremonies of his own religion.

Similarly, Bachtesu, son of Gabriel was the personal physician of Mutawakkil, and held a high position at his court. This person rivalled the caliph himself in the abundance of riches and magnificent dresses and pomp and glory.

No Discrimination

Closeness to the rulers and conferring of honour by them was more or less the same with the literati and the poets. The poets and literati were honoured at the court of Hams Ummayyah and Banu Abbas and other Chieftains, without any discrimination, the only condition being excellence and expertise. We all know what position Akhtal held at the Ummayid court. He had the permission of the caliph to approach him any time he was pleased. So he came to see the caliph Abdul Malik any time of the day or the night, when he was seen dressed in a silken gown and a cross, amulet fashion, suspended by a golden chain from his neck and droplets of wine rolling down his beard. He is the same person who had reviled the Ansars of Madinah in which he had said, "And disgrace and reproach lie beneath the turbans of Ansars." At this the Ansars (helpers) of the Prophet were very much grieved, and they sent one of their elderly men, N'oman bin-e-Bishr, who had the honour of being a companion of the Prophet, to Abdul Malik. He saw Abdul Malik and taking off his turban showed its interior and his own scalp to him, saying, " Where is 'disgrace and reproach' here?" Abdul Malik himself apologised for this insult and pacified him with earnest supplication, but did not call Akhtal to account for his arrogance and insolence.

In this matter of religious tolerance the outstanding persons were also open-hearted like their caliphs. Their circle of friendship and religious co-operation were not limited to their co-religionists. For example, Ibrahim bin-e-Hiiai who belonged to a particular sect Sabian of the Magians got appointed to a high position in the government and who welcomed and valued poets very much. But his social circle was not limited to his co-religionists. Rather, he was on very good terms with the Muslim learned men and men of letters, an idea of which can be had by the fact that on his death, Sharif Razi wrote a long poem known as "Qasidah waliah", when it is well-known that Sharif Razi was the leader of Hashimites and head of the Shiite community. He says in his Qasidah (Eulogy):

"Did you notice whom they took away on planks,

And did you see how the fire was extinguished."

"I did not know before thy burial,

That mountains could also be buried in graves."

And Sharif Razi kept remembering him even after that and wrote elegies on proper occasions. Once he passed by his grave (were the Magians given burial to its dead? Or only their Sabian sect buried its dead? The issue is open to contention and needs some research work), and burst into tears. Some of the verses of the elegy written on this occasion are given here:

"I say to the way-farers passing this way to come to this (grave) that I may show them a seclusion-loving branch of greatness and eminence."

"I mourned your loss to lighten the burden of my grieved heart, but the pain increased; the elegies do not lessen the grief of calamities."

"I know it is not gainful to mourn your loss, but the longings have made me all the more aspirant."

The Court of the Learned Ruler

Under the patronage of the caliphs, the academic circles always attracted men of learning of various creeds. Mamun-Rasheed had an academic circle of his own in which he met men of learning of many creeds. He had advised them to keep their discourses and discussions confined to the learning and art, and not bring in their religious scriptures to their aid in reasoning, which was the source of rousing communal passions and creating untold difficulties.

Popular Appeal

The same is true of general national academic circle. Khalaf binal-Muthanna says that he happened to attend, in Basarah city, the meeting of an academic circle comprising ten persons, each one of whom was unique in his own branch of learning having no rivals far and near. These ten persons were:

1. Khalil bin-e-Ahamad, the well-known Grammarian, belonging to the Sunni sect of the Muslims.
2. Humairi, a poet and a Shiite,
3. Swaleh bin-e-Abd-al-Quddus, an atheist.
4. Sufyan bin-e-Mushaji' belonging to the Safwi sect of the Kharijites.
5. Bishar bin-e-Burd belonging to the Sho'ubi sect.
6. Hammad 'Ajrad who was a nationalist atheist.
7. Ibn-e-Ras-al-Jalut, the well known poet who was a Jew.
8. Ibn-e-Nazeer, a philosopher who was a Christian.
9. 'Umar bin-e-al-Mu'ayyid, a Magian.
10. Ibn-e-Sanan Al Harrani, a poet and a Sabian.

These people used to sit together, discussed various problems, poems were recited, historical events were discussed, in such a friendly atmosphere that nobody could suspect that they belonged to conflicting creeds.

Domestic Life

This religious tolerance was common in families and homes also. So often it was witnessed that out of four brothers living in the same house, one professed the Sunni Creed, another was a Shiite, a third was Mu'tazalite and the fourth was a Kharijite, and all the four were living in a spirit of perfect unity, love and concord. Similarly this situation was also witnessed that out of the two brothers living in the same house, one remained occupied with his devotional acts and the other in his ludicrous fun and frolic. In this connection a very interesting event has been narrated in literature. Two brothers lived together in the same house, one a very pious person, putting up on the ground floor, and the other an impious transgressor living on the first floor. Once it happened that some equally impious friends of this drunkard gathered together at his place and made such a din and noise with their songs and music and kept it up so long that the pious brother of this transgressor could not sleep the whole night. He came out of his apartment and called out his brother saying:

> Do then those who devise evil (plots) feel secure that God will not cause the earth to swallow them up.
>
> (AI Quran XVL: 45)

> To which his brother said:

> But God was not going to send them a penalty whilst thou wast amongst them. (Al Quran VIII: 33)

Respecting Others' Culture

Similarly, on the occasion of the festivals of other religions and sects, the Muslims participated with great enthusiasm. After the Ummayid dynasty, the Christian held their religious meets beside the public thorough-fares and went in processions on public roads. In these processions some people bearing crosses led the procession and their religious leaders in their peculiar dresses accompanied them. Once patriarch Michael entered Alexandria at the head of a magnificent procession. The front rank was occupied by crosses, torches and Gospels, and the priests were raising the slogans: "God has sent us a saviour, a pastor who is the modern St. Mark." This incident relates to the period of Hisham'bin-e-Abd-al-Malik. During the period of Rasheed, the Christians on the occasion of Easter came out in the form of a big procession holding aloft big crosses on pedestals. AI Maqdisi mentions in his book *Ahsan-al-Taqasim*, that on the occasion of the Christian festivals the markets of Shiraz were decorated. And when the Nile rose in flood and the Christians celebrated their festivals of the cross, the Egyptians also participated in celebrations with gusto.

Maqrizi writes in his book *Khitatah* that during the period of Akhshidis, the common people made great rejoicing on the occasion of the festival of Baptism. In 330 A.H. this festival was celebrated with great pomp and munificence. Mahad bin-e-Tafaj Akhshidi's palace in Amneel island was decorated with one thousand chandeliers. The nation also followed suit and countless torches, candles and chandeliers were lighted. Thousands of Muslims and Christians gathered round water tanks and reservoirs. The house tops and the banks of the canals were packed to capacity. People put on their best dresses and vituals were brought in silver and gold vessels. That night the gates were not closed and most people bathed and dived in tanks under the impression that bathing on the night of the festival of Baptism was beneficial to countless maladies.

The Tolerant Regime

And still more amazing is the fact that these manifestations of tolerance and love were conspicuous even during the period when crusades were raging. And this behaviour continued unaltered although the western powers had risen against the Islamic countries and had assaulted them with great fury. AI-Rihalah Ibn-e-Jubair says:

"What was most curious about this period was the fact that the Muslims and the Christians were engaged in a deadly war, and on many occasions it had been witnessed that both armies were facing each other in perfect battle array, but the delegations of the Muslims and the Christians were moving from one place to another in perfect amity and meeting people and nobody objected to this trend. The caravans were moving from Egypt to Damascus and from there to the European countries, the Muslims were paying out taxes to the Christians in their lands willingly, and the Christian traders were paying the custom duty or octroi for their merchandise in the Muslim countries and full justice and equity were being observed in these dealings. While their armies were grappling with each other, the people were living in perfect amity and peace, and the world belongs to one who dominates."

In short, the standard of religious tolerance in the Islamic civilization attained a height which has no parallel in the past history of mankind. And even the truth-loving historians of the west are in accord with this view and bear witness to it.

The well known American writer, Drapper, says: "During the period of the caliphs the learned men of the Christians and the Jews were not only held in great esteem but were appointed to posts of great responsibility, and were promoted to the high-ranking jobs in the government. Haroon Rasheed appointed John, son of Mas-waih, the Director of Public Instruction and all the schools and colleges were placed under his charge. He (Haroon) never considered to which country a learned person belonged nor his faith and belief, but only his excellence in the field of learning."

The well known historian of our own days, Wells, under the head Islamic teachings, writes:

"The Islamic teachings have left great traditions for equitable and gentle dealings and behaviour, and inspire people with nobility and tolerance. These are human teachings of the highest order and at the same time practicable. These teachings brought into existence a society in which hard-heartedness and collective oppression and injustice were the least as compared with all other societies preceding it." Again, he continues:

"Islam is replete with gentleness, courtesy and fraternity." Sir Mark Syce, writing on the qualities of Muslim imperialism during the period of Haroon Rasheed says:

> "The Christians, the idolators, the Jews and the Muslims as workers running the Islamic state were at work with equal zeal."
>
> Tirnoon says:
>
> "The faith of the Muslims did not interfere in the affairs of the poets and the musicians."
>
> Liefy Brutistal writes in his book *Spain of the Tenth Century*:
>
> "So often the scribe writing out the terms of a treaty was a Jew or a Christian, just as many Jews and Christians were holding charge of important posts of the state. And they were vested with authority in the administrative departments, even in matters of wars and peace. And there were several Jews who acted as the ambassadors of the Caliph in the European countries."

Reno writes in his book *The History of Saracenic wars in France, Switzerland, Italy and Mediterranean Islands*:

> "In Andalusian cities the Muslim meted out the best treatment to the Christians. And likewise the Jews and the Christians had full regard for the feelings of the Muslims. For example they got their offspring circumcised and abstained from taking pork."

Arnold discussing the religious thought of the Christian religious sects writes:

"But the principles of the Islamic religious tolerance do not allow such things which culminate in oppression and tyranny. Therefore the behaviour of the Muslims remained quite different from that of the followers of other religions. Rather, the Muslims did not approve of the injustices of the various sects of other religions which they had meted out to one another due to religious prejudices. This we can vouch for since we have before us the evidence of history that where the various Christian sects living as subjects of the Islamic state were concerned, the Muslims never faltered in the maintenance of balance of justice between them. A manifest example of it is that after the conquest of Egypt, the Jacobite sect of the Christians to avenge themselves of the tyranny of the Byzantine Christians of the past, took possession of their properties and churches by force. But the Islamic state meted out full justice to them, and all the properties and churches of the conservative Christians to which they could prove their just claims were duly restored to them."

Arnold goes on to say:

> "When we witness the justice and equity and religious tolerance of the Muslims to their Christian subjects in the early days of the Islamic state, it becomes very evident that the propaganda of the west regarding spread of Islam by means of sword is not credible and worthy of attention."

In our discourse on the theme of religious tolerance and freedom of religious thought in the Islamic civilization, we have brought in detailed arguments and evidences so that the prejudiced western historians may be fully exposed in their nonsensical accusation that "Islam has been propagated and spread by means of sword, and the Muslims have forced people to enter the fold of their faith, and also that we (the Muslims) have always meted out debasing treatment to the non Muslims."

It would have been better for these prejudiced western historians to have looked into the record of their black deeds before all this hubbub and noise, lest their own guilt should come to lime-light and blacken their faces. Here, on the other hand, every thing is in broad day light in which even the myopics can see clearly how much we stand free of this mischievous charge. However, the conduct of our accusers is so disgusting that sweat should stand out on their brows with shame. For example, during the crusades (in West Asia, Tr.) and in Spain, the cruel way they manifested their religious prejudice against the Muslims, was enough to bow down the head of humanity in shame for all time to come. Rather, their oppressive crimes even against one another, no student of history dare deny. The Protestants killed and plundered the Catholics. Particularly, the bloodshed of Bartholomew is horrifying in its nature and magnitude. Again, those wars also stand to their shame and ignominy that were waged between the supporters of the Papal Order and their adversaries, the European nations. Likewise, during the Middle Ages, the barbarity of the officers of the Inquisition, who perpetrated hair-raising tyrannies on the people, are in themselves extremely disgraceful. All these events are evident of the fact that the European nations have ever been extremely prejudiced and malicious, and could never tolerate any opinion against their own and any alien creed, even if the contenders were their own countrymen and belonging to the same lineage. During their past history, there is not a single example of religious prejudice and narrowmindedness that are really at work in the background of political ascendancy and colonial policy.

Finally I would like to present the evidence of a great learned man and leader of Christianity about the Islamic policy of religious tolerance. And that witness is no other than the patriarch of Antioch, Michael, of the latter half of the twelfth century. And this is the period when the Eastern Churches had been under the Islamic rule for about five hundred years. This pariarch, writing about the religious tolerance of the Roman Christians (western

Ecclesiastical Wing Tr.) perpetrated against the Eastern Churches, goes on to say:

"This is the reason that when God Almighty, the owner of all Power and Omnipotence and One of Whose attributes is also the Lord of Retribution and Who confers the rule of the land on whomsoever He is pleased and at times honours those who have been in disgrace .... When He saw that the mischievous Christians of Rome, after coming in power, ravaged our (those of the Christians of Antioch) churches and plundered our homes, and this pillage and devastation were widespread and on a large scale. And divesting themselves of humanity they inflicted on us most grievous injury and torment. This was the time when God sent Banu Ismail from Arabia to release us from this painful torment in which Rome had placed us. Correct, that we suffered some losses also due to the domination and authority of the Muslims, such as the slipping away of several Catholic Churches from our hands and going to the people of Khalqiduniah, since they had been in their possession since long, whereas when the Muslim rule was established, whoever held a church it was allowed to remain in his possession. At that time we lost the Great Cathedral and the Church of Huran. But as compared with this petty loss what great advantage it was to be freed from the revenge of the Romans, their prejudice, their torments and their oppression and tyranny, and we are living now in a haven of peace."

And do you have in view the judgement of Gustav Le Bon?

"History is not acquainted with any nation of conquerors, kindhearted and tolerant like Arabs. Nor can history present any faith, so clear, simple, and harmless like that of the Arabs."

In this just saying of his, Le Bon has, in reality, done full justice to the truth.

FOUR

Magnanimity of the Faith

Perfection and Scope

Islamic legislation takes its philanthropy to perfection when it brings men, animals, plants, inanimate objects, the earth and the heavens to slavery of God and obedience to the laws of nature. The Quran reminds every believer in a beautiful manner in every unit (Rak'at) of the prayer:

> Praise be to God, the Cherisher and Sustainer of the worlds; Most Gracious, Most Merciful. (Al Quran I: 1-2)

And in this way it demands of every Muslim that he must always keep it in view that he is a part of the universe which is the creation of the Most Gracious, Most Merciful Creator, Whose Mercy extends to every one and everything. Therefore every Muslim ought to make himself the manifestation of His attribute of Mercy in this universe of His in which he is living and depends on it too for his needs, although God does not in the least stand in need of his devotion and service.

Hollow Claims

These were the manifestations of the philanthropy of our civilization, at work in its basic concepts also and manifest in its laws when they were proclaimed for the people. Now the question arises whether it factually behaved like that when it came in power. Or this principle just remained on paper like the Charter of Human Rights of the United Nations, whose anniversary is celebrated every year with great pomp and show, but the great powers of the world are trampling them under their feet every day, every hour throughout the year. Again, were these proncipals confined to the countries in which they had been proclaimed like the principles of the French Revolution that remained limited to the confines of France only, and those in the French dominions, colonies and those under mandatory rule were denied the privileges of liberty, equality and fraternity? Has any statue of liberty been erected anywhere else in the world like the one standing on the sea shore in New York that every one entering that country witnesses? And in the world outside, American policies and activities are practically chiding liberty, and the lovers of peace and liberty are being oppressed and crushed.

No. It was not so with the Islamic civilization. It accomplished what it professed. We ought to ask history since that is the only true witness. We ought to look at the brilliant aspects of the philanthropy of our civilization and see for ourselves what the facts, attitudes and acts of those in authority and ordinary individuals of our civilization, that are deeply impressed on the pages of history, are proclaiming loudly.

Evidences to Prove

Abu Zarr of the Ghifar tribe somehow got angry with the freed slave of Abu Bakr, Bilal of Abyssinia. Both of them were the companions of the Prophet. The altercation became prolonged and Abu Zarr in his fury called Bilal the son of a black skinned mother. Bilal complained to the Prophet, who addressed Abu Zarr saying, "Did you call him a name reviling his mother? It appears you still retain vestiges of Jahilryah." Abu Zarr took it to signify, some sort of sexual immorality, and meekly questioned in surprise, "At this ripe age, O Prophet of God?" The Prophet said in reply, "Yes, you are his brother (and should be considerate and kind to him)". Abu Zarr who had by now understood the significance of the Prophet's remark, was ashamed and repentant and out of extreme repentance and humility requested Bilal to trample his face with his feet.

It happened once during the period of the Prophet that a woman of the Bani Makhzoom tribe, Fatimah, was found guilty of theft. She was brought to the Prophet so that she might receive her due according to the Shari'ah. The Quraish very much resented it since it involved their tribal prestige and dignity. So they thought of intercession by somebody for the remission of her punishment.

It was therefore decided after deliberation to send Usamah bin-e-Zaid for such intercession since he was very much in favour with the Prophet. So he was approached, prompted to intercede and he talked to the Prophet on this issue. The Prophet was very angry and said to Usamah, "You intercede in the matter of the limits prescribed by God?" Then he had the people called and harangued to a big gathering of the believers in a touching manner, saying, "The people before you who met their doom, discriminated between the patricians and the plebians in the dispensation of justice for crimes like theft. The high-placed were spared while the weaker elements of society were readily punished. By God if Fatimah hint-e-Muhammad had committed theft, I would have amputated her hand also. "

Qais bin-e-Mutatiah, a hypocrite, once came to a gathering where Salman Farsi, Suhaib Rumi, and Bilal Habashi were also present. He remarked tauntingly, "Aus and Khazraj have rendered some service to this person (the Prophet, Muhammad Sal'am), but I fail to understand what have these people (Bilal, Suhaib and Salman) done (to deserve this honour). Mo'az bin-e-Jabal was there in that gathering, and catching hold of. him by the scruff of his neck, he dragged him to where the Prophet was seated and told him what he (Qais) had uttered. The face of the Prophet became ruddy with anger, and dragging his sheet after him, he proceeded towards the mosque. The usual summons for the gathering of the believers in the mosque were given and the Prophet harangued to them saying, "O ye people ! Always remember that your Lord and Cherisher is one and your supreme ancestor is one, and your faith is also one and the same."

Adi Bin-e-Hatim came to Madinah before embracing Islam and found the companions sitting around the Prophet. They had just returned from some skirmish and some of them still had the armours and helmets on. Adi witnessing the awe of the Prophet and their reverence for him was himself inspired with awe. Meanwhile a humble woman of Madinah came to the Prophet and requested to see him in private. The Prophet readily agreed to talk to her in any street of Madinah named by her. Then he got up and at some distance from the gathering talked to her for a sufficiently long time, and having finished with her came back to the gathering. When Adi witnessed this state of affairs, he was very much touched by this inconceivable concept of philanthropy and embraced Islam.

When after twenty-one years of hard struggle, the Prophet conquered Makkah and those who had falsified him, had driven him out of his home and had been waging a war with him, were brought before him vanquished, even then he called them to the same thing and kept in view those principles which he had preached bare footed in the vales of Makkah or had enforced in Madinah as a ruler when he was laying the foundations of a new civilization in the Islamic history. That day he proclaimed those principles which he had been preaching while he had not yet gained his final victory. Standing at the gate of the Ka'bah he said, "O ye people of Quraish ! Allah has, this day, put an end to your pride of the *jahilyah* and also the pride of your ancestry. Keep in mind! All men are the offspring of Adam, and Adam was fashioned out of clay". The Quraish who held an exalted position in the Arabian society, and had a high opinion of themselves, listened to him in silence with bowed heads. On this occasion he recited the following Quranic Verse which he had been reciting off and on:

> O Mankind, We created you from a single (pair) of a male and a female, and made you into nations and tribes, that ye may know each other (not that ye may despise each other). Verily the most honoured of you in the sight of God is (he who is) the most righteous of you. (Al Quran XLIX: 13)

When it came to the period of the Caliphate of Abu Bakr, he came forward as a ruler whose heart was full of sympathy for mankind. Notwithstanding his position as the head of the Muslim state he came to the girls of the locality whose fathers had become martyrs in religious wars. He milked their goats for them and assured them that his new responsibilities would not stand between him and his routine of benevolent acts such as that.

'Umar comes as a glorious Caliph. He is sympathetic to the weak, is firm in his stand by the truth, and all are equal in his sight. He goes without food to feed others, and keeps himself deprived to give to others. He goes from door to door asking people about their conditions of living, and is well known for his activities in this behalf. For example, once he saw an old man begging in the market-place. He questioned to ask him about his identity. He said that he was infirm and old (unable to work for his sustenance) and was therefore begging to pay Azyah and keep something for his daily bread. He was from the Jews living in Madinah. 'Umar said to him, "Old man! We have not done justice to you. In your youth we realized Azyah from you and have left you to fend for yourself in your old age". Holding him by the hand, he led him to his own house, and preparing food with his own hands fed him and issued orders to the treasurer of the Bait-al-mal that that old man and all others like him, should be regularly doled out a daily allowance which should suffice for them and their dependents.

'Umar was going through a lane in Madinah, when he saw a very lean and thin young girl moving along shakily. He said, "In what a sad plight this child is ? Does anyone of you (his companions) know who she is ?" Abdullah bin-e-'Umar being closest to him said, "O Amir of the believers! you do not recognize her." 'Umar said, "No, I do not." He told him that she was his own daughter. 'Umar'again asked him, "Which of my daughters is she?" Abdullah bin-e-'Umar said in reply, "She is such and such of my daughters (meaning that she was his Umar's own grand-daughter)". 'Umar asked him, "Why then is she in this pitiable condition!" Abdullah said in reply to his father, "Whatever is in your charge, you give us nothing from it: This indigence of mine has brought her to this sorry state". 'Umar said in reply to his complaint, "By God! I have nothing for you more than I can give out to the believers in general, whether it meets your needs or not. The Book of God stands to decide justly between us."

Once a caravan came to Madinah. It had women and children too with it. 'Umar said to Abdul Rahaman bin-e-Auf, "Can you stand guard on them tonight?" So 'Umar, the second Caliph, and he, kept awake that night together and kept vigil over the caravan. During that nighly vigil they both offered Tahajjud (late night and early dawn) prayer also. 'Umar on hearing a baby's cry and approaching, said to the mother, "Fear God and do look after your child carefully." Saying this he came back to his own position. Once again he heard it crying, and going over to her mother once again gave her the same advice. When during the last part of the night the child cried once again, "Umar came to its mother and said, "Woe to thee! Thou appears not to be a good mother. How is it that thy child could not sleep peacefully during the night." The woman little suspecting that she was speaking to the Amir of the believers, said in reply, "God bless you man, you have pestered me several times during the night. I want to wean it forcefully (before time), but the child is intractable." `Umar asked her, "And pray, why wean it forcefully?" She said in reply, "Because `Umar grants allowance only for such children that have been weaned. " Umar asked her, "How old is your child?" And she told him it was only a few months old. And `Umar asked the woman not to be hasty in weaning her child. and then he led the morning prayer in such a state that his weeping made the recital of the Quran inaudible and unintelligible. At the end of the prayer he said, "Umar is ruined. He killed the children of the believers!" And at this, he ordered the crier to proclaim in the town of Madinah that the mothers should not wean their children only for the sake of the allowance for the suckling. From now on, every child, suckling or weaned, shall receive a stipend. And it was also proclaimed throughout the length and breadth of the Islamic state.

The Mankind to Learn

By God! The entire history of mankind is unable to produce such a brilliant and glorious incident. None among the civilizations of the world can present any personage like 'Umar. He kept awake the whole night, keeping guard over the caravan and the caravan slept in peace. And we should keep in mind that he was the head of the Islamic state, and wielded great authority and power that had conquered the then mighty empires of Rome and Iran. And in spite of all that, he did what even a petty guard detailed to patrol the vicinity of a caravan in its sojourn would not do. He drew the attention of the crying child's mother to her babe and asked her to quieten it. Is there any one who can mete out that treatment to the children in a passing Caravan, like 'Umar? Who is there among the greatest personages of the history of mankind who can even touch the great human consciousness of Umar?

And this is not all. Our civilization has still more glorious incidents to present. 'Umar's servant Aslam relates that he came out with 'Umar one night, and went far out on a fact finding mission to distant hamlets on the outskirt of Madinah.

From a distance we observed fire aglow far off. 'Umar said, "I believe the darkness of the night and the cold have compelled some horsemen to sojourn here. Let us go and see." We proceeded at a brisk pace and reached that spot. We saw a woman sitting there with some children around her, a pot boiling on fire, and the children crying. 'Umar greeted her and asked the woman about her condition and also what was going on there. The woman told him that the darkness and cold had forced her to stay there for the night. 'Umar asked her, "Why are these children crying?" And the woman said in reply, "They are hungry". Then 'Umar asked her, "What is there in that pot on fire?" The woman said, "Only water to console the children so that they may remain quiet and go to sleep. And God alone shall judge between us and 'Umar". What the woman wanted to convey was that 'Umar was not fair and just to them. 'Umar said to her, "My good woman! What does 'Umar know about your state of affairs?" To which she retaliated, "Why then should he hold the high office of the Caliph when he is unaware of our condition?" Aslam relates that 'Umar said to him, "Let us go now". "And we started from there with all haste," Aslam goes on to say, "and reached the godown of provisions (of the Bait-al-mal) and 'Umar took a bag of flour and container of fat and asked me to load the bag on his back. I offered my services but he angrily brushed aside my offer saying 'Can you relieve me of my burden on the Day of Reckoning also?' So I loaded the bag on his back, and then we hastened towards our destination at a fast enough pace and soon he put down the bag and taking out some flour from the bag gave it to the woman and asked her to knead it while he himself offered to fan the fire to a flame. So he started blowing the fire below the pot. His beard was thick and I saw smoke percolating through his beard. He went on blowing at it until the food was ready, and he asked the woman to bring some vessel. And when she brought a platter, he poured out the contents of the pot into it and asked the woman to feed the children while he himself fanned to cool it. We sat there until all of them had eaten to their fill. What was left of the flour and fat was handed over to her and then 'Umar got up and I followed suit." The woman said, 'God bless you. You are more deserving of that high office than the Amir of the believers.' 'Umar said to her, 'Say only a good word. When tomorrow you come to see Amir of the believers, you will find me there, God-willing.' After that 'Umar went to some distance and retraced his steps and hid himself close to their place of stay. I said to him that it was not proper on his part to observe them from the place of his concealment. But he kept quiet. We saw that the children were playing merrily and then they went to sleep. 'Umar thanked God and got up and turning to me said, 'Aslam! Hunger was gnawing at their stomachs and they were miserable and could not go to sleep. I would not have been at ease until I had seen them happy and comfortable. So I looked at them from my position of vantage. You have also seen that they have gone to sleep perfectly at ease."

One of the unique incidents relating to sympathy and equality in the history of mankind is that 'Umar came by one night. It was usual with him to go out during the nights to see with his own eyes the conditions under which people were living. One night he found himself in one of the many valleys of Madinah. All of a sudden he heard somebody crying in a nearby tent, at whose door was standing a man. 'Umar greeted him in the proper manner and asked him who he was. He said in reply that he was a beduin who had come to Madinah to ask the Amir of the believers for help. Then 'Umar asked him about the crying and wailing inside the tent, which question the beduin tried to evade, saying that since it did not concern him, he should not interest himself in it and go his way. Little did he know that he was talking to the Amir of the believers. However, on the insistence of 'Umar he told him that his wife was in labour pain and had no one to help her with the delivery. 'Umar came back home and asked his wife, Umme Kulsum bint-e-Ali, whether she was interested in the reward from God which He might have brought her way. And on her asking what was that, he told her in some detail, and asked her to take with her the requisites of a new born and the delivered mother and also some provisions for food. He took all those things from her and started, Umme Kulsum following him. Soon they came to the beduin's tent and 'Umar sending his wife inside, himself sat with the husband, and lighting a fire started cooking food with the provisions he had brought with him. The beduin was even now unaware that he was sitting beside a great man of the world. Meanwhile the woman in the tent was delivered a babe and Umme-Kulsum called him from inside the tent, addresing him as Amir-al-Muminin, and asked him to congratulate his friend on the birth of his child. The beduin on hearing her words became conscious of the fact that he had been with the head of the Islamic state all this time and had been rude to him, and was awestruck and began receding from 'Umar. But 'Umar reassured him and asked him to keep sitting where he was, unceremoniously. And then he asked Umme Kulsum to offer the mother the food that he had cooked. And when she had eaten, he offered food to her husband, saying "Partake of it, you have kept up the whole night and have been inconvenienced. Come to me tomorrow and I shall see to it that your needs are provided." When he came to him ('Umar) the next morning he granted an allowance for his new born babe and he too was liberally helped.

No Parellel

So far as my information is concerned, I can say with certainty that there is not a single incident as glorious, outstanding and based on the sentiments of fraternity as the one cited above, anywhere in the lives of the greatest men in the history of mankind. There is an incident connected with George Washington the savour of America that he was once going along the road when he saw that some soldiers were trying to lift a stone but were unable to do so. Their supervisor was standing close by but not lending a helping hand. George asked him to come to their help, but he refused saying that it was below his dignity. Washington kept his sheet on one side of the road and helped them lift the boulder, and said to them when departing that whenever they needed help in difficulty of that type they could enlist his help at such and such address.

Certainly this is a unique incident and is an example of a high standard of morality. But it stands no comparison with the incident of 'Umar cited above. 'Umar sacrificing his sleep and comfort of the night came out to find out the condition of the people, when he found a woman passing through the pangs of labour, having no one to help her, he came home, took his wife with him and loaded with provisions himself and the wife with the needs of the mother and the new born infant, to go to the tent of a beduin far from the town in the darkness of the night. The wife, who, in our present day terminology, was the queen, plays the role of a maid-servant, a mid-wife, and he himself takes up the role of the cook. Is there a single example of this height of man's psyche? The height which was never attained by any ruler of a state on this globe. This is one of those brilliant incidents that go to make 'Umar so great, and also one of the dazzling aspects of our civilization that it moulded a simple beduin Arab like 'Umar into a personage that even today occupies the highest stand among the great men in the history of mankind, just as our civilization stands out among the civilizations of the world, topping the list.

Here we must also mention that 'Umar is not an isolated example presented as a perfect and affectionate person by our civilization. There are many-rank after rank. The lives of Abu Bakr, Uthman and 'Ali (God be pleased with them all) were also moulded in the mould of perfect humanity, brimming over with mercy and affection. Also the lives of 'Umar bin-e-Abd-al-Aziz, Salahuddin Ayyubi and many other big personages, the 'ulama', the legists, philosophers and leaders also present countless immortal examples, which is a brilliant evidence in favour of our glorious civilization from every aspect.

The Ideal Culture

Some authors have defined civilization as a collective system which helps man to the utmost in collecting the fruits of culture. Civilization is composed of four elements, economic means, political setup, moral principles and regulations and consolidation of sciences and arts. For the organization and development of civilization certain geographical, economic and physical elements are inevitable. For example faith, language and education and training. And for the demolition of the edifice of civilization too there are certain elements which are just the opposite of the former (ensuring its building up). Some of them are moral and ideological infirmity, disturbance of law and order, spread of tyranny and poverty, rampancy of wretchedness and indifference, and paucity of sincere and capable leaders. The story of civilization begins from the time when man got peacefully settled on earth. The links of civilization are interconnected, without interruptions, which every nation has been transferring to its successor through the ages. Rather, the above mentioned elements are responsible for its existence. Perhaps there has been no ummah in the history of the world which has not made additions to the pages of the history of civilization. However, what distinguishes one civilization from another is the strength of the foundations on which these civilizations have been founded, and the effects which this civilization has come to bear on humanity as a whole and the benefits conferred by it. The more philanthropic according to its universal nature, the more moral in keeping with its leanings and the more realistic in its principles, the more lasting and immortal and respectable it will be regarded.

Our civilization too is a link in the chain of human civilizations. Many civilizations have preceded it, and many more shall be following it too. There were some factors responsible for the establishment of our civilization and there were some causes of its degeneration. But those causes and factors are outside the ambit of these discourses, since we have limited ourselves in these talks to what it was when once it was established. But before coming to talk about the attraction of this civilization, we ought to mention a little of the magnificent part played by it in the history of man's evolution, and its beneficence of a perpetual nature to the nations of the world in the fields of beliefs and learning, art and literature, rule and the state-craft. So we see that the most outstanding peculiarities that attract a person studying our civilization are the following:

This civilization rests on the foundation of the creed of the unity of God. So this is the first civilization on the stage of the world that calls man to the One and Only God, Who has no partners in His sovereignty and rule. Only He must be worshipped and He alone must be taken for the goal, and refuge must be sought in Him alone.

Thee do we worship and Thine aid we seek.

(Al Quran 1: 4)

He it is who endues with honour or brings low. In His hand lie all beneficence and bounties.

There is nothing between the heaven and the earth that is not under His Power and in His Grip. This was the miracle of absorbing the sense and the demand of the unity of God which elevated man's position and freed the common people from the oppression of the kings and the chieftains, and the hold of Papacy and Brahmanism over them. It set right the relationship of the ruler and the ruled and turned their eyes to the One and Only God Who is the Creator of all the created things and Cherisher of the Worlds.

This creed had such a profound influence on the Islamic civilization that it stood out among all the former civilizations of the world, and in its creed, administration and poetry and literature it became free of all manifestations and manners of idolatory. That is why the Muslims have abstained from translating *Iliad* and other heathenic pieces of Greek literature, and in spite of being experts in engraving, painting and other types of decorative arts, mosaic and other patch works, and architecture, they did not go far into the field of portrait painting and idol-making. Islam has openly declared a war against idolatory and did not permit making the statues of the leaders, the virtuous, the prophets and the conquerors, whereas such statues are regarded as the most outstanding manifestations of old and new civilizations, since none of these civilizations attained the position of Islam in the creed of the unity of God.

This creed of the unity of God created that colour of unity and uniformity whose stamp is borne by all the impressions and effects of our civilization and the phenomena in its minor details. That is why here there is unity in the message and goal, unity in legislation, unity in the enterprises relating to the masses, unity in the collective from of social intercourse, unity in the means of subsistence and way of life, unity in the pattern of thought, so much so that those studying the Islamic arts have observed the unity of style and taste at work in the various kinds of the Muslim creations of art. You may take a piece of ivory from Andalusia (Spain of the Islamic days), Egyptian cloth, an earthen-ware made in Syria and a piece of jewellery fashioned from Iranian minerals, notwithstanding the variety in form and design, appear to bear the same stamp (of the unitarian culture).

The second peculiarity of our civilization lies in its embracing the entire humanity according to its leanings and trends, and the universality of its message and mission. The Quran had declared the unity of mankind in spite of the variety of race, family and homeland, in these words:

> O mankind! We created you from a single (pair) of a male and a female, and made you into nations and tribes that ye may know each other (not that ye may despise each other). Verily the most honoured of you in the sight of God is (he who is) the most righteous of you. (Al Quran XLIX: 13)

When this declaration of the Quran laid the foundation of the unity of mankind on truth, good and the fear of God, in the thread of its civilization were strung all the intelligent and shrewd persons of every ummah and nation conquered by Islam. That is why every other civilization can only take pride in the renowned persons of only one nation (or race or region). But the Islamic civilization can take pride in all the distinguished sons of all those nations and tribes who had joined hands in building the edifice of this civilization. Abu Hanifah, Malik, Shafi'i, Ahmad, Ai-Khalil, Sebawaih, AI-Kindi, AI Fara', AI Farabi, Tbn-e-Rushd and many other renowned men, notwithstanding their alien racial and regional affiliations were all regarded the sons of Islam, through whom the Islamic civilization had presented the best results and fruits of healthy thought before humanity.

The third characteristic of our civilization is this that it has assigned priority of place to the moral principles in its entire system and all its activities. It has never lost sight of these principles and never made them the means of the material benefits for the rulers, parties or individuals. Application of moral principles has always been kept in view in governance, learning and arts, legislation, peace and war, economy, and familial affairs. Rather, the height of perfection and excellence attained by the Islamic civilization in this behalf has never been reached by any old or new civilization, and the traces and impressions left by this civilization in this connection are marvellous. Rather, this is the one and only civilization which has guaranteed only prosperity and good fortune for mankind and has kept it away even from the shadow of wretchedness.

The fourth peculiarity is this that this civilization has faith in the true principles of knowledge and learning, and makes the chaste principles and the tenets of belief its nucleus. It has addressed intellect (thought) and heart (sentiments) simultaneously. From this point of view it stands out among other civilizations. Again, it is a peculiar characteristic of our civilization that it has designed a system of statecraft based on faith and belief without their being any impediment in the growth and development of the state and the civilization. Rather, the faith is the most important factor in their development. The radiation emanating from the mosques of Baghdad, Damascus, Cordoba and Granada had illumined the then known world. Islamic civilization is the one civilization which does not separate the faith from the state. But in spite of this intimate mingling of the two it experienced none of those evils which had overtaken Europe during the middle ages. The Muslim state is headed by an Amir or Caliph (President). But the rule is not in his own right or the eminence of his person. It is, on the other hand, for the establishment and the maintenance of the Truth. Undoubtedly, the president is the caliph or Amir of the Muslims and legislation is the business of the experts of the law and every category of the learned men has a particular service of the state assigned to it. But all stand equal before the law, excellence and superiority, if any, depending on an individual's fear of God and service to mankind. A certain woman, Fatimah by name, is brought to law for the crime of theft, and when intercession on her behalf is sought, the Prophet of God is filled with righteous anger, and tells the intercessor:

> "By God, if Fatimah bint-e-Muhammad had been found guilty of it, I would have cut off her hand (unflinchingly)."
>
> (Bukhari and Muslim)

Once the Prophet said:

All mankind is the family of Allah. So the most beloved of God is he who is the most beneficent to His children.

This is that faith on which our civilization is founded. And herein there is no distinction or special privilege for any ruler., religious leader, any aristocrat or a wealthy person.

The Quran says:

Say, "I am but a man like yourselves".

(AI Quran XVIII: 110)

And finally, the remarkable peculiarity of this civilization is its marvellous religious tolerance which. has never been witnessed in a civilization based on the religious foundations. However, it is possible for one not reposing faith in God and any known (revealed) faith, to regard all religions equally respectable and treat their followers on an equal footing. But the follower of a faith who is convinced that his faith is true and his creed is the truest and most accurate. And then he is afforded a chance of lifting the sword, conquering lands, and ruling and sitting in judgment over them, and even then his faith and beleif do not allow him to be a tyrant in his rule, to pervert the administration of justice and to compel people to enter the fold of his own faith, such a person would really be regarded a strange creation. Therefore how amazing and isolated would be the situation that there was an entire civilization founded on religious bases and built on these principles, but in spite of all that it might have adopted the behaviour of utmost tolerance, justice and equity, and humanity. This feat has been accomplished by our Islamic civilization, and many examples of this behaviour will come before the reader in the discourses we are going to present in the following pages. It is enough for us to learn that our civilization is unique in this behalf, that it established only one faith, but its blessings benefited all other religions.

These are some of the peculiarities and distinctions of our civilization in the history of civilizations which had amazed the world, and were the cause of attraction for the serious and intelligent people of every religion and *millat*. That was about the time when this civilization dominated the world, was in power, was in a position to turn the world round in the right direction and could and did educate and train the world. But when this civilization was on the decline and another civilization took birth, there was some difference of opinion about the worth of our civilization. Somebody looked down upon it, some one else praised it. One man recounts its merits and excellence and another exaggerates in finding faults with it. The professional critics of the west are divided in their opinion about our civilization. They were not competent to arbitrate and sit in judgment on our, civilization. But what to do. They hold the norms of judgment these days, and their opinions are accepted. They hold sway over the world and the reins of civilization are in their hands. And the people and their civilization on whom they are pronouncing judgments are so infirm that the powerful nations have covetously fixed their gazes on them so that, what little remains with them, they may snatch away from them and holding sway over their land they may quench the fires of their avarice. Perhaps this is the stand taken by the strong against the weak that the former disdains and finds faults with him. That is what the mighty have done with the helpless in every age, with us as the only exception that when we were powerful we dealt equally justly with the strong and the weak, and had recognized the excellence wherever it existed whether in the East or the West. Who can come up to us in the matter of just rule, the purity of objectives and constancy of conscience in the history of the world.

It is really regrettable that we are not aware of prejudice of the powerful nations of the world and their unjust opinion about our civilization. Many of them are blind-folded by the religious bigotry and they are unable to witness the truth. Or else the national prejudice at work in them does not allow them to recognize the excellence of any other nation. But that we ourselves are influenced by their opinions of us is not understandable. We are unable to understand why some individuals of our own *millat* look derisively at this civilization which is their own, and at whose feet the whole world has bowed down for centuries.

Process of Deterioration

Perhaps the argument of those who make light of the worth of our civilization, is this that in comparison with the inventions and conquests in the practical field of the modern civilization our own civilization stands nowhere. But even if this assertion be accurate, it does not lower the dignity and exalted position of our civilization on two accounts. The first reason is this that every civilization comprises two elements, a moral and spiritual element and the other a material element. Where the material element is concerned, the succeeding civilization undoubtedly has superiority over the preceding one. This evolution in life and its resources are in accordance with the Divine law, and it is in vain to expect the preceding civilization to have all that the succeeding one has acquired in this behalf. If this had been justifiable we would have been justified in looking down upon all those civilizations preceding ours, since our civilization too had invented such resources of life and phenomena of civilization of which the preceding civilizations had no trace. So the material element is not the true basis for the determination of any lasting and abiding excellence among the various civilizations.

As for the moral and spiritual element, it is this that makes any civilization immortal, and through which humanity comes by good fortune, and is safeguarded against all hazards and griefs. In this field our civilization has left behind both the preceding and the succeeding ones, and has attained a stage of evolution unparalleled in the history of cultures and civilizations. This one fact is enough to make our history everlasting. The real purpose of civilization is this that man may attain the height of blessings and good fortune, and the service our civilization has rendered towards this end has not been achieved by any other civilization in the East or the West.

The other reason lies in the fact that civilizations are not compared on the strength of material standards. The paraphernalia of a civilization and its material monuments are not the proper basis for comparison. Taking rich food and passing a life of luxury is no argument in support of cultural superiority. In this matter the true norm of finding the excellence of a civilization is the assessment of its lasting influence on the history of mankind. The same is true of wars and empires. They too are not compared on the basis of the areas of their empires or the number of fighting men that took part in any war. If the wars waged during the distant past and the middle ages are compared with the second world war in the matter of the number of fighting forces and the military hardware, the former pale into insignificance. But those old wars too have great importance and historical significance, since they. have resulted in farreaching effects on the history of mankind. The battle at Caunae (Italy-216 B.C.) in which the world-renowned Carthaginian general, Hannibal, had badly defeated the Romans, is on the list of those wars which are taught in the military schools of Europe (from the point of view of military strategy).

The great feats of Khalid bin-e-Waleed in the conquests of Iraq and Syria are still under study of the Western experts of warfare and they still marvel at it (his military genius, strategy of wars and temerity): And these wars are the brightest chapters of our wars and conquests. The battles of Caunae, Badr, Qadisyah and Hittin cannot be lost sight of, just because they belong to the distant past, since they are the milestones in the history of mankind.

After this brief discourse, I am sure, the eyes must have been lifted to witness the beautiful manifestations of our civilisation that I am going to present, although justice cannot be done to the theme here. It suffices for me now to present in my ensuing talks the fascinating aspects of our civilisation, and argue in support of the immortality of this civilization, established and consolidated by the Muslim ummah, and on which has been conferred the title of the "Best Ummah", by the wisest of the judges, that has been brought into the field of action for the good of humanity.

FIVE

Universal Impact

In an earlier discourse of mine pointing out the outstanding peculiarities of our civilization, I had stated that the more abiding the ideological, moral and material impressions left by the civilizations in the history of mankind, the greater their perpetuity. Our civilization played a magnificent role in the history of the evolution of man, and has left farreaching effects and strong monuments in the fields of creed and ideology, learning and arts, state-craft, philosophy and literature. Let us see what are those impressions and monuments and what is their significance.

We can take up the eternal impressions of our civilization under five different categories:

Basic Principles

The principles and preliminaries of the Islamic civilization have left a very deep impression on those reformative civilizations of Europe which have been rising from the seventh century of the Christian era to the modern times. Islam is that faith that imparted the lesson of the unity of God and forcefully impressed that He has no partners in His Sovereignty and Authority, and also that He is free from anthropomorphism, injustice and tyranny and defects and shortcomings. Islam has also made it very clear that man in his devotional acts, in strengthening his relationship with God and to understand the Divine Laws, does not stand in need of the mediation of priests or the clergy and such other classes (of professional men who have insisted on interposing themselves between man and God and even false claims of intercessing with Him on his behalf, for their own personal ends and enslaving man in every age, Tr.). In opening up the minds of the nations and guiding them to these firm principles, Islam has acted as a powerful factor. Before this the nations of the world were in the strong grip of the most violent kind of religious despotism and leadership, which had held their thought and opinion incarcerated, and their bodies and their goods too were in their possession. It was the natural consequence of the conquests of Islam in the East and West that the nations around the lands directly under the Islamic rule, must be first of all influenced by the creed and ideology of Islam. And that was what actually happened. So in the seventh century of the Christian era many reformers arose in Europe who were against idolatory and image worship. In later times arose such people who refused to take men as mediators between God and His slaves, and invited people to understand the holy books totally independent of the clergy and the Pope. Many researchers have vehemently asserted that Martin Luther, (1483-1546, leader of the Protestant Reformation in Germany) in his reformation movement was influenced by the Arab philosophers and Muslim learned men in the religious lore. Long before this the writings of the thinkers of Islam had been translated into Latin, and during Luther's time the European Universities depended on and reposed trust in them in their educational programme. We can also say that the state set afoot during the course of the French Revolution, was the product of those powerful ideological movements which pervaded Europe for three hundred years or even longer, and our civilization had influenced these movements through crusades and through (the Muslim rule in) Andalusia or Spain of today.

Source of Knowledge

In the fields of Medicine, Mathematics, Chemistry, Geography and Astronomy too our cultural impressions are outstanding. The awakening in the field of learning in Europe was the result of that instruction that the Europeans had received from our 'Ulama and philosophers in Isabella, Cordoba and Granada as their students. The students from the West, when coming to our centres of education, were amazed to find that the doors of these sciences and arts were open to every person (without any discrimination Tr.) and every one could benefit from these sciences and arts devoting himself to them with great enthusiasm and concentration in a free atmosphere, since there was no parallel in their own land. At the time our 'Ulama were dealing in their lectures and in their compilations the scientific facts like the revolution of the earth and its spherical shape and the movements of the heavenly bodies, the minds of the Europeans were filled with lot of nonsensical ideas about these facts. It was here that the movement of rendering into Latin of the Arabic texts started and the books written by our 'Ulama were being taught in the European educational institutions. *Al-Qanun* on the theme of Medicine by Ibne Sina was translated in the twelfth century. Razi's *Al-Havi* which is much more voluminous than Avicenna's *Canon*, got translated about the end of the thirteenth century. Upto the sixteenth century Europe depended on this material on Medical Science from the Arab sources for their teaching and practice of Medicine. Where the profuse literature on philosophy is concerned, its teaching continued there even longer, and Europe got acquainted with Greek philosophy through our compilations and translations. That is why many European writers confess that during the Middle Ages we have been the teachers and instructors of Europe for at least six centuries.

The learned author, Gustav Lebon says, "for five to six hundred years books in Arabic language and particularly on various disciplines have been almost the only source of learning and teaching in the European universities. And we can safely assert that in certain disciplines like Medicine the impressions of the Arabs are still at work in Europe. The Medical writings of Ibn-e-Sina have been explained about the close of the last century in Monabiliah". The same author says further, "Roger Bacon, Leonard, Erno A1 Felquni, Raymond Lot, San Thoma, Albert and Azfonish Qashqani have solely depended on Arabic books". Monsieur Renan says, "Albert, the Great, is indebted to Ibn-e-Sina and San Thoma owes it all to Ibn-e-Rushd." The famous orientalist Sideo writes, "During the middle ages, the Arabs alone were the standard-bearers of a civilization". The Europe that had been ravaged during the onslaughts of the northern tribes, its barbarism had been removed by the Arabs alone. The Arabs gained access to the ancient Greek philosophy and not contented with acquiring this knowledge, extended its scope vastly and opened up new avenues for the study of the Universe. The learned author also says, "When the Arabs gained expertise in Astronomy, they paid special attention to Mathematical sciences and gained a high degree of excellence and they were really our teachers in this field." He tells us that when we take stock of all that got transferred from Arabic to Latin, we find that a great doorway was made in the name of Gerbert Salifster II, through which during the period between 970-980 A. D., all those sciences he had acquired in Andalusia had entered Europe. And the learned English author O' Hallard toured Andalusia and Egypt, some time between 100 and 1200 A. D. and translated from Arabic *Al-Arkan*, by Euclid, which had been unknown to the West so far. Another learned person Plato Taiquli, translated *Al-Arkan* by Theodosius, from its Arabic version. Rudolf Bnsgie translated from Arabic Ptolemy's book on Geography of the inhabited Earth. Leonard Baige, wrote out about 1200 A.D., a treatise on Algebra which he had picked up from his Arab teachers. Kunbanos Nausy has done the best translation of the Arabic text of Euclid during the thirteenth century. Also Fastaloon of Bologne drawing upon Hasan bin-e-Haitham's book *Al-Basariyat* propagated the astronomical science in the West. In 1250 A.D., Azfonish Qashqani ordered the publication of astronomical almanac which took its name from him. During this period on the one side, Roger I ordered the study of Arabic sciences and arts, particularly those written by Idrisi, and on the other, Frederick II, highly stressed learning of sciences and manners. The sons of Ibn-e-Rushd were always with him at the court and taught him the natural history of the plants and animals. Homeld writes in his book on Science, "It was the Arabs who for the first time invented the method of the chemical preparation of medicines, and it was from this source that sound advice and the procedure of experiments came to us, which were taken up by the School of Sairnm and from there after a long time spread to Southern Europe. Then the medicinal and natural elements on which medication entirely depends became the cause of the study of plants'

Chemistry. In this way both these studies went on simultaneously in two different ways and thus the door on a new era of the study of this science was opened by the Arabs. There was sufficient proof of the vast Arab knowledge of the plant kingdom that they made addition of two thousand herbs to those of Zulefuredas. There were many herbs in their pharmacy that the Greeks had not even dreamt of. Sideo says about Razi and Ibn-e-Sina that both of them pervaded the educational institutions throughout Europe for a sufficiently long time. Particularly so, Ibn-e-Sina who got introduced to Europe as a physician. For full six hundred years his works held sway over the educational institutions of Europe. His book *Al-Qanun* (Canon) was translated in five volumes and had repeated reprints, since the instruction in the universities of France and Italy totally depended on it.

Promotion of Literature

The western people and particularly the Spanish poets have been very much impressed by the Arabic literature. Horsemanship, chivalry, metaphor and fine and unique topics have found their way to the western literature through the Arabic literature of Andalusia. The famous Spanish writer Abanese writes: "Before the entry of the Arabs into Spain and the spread of their stables, horses and horsemen throughout Southern Europe, horsemanship and chivalry were unknown in Europe." In the book written by Dousie on the topic of Islam, he has quoted a letter of Algharu, a Spanish writer, who has lamented very much the indifference of the Europeans to Latin and attachment to the Arabic language, which shows that in those days the western men of letters were very much impressed and given to the Arabic learning and literature.

He says:

"The intelligent persons and men of tastes have been bewitched by the Arabic lyrics. So they look down upon Latin, and leaving aside other languages communicate in the official language. A contemporary surging with patriotic zeal has regretfully stated that his Christian brethren have been fascinated by the Arabic lyrical poetry and tales, and study the books written by Muslim philosophers and legists. They do not study them to prove them wrong or to refute them but to pick up eloquent Arabic style. Who else, save the clergy, studies the commentaries on Torah and Injil (Old and the New Testaments)? Who is there to recite the gospels and the books of the prophets and the apostles? Alas! the younger generation with the new trends of thought does not look approvingly at any save the Arabic language and literature. They derive light of guidance from the books written by the Arabs, establish libraries comprising these books and sing praises of the Arabic treasures of learning and literature everywhere. When they hear of the Christian literature, they scowl and argue that it is not worth their time and attention. Alas ! the Christians have forgotten their own language. You will not be able to find one in a thousand who writes letters to his friends in his own tongue. But where Arabic is concerned, there are many who express themselves in its best style and write poetry in it which may excel even that written by Arabs in accuracy of idiom and eloquence."

During the fourteenth century and later there have been many renowned men of letters whose literary writings and style bear the lasting impress of the Arabic literature. In 1349 A.D., Boccaccio, (1313-75 - Italian novelist, poet and humanist, author of *Decameron*), has written stories under the Caption 'Ten Morns' (*Decameron*), in which the style of world renowned stories, *The Arabian Nights*, has been imitated. Shakespeare has derived the theme of one of his plays from this source. And the German playwright Lissing has borrowed the plot of his drama *Natan, the Physician* from the same source. Chaucer (1340-1400), the father of modern English poetry has drawn upon Boccaccio most. They had met in Italy, and it was after that he had written his *Canterbury Tales*. Similarly, the famous poem of Dante (1265-1321), *Diving Comedia* in which he has recounted the tales of his journey to the other world. It has been said that Dante, at the time of writing this poem, had on his mind deep impressions of the treatise "Gufran" by Abul-ula' AI-Mu'arri and all that Ibne-Arabi had written about the Genii. The reason is to be sought in the fact that he had lived in Sicily during the rule of Emperor Frederick II. This monarch was fond of cultural pursuit and pastimes, studied the cultural literature in the Arabic language. And he used to have discussions with him (Dante) on the Aristotlian theories. Their sources of information were the Arabic books. Dante was acquainted with the life of the Prophet Muhammad (Sal'am) and the details of the Ascent of the Prophet and the accounts of the heavens furnished by the holy traditions.

The period of the life of Peter of York corresponds to the period when the Arabian culture held sway over France and Italy. He had been educated at the universities of Monabliyah and Paris. And both these universities had been founded by learned men who had received instruction and training at the Andalusian universities, and the books compiled by the Arab authors were taught there. The stories rife among the Arabs during the middle ages had a deep impact on Europe during the renaissance. These include stories of chivalry and horsemanship and other feats of strength and valour that the renowned Arabs had performed for the sake of love and magnificence. In this connection the translations of *The Arabian Nights* into European languages had a profound effect on the European fiction. More than three hundred editions of this book have been published in the European languages. So much so, that several critics of Europe are of the opinion that the travelogue by Swift and Defoe's *Robinson Crusoe*, are both indebted to the *Arabian Nights* and *Ha'i bin-e-Nafeezan* by the Arab philosopher Ibn-e-Tufail. Nobody can entertain any doubts about the fact that the repeated publication of *The Arabian Nights* reveals that the Europeans have made it the centre of their attention and have been very much impressed by it.

Here it hardly needs mention that in various European languages, many Arabic words relating to the necessities of life, are used in almost their original form. For example Cotton, Damask, Musk, Lemon, Zero are really the Arabic words *Qutn, Harir-e-Damishqi, Limmun* and *Sifar*. And there are innumerable other words of that sort. Without going into details in this connection it would be enough to quote Mr. Michael: "Europe for its finest literature is indebted to the Arab countries. Similarly, the spiritual and ideological recollection during the Middle ages, had certain forces at work at its back, and the Arab nation had a great deal to do in putting them into action."

Law and Law Making

The European students who were being educated in the educational institutions of Andalusia, had translated the Muslim literature on Fiqh and enforcement of the Shari'ah. Europe at this time had no firm political system, nor were there any laws based on equity and justice in force there. When Napoleon conquered Egypt, the well-known compendiums of Fiqh of the Malikite School were translated into French. To begin with, *Kitab-e-Khalil* was translated which served as the seed (basis) for the French Law. So we find that the French Law of that period was to a great extent resembling Fiqh of the Malikite School. Sideo says : "Our searching gaze rests on the Malikite Law, since we have had contacts with Africa, and France had ordered its competent learned men to translate into French the short compendium on Fiqh compiled by Ishaq bine-Yaqub (D. 1422 A.D.)."

In ancient times and even during the middle ages the right of common people to call their rulers to account was not recognized. The relationship of the ruler and the ruled was that of the master and the slave. The ruler was a despot and treated the people as he pleased. The dominion was regarded as inheritance which got transferred along with other effects of the passing out monarch. So much so that if a princess inherited the throne and got married to another ruler in an alien kingdom, the two countries found themselves at war for their shares in the land of the princess.

Again, when two kingdoms were engaged in a war, the conqueror came in possession of not only the conquered land but also the lives, property, honour and dignity and freedom of the vanquished people became permissible to him. These conditions lasted for a long time until the era of the Islamic civilization dawned and it became dominant, and along with other principles propagated by it, it also declared that the people have a right to criticize and call to account their rulers, and the latter are only the trustees and employees whose duty it is to honestly guard the interests of the people. So it was for the first time in the history of the world that the subject publicly asked the ruler to account for the dress he had on at the moment. And the ruler neither condemned him to be hanged for his impudence nor imprisoned him, nor exiled him. On the contrary, the ruler explained his position and rendered account of the cloth that went into his mantle, which satisfied the objector and the rest of the assembly.

And this also happened for the first time in the history of mankind that an individual from the common people addressed the president of the state thus, "*Assalamu-Alaikum* (Peace and blessings of God on you, O you (our) employee!" And the Amir admitted that he was certainly an employee and like one it was his bounden duty to serve the nation sincerely and to render his due relating to this trust. The Islamic civilization declared this principle and practically demonstrated its application and enforcement.

It was this spirit of the freedom of thought and conscience which was infused into all the nations that existed around the Islamic society. All these nations took a turn, became dynamic, prepared themselves for a revolution, and at last breaking their chains became free. Throughout Europe this process was repeated. During the crusades the Europeans entered Syria. Before this they had witnessed these phenomena in the caliphate of Andalusia that the people kept a strict watch over their rulers, and they were responsible to their own people and not to any one else. The European rulers observed that the Muslims in every period looked to Islam and their rulers instead of being subservient to any particular individual or class were accountable to the entire nation. And as against this, they themselves were dominated by the Roman Emperor. And unless they recognized the religious dominion of Rome they had to face failure and disappointment. So when these rulers returned to their own lands they rebelled against the Roman authority and finally became free of vassalage. And as the next step the peoples of these lands rose in revolt against these monarchs and breaking the shackles became free. The French Revolution came much later. And it declared no such principle that had not been declared by our civilization twelve hundred years earlier.

The principles that our civilization had declared are that the treaties must be respected, there must be complete freedom in the matter of creed and the places of worship must be allowed to remain in the possession and under control of those worshipping in them. The personal freedom and honour and dignity of people should not be violated. It was the observance of this principle which helped create in them a spirit of dignity and self-respect and the basic traits of nobility and humanity were awakened in them. So, the history witnessed for the first time the scene that an individual of the non-Muslim subjects complained to the head of the Muslim state that the son of his governor had flogged his (complainant's) son. The president of the state became infuriated on hearing this complaint he called the governor's son to account and he was flogged by the oppressed. Then he scolded the culprit's father, (the governor) saying, "Since when you have enslaved them when their mothers had borne them free."

This was a new spirit that our civilization infused in the nations and the individuals. Otherwise the father who had boldly taken his grievance from Egypt to Madinah completely certain of its redressal, was mercilessly beaten, his possessions were plundered, and force was used in the matter of his creed, before the advent of our rule and civilization redeemed him. But what to say of rebellion, he dared not stand in protest or express grief on being oppressed. Rather, the sense of self-respect was lacking in him. When the sun of our civilization rose on him, his voice was raised and addressing the Amir of the Believers, he said, "I seek refuge in Allah against your oppression." What was this oppression? It was neither blood-shed, nor violation of chastity, nor compulsion in the matter of faith, nor confiscation of property. It was a minor issue of one boy having given another boy a few cuts of lash.

The western people got introduced to our civilization through Syria and Andalusia during the middle ages. Before this the monarch dared not say a word against the religious leaders and the people against the monarchs. They lacked a sense and knowledge of the fact that calling the ruler to account, or the support of oppressed is their basic right. They were used to slaughtering each other like butchers slaughtering goats, on the basis of the difference in creed. When they came in contact with us, the sentiment of awakening and freedom was created in them, which at last obtained liberty for them. Is it possible even after all this to deny the part played by us in liberty, humanity and freedom of action. If these are some of the ever-lasting traces of our civilization in five different major departments of life - and these are the most outstanding manifestations in the life of nations and civilization - we can justly assert that the nations in whom our civilization has infused the spirit of liberation from bondages, are indebted to us. But we would not like to square this deal by false boasts of the past glory and nursing equally false hopes and longings. All that we want is that we may be able to create self-recognition in ourselves so that we became aware of the worth of our civilization and the importance of our inheritance. And once again we may create in ourselves the capability of becoming the "Best Ummah", which may discharge the duty of being witness to the truth, and may show humanity the way to goodness, truth and nobility. And God willing, we shall be able to do it.

And the grace to do things comes from God alone.

It is not possible for a person discussing our immortal civilization and its impressions, to lose sight of one such peculiarity of our civilization in which it stands out among civilizations. This peculiarity is the love of man. Our civilization, while ridding mankind of hatred, malice, dissention, has taught it the lesson of love, generosity, co-operation and equality. In keeping with the Islamic law and the Islamic social principles, no question of superiority on the basis of race, class, or nationality arises. This principle is conspicuously at work in the bases of our civilization and its finer details.

Where the Islamic principles and elements are concerned it has declared that all men are the offspring of a single pair, Adam and Eve:

> O mankind! reverence your Guardian Lord, who created you from a single Person, created, of like nature, His mate, and from them twain scattered (like seeds) countless men and women. (AI Quran IV: 1)

So humanity comes from the same origin. And it was from this common origin that people got divided into tribes, countries and classes. Their example is that of different brothers and sisters born out of the same parents. Such being the fact, the variation of classes and nations should only be a means of mutual recognition in good deeds. The Quran says:

> O mankind! We created you from a single (pair) of a male and a female, and made you into nations and tribes, that you may know each other (not that ye may despise each other). (Al Quran XLIX : 19)

After that some individuals advance in life and others lag behind. Some become prosperous and others indigent. An individual becomes the ruler and a nation becomes subjugated. Some are white-skinned and others get tanned or even become black.

And now all this is in accordance with the natural laws and the unchanging system of life. But certainly it does not mean that these discrepancies and this unevenness should be allowed to become the cause of distinctions and dissentions. The prosperous have no superiority over the indigent, the ruler over the ruled and the white skinned over the black. At the basic level of humanity they are all alike. Superiority, if any, lies in Taqwa or the fear of God:

> The most honoured of you in the sight of God is (he who is) the most righteous of you. (Al Quran XLIX : 13)

They are all equal in the sight of law and the law equally holds sway over and is superior to them all. Distinction shall be made on the basis of truth and justice only. The Quran says:

> Then shall any one who has done an atom's weight of good see it! And any one who has done an atom's weight of evil, shall see it. (Al Quran XCIX : 7-8)

In the collective form all have an equal position. The powerful of them supports the weak. And in this way the entire society serves every individual. A tradition of the holy Prophet, says:

"The powerful of them supports the weak. And in this way the entire society serves every individual." Another tradition of the holy Prophet, says:

> "The example of the Muslims in the matter of mutual love and affection is that of a body. When one of its organs is

> affected with disease, all other organs suffer from fever and sleeplessness in sympathy." (Muslim and Ahmad)

Thus, Islam has been constantly proclaiming that humanity is a unity, and all its individuals are the offspring of the same parents. Human society is like a tree that when the wind blows all its branches at all levels, high and low, without distinction, move to and fro. From this it can be easily understood that the Quran addressing mankind as "O ye men" or "O ye children of Adam", is for the reason that it wants to create and impress the concept of the unity of mankind. Similarly, the followers of Islam have been addressed as, "O ye who believe" and "O ye believers", and no racial or class distinction were allowed.

Islam for Equality

Where the laws of our civilization are concerned, every aspect of them is pervaded by man's equality. In prayer they all stand before God in the same capacity (as slaves of God), there being no place of distinction reserved for any monarch, chieftain or a learned person. In fasting too, they all abstain from food alike, there being no distinctive facility for the rich. And on the Hajj pilgrimage, people are all clad alike (in a white shroud) and stand alike. And there is no distinction of any kind whatsoever made between (those living) far and (those living) near, the strong and the weak, and the classes and the masses. Then if we look at the civil code, we find that one and all are treated on the basis of the truth and justice. The main objective of legislation is dispensation of justice. The law lifts its banner to check people from injustice, so that all aggrieved and deprived persons may find refuge under its shade. Again, when we come to study the criminal law, we see that all men are equally liable to punishment in case of violation of the legal limits. The murderer gets murdered, the thief gets punished for theft and whoever is guilty of violence is admonished and corrected. The murderer may be a learned person or an ignorant clod and the murdered person may be rich or poor "whoever has been oppressed may be an Arab or a non-Arab, may belong to East or West, they are all equal in the sight of Law."

> The free for the free, the slave for the slave, the woman for the woman. (AL Quran II: 178)

The Islamic Law is still more magnanimous, and irrespective of faith, race and colour, it honours the entire humanity. The Quran declares:

> We have honoured the sons of Adam. (XV1I: 70)

This honour is the birth-right of all persons, and with respect to creed and knowledge and the mode of living provides the same opportunities for all men. It is the duty of the Islamic state to support them in all these matters without distinction. The Islamic Shari'ah takes man to an even higher plane, and says that decisions shall be taken by God in matters of the rewards and punishments not on their outward appearances and acts but in accordance with their intentions (*niyat*).

The Prophet says:

> Certainly, Allah does not look to your forms and countenances but to your hearts. (Muslim)

Rewards and punishments depend on intentions. So we find the following tradition of the Prophet, which has been reported by all the Traditionists:

> All acts depend on intentions and there is for everybody what he intended. (Unanimous)

And along with that Islam has also pointed out that the intention agreeable in the sight of God is that doing good, beneficence and seeking the countenance of God must be intended and no material or commercial objectives must be in sight. The Quran says:

> And adore your Lord; and do good; that yet may prosper.
> (Al Quran XXII : 77)

For this good turn that is done only to seek the countenance of God, it is not right to expect any return form the person benefited. The Quran has said:

> And they feed for the love of God, the indigent, the orphan, and the captive, (Saying), "We feed you for the sake of God alone; no reward do we desire from you, nor thanks. "
> (AI Quran LXXVI: 8-9)

SIX

Justice for All

Another aspect of the philanthropy of our imperishable civilization is that it strengthened the bases of real equality irrespective of colour and race. So after the proclamation of the Quran, "Verily the most honoured of you in the sight of God is (he who is) the most righteous of you, (XLIX-13), the Prophet said in his last harangue on the occasion of Hajj before his departure from this world:

"All men have sprung up from Adam, and Adam was fashioned out of clay. No Arab has any, superiority over the non-Arab, nor a white-skinned person over a black-skinned one, save for Taqwa (fear of the displeasure of God)."

Practical Example

This equality was not one which would have been proclaimed on a few formal occasions, as is customary with the sons of the western civilization. Rather, it was real equality applicable to various situations in life, which was at work like the routine of life which neither amazed anyone nor any affectation or show found any place in it. So this equality stepped into the mosque where people came for a devotional act and to humble themselves in the extreme before their Lord, Most High. Those who attended the mosques were a medley of men of every colour and race and stood shoulder to shoulder on the same floor in an attitude of extreme humility and devotion. And never a white-skinned person was afflicted in mind that a black-skinned nigger was standing by him. Similarly, this equality got infused in Hajj ceremonial also, where different classes of men, white and black gather there around the sanctum sanctorum of Ka'bah. They perform the ceremonials together, in the same dress (a white shroud), without any distinction between the white and the black or any superiority of the white over the black. And history has witnessed and recorded the scene of the height of equality when on the occasion of the conquest of Makkah, the Prophet ordered Bilal of Abyssinia to mount the roof of Ka'bah to proclaim the Truth and call the faithful to prayer. We can well imagine, that Kabah which is called the Abode of God, which was a sanctum even during the days of Jahiliyah and has the most privileged position of being the Qiblah of the believers, a negro slave has the same sanctum under his feet. This is an instance which is unimaginable even in this (so called) age of enlightenment and the civilized world. For example, in America (where the blacks have segregated colonies and schools, churches and hotels, and the whites and blacks do not mix at all). But Islam, not today, but fourteen hundred years earlier, had demonstrated it practically. Bilal's mounting the roof of Ka'bah was really the general proclamation of the fact that man has superiority over every thing in the universe. And man becomes deserving of this honour and dignity on the basis of his belief, his knowledge, his morality and his intellect and not on that of his flesh, bones or race and colour. Therefore the colour of the skin of a person cannot advance him if his record of deeds has thrown him back. Nor can any one's black skin push him backwards if his intellect, discernment and power of interpretation and decision have advanced him forward.

That is why Abu Zarr Ghifari notwithstanding his position as a high ranking companion of the Prophet, when, once in a rage called Bilal 'O son of a Negress', the Prophet did not tolerate this much of intemperance on his part, admonished him and said, "You still smack of the evil traits of Jahiliyah, (that you tried to disgrace him by lowering the dignity of his mother on the basis of colour)".

This is the point which marks the line of demarcation between knowledge and ignorance. In other words it demarcates the real human civilization and the civilization of the Jahihryah (un-Islam).

Only a far-sighted man of superb nature can establish and develop such a civilization, in which no one race has any superiority over another race. And only this civilization can become a cradle of good fortune for the honourable and dignified humanity. And the civilization in which the whites have superiority and the blacks are despised and wretched, the whites are deemed fit for all the comforts and luxuries of life and the blacks are distressed and helpless, is a civilization of the Jahihryah, which pushes man thousands of year back, into the dark ages This is a blind, ignorant, arrogant civilization steeped in stupidity. Although the Prophet said to Abu Zarr "You (still) smack of (the evil traits of) Jahihryah," but what this sentence really signifies is that conscience which goes into the making of every civilization of Jahiliyah that discriminates between man and man on the basis of the land of birth, blood, tongue and colour. It was such civilizations that the Islamic civilization confronted in every walk of life, in the mosque, in the courts, in the field of leadership, and has treated the friends and foes alike in this matter.

When the Muslims invaded Egypt and advanced far into the country until they reached the fort of Bablion, Maquqas, the ruler of Egypt sent a delegation to talk to the Muslims and find out what they wanted. He also expressed a desire to receive a delegation from the Muslims. Therefore, 'Umro bin-al-'As sent a delegation comprising ten persons. This delegation was led by 'Ubadah bin-e-Samit and he alone was authorized to talk to Maquqas. 'Ubadah was extremely swarthy and he was of a very tall stature. When this delegation approached Maquqas to talk to him, he was over-awed by his appearance alone, and he said to the members of the delegation, "Keep this black person away from me, and bring forward some-body else to talk to me." The members of the delegation with one voice said to him, "He is superior to us in intellect, opinion and insight and in every other way. He is our leader. We all turn to him for his opinion and advice. Moreover, our Amir has given him some particular instructions, and has ordered us not to go against him in any matter whatsoever." At this Maquqas said to the delegation, "How could you agree to make him your leader and superior, whereas he ought to have been your subordinate?" To this the delegation replied, "How is it possible when he is superior to us in knowledge and nobility, as well as in opinion and insight? As for his swarthiness, we do not mind it, and as such it is no disqualification for leadership." Maquqas was confuted and said to 'Ubadah, "Come forward, you swarthy one, but talk to me in a gentle tone. Your mere sight sends a shiver down my spine, and if you were to talk to me in a harsh tone, my distress shall be all the greater." 'Ubadah noticing this much fear of himself said to him, 'My brother! There are a thousand persons in our army more swarthy than I."

Just think over, how bright is this aspect of the Islamic civilization, and how lofty is the position of man in it. People, one and all, regarded swarthiness a defect (and the so-called civilized men of today regard it a blemish even in this age of enlightenment and intellectualism), and behaved in a manner as if the black-skinned men were not human beings, and advancing them and conferring on them a high position in knowledge and opinion was simply unimaginable to them. But when our civilization came up, it put an end to all such false notions and norms. False ideas were looked upon with derision, and if his knowledge, sound opinion and daring could advance a person of swarthy skin, the Islamic society was not found niggardly in advancing him. 'Ubadah bin-e-Sarnit was no isolated example, whom the Islamic civilization exalted to the position of the leader, but hundreds of such examples can be cited.

Abdul Malik bin-Marwan used to have it proclaimed during the Hajj season that no other but Ata' bin-e-Abi Ribah who was the religious leader, learned man and legist of the Meccans, should pass religious verdicts. Shall we tell you what Ata' looked like? A black skinned, squint-eyed, lame and flat-nosed and curly-haired person (like .the negroes), whose sight even for a short time may be disagreeable. And when he was sitting among his students it appeared as if a crow was sitting in a field of cotton. But it was this black, squint-eyed and flat-nosed person whom our civilization made a religious leader (Imam), and people turned to him for his religious verdicts. He was in his own person a school of thought from whom benefited myriads of bright faced learned men. And to these disciples of his, he was honourable, lofty and lovable.

In our civilization and society there have been several such experts of superb excellence who racially belonged to the Negroid group and were black-skinned. But their black skin did not prevent them from making headway in the field of learning and literature and become such literati who became the courtiers or associates of the extremely fine tastes, or from becoming legists and writing such books to which may turn all those working in the fields of Islamic learning and literature - for example' Uthman bin-e-Ali Zela'i who wrote a commentary on Kanz-al-Daqa'iq, of the Hanafi school of jurisprudence. Or Jamaluddin Muhammad bin-e-Abdullah bin-e-Yusuf Zela'i, (D. 762 A.H) who wrote an authentic and famous book like *Nasib-al-Rayah*. Both these men hailed from "Zela," in Abyssinia. Again Kafur Akhshidi is also a well known person. He was a black-skinned slave who ruled Egypt in the fourth century A.H., and whose name has been immortalised by the famous poet Mutanabbi through his satire and eulogy.

Dignity of Action

In short, our civilization never discriminated between the blacks and the whites placing them in different classes or in conferring distinction otherwise. Nor was there any colony established for the blacks totally segregated from those of the whites, nor the rights of the blacks were so curtailed which could give the whites the upper hand, and they might be compelled to put up with the violence and excesses of the whites. Rather, ours is such a real human civilization which values humanity. It looks upon all men under the norm of the truth and good, and in its sight the blackness and whiteness of their acts counts and not that of their skins. The Quran has said:

> Then shall any one who has done an atom's weight of good, see it And any one who has done an atom's weight of evil, shall see it. (Al Quran XCIX: 7-8)

A Great Lesson

Correct, that after the period of the past fifty years the fact that discrimination between man and man on the basis of the colour of their skins is foolishness, and no developed civilization can tolerate it in its society. And our society, in particular, well-known for its love and equality among the civilizations of the world, can never tolerate it. So our dilating on this peculiarity of our civilization appears rather odd. But it is a tragedy that in this era of progress, and in spite of formation of the United Nations Organization and proclamation of the Charter of Human Rights we are constrained to write on such problems, since the curse of the racial discrimination (apartheid) in South Africa is before us and we keep hearing vexatious things about it day in and day out. The fearful tyrannies of colonialism in Kenya are before the world. The sad plight of Negroes in America is no secret, and still more amazing is the fact that not a single individual of those upholding apartheid in South Africa, those perpetrating economic crimes on the blacks of Kenya and those severely tormenting the Negroes in America, belongs to the East who could be taunted for conservatism, backwardness and foolishness. They are all the sons of the self-styled cultured and developed nations of Europe and are regarded the outstanding members of the United Nations Organization. These so called sons of the civilization of Europe are never tired of ridiculing the men of the East for backwardness, conservatism and prejudice. But what they themselves are doing is not hidden from the public view. The governments guilty of these crimes are those that are regarded the important observers of the United Nations. America controls the entire institution of U.N.O. Britain is that big and important (it is neither big nor important now and is unable to solve its own problems both political and economic Tr.) power in Europe that is proud of its democracy (and oldest democratic institutions. South Africa is their African outpost that is acting as the agent of the colonialism of white Europe in that part of the world. And it is the Britishers that are ruling over it (South Africa). This too is counted among the civilized nations of the world. South Africa is also an important member of the U.N.O., and among the middle class member governments of this body it has a say. As the standard-bearers of civilization, these are some of those governments that are perpetrating the worst crime of the history of mankind right in the twentieth century, which is nowhere traceable in man's history. The crime of man oppressing man, his own brother, not because he is infirm and ignorant but only because he is black.

The government of South Africa has adopted the policy of apartheid, and has aportioned separate rights and obligations for the black and the white nations, and notwithstanding the constant protest and strong opposition of the Afro-Asian group of the U.N.O., insists on that policy. Britain is crushing the patriotic and freedom-loving movement, Mao Mao, in Kenya and resorting to their massacre. There it is insisting on the Land Reforms Act of 1915, according to which only twenty nine thousand white men have been made the owners of more land than four million and fifty-five thousand Africans. And these Africans are attacked in their homes, while at work in their fields, when it is they who are the real owners of that country and rightly deserve to have all the wealth and the government in their hands. Mr. Seer Eliot, the first and independent delegate, appointed in 1955, explains the policy of the government of Kenya, in a statement of his, like this: "The existing condition in Kenya under mandatory rule is this that all land there belongs to the white men. And it will be hypocratic on our part not to say in plain language that the whites have perfect domination in Kenya. The politics, policies and legislation in Kenya clearly show that a white colony is being established there. Even today the Western rulers of Kenya are pursuing a policy whereby all lands may go to the white men, and they may utilize their produce and the rest of the bounties as they please."

"One of the queer laws of land of that country is also this that if the area of the land does not exceed five thousand acres, the rulers have the powers to allot that piece of land on 999 years lease for a mere pittance. And this has resulted in every European having on an average five hundred acres per head. But as compared with it the real citizens of Kenya have only 8 acres per head when they are the real owners of all land in that country. Moreover, to keep the blacks and the whites segregated, totally separate residential areas have been allotted to the black population they can never visit the colonies of white men. And when the latter stand in dire need of the bonded or very cheap labour they take work from them but drive them away from their lands as soon as the work is over. They would not have put up with even this much of contact with the blacks if they could do without this cheap, almost bonded labour." (Things have entirely changed long since this was written. Tr.)

The Face of the West

When we take stock of the American blacks we come upon pathetic conditions of tyranny and oppression and for once the observer is terrified. America is a new continent and claims to be civilized. Every one on landing at the New York port of America, comes in view of the Statue of Liberty that greets every visitor to this land of George Washington and Abraham Lincoln. Below the statue the visitor finds engraved the following words:

"Hand over your helpless, afflicted and enslaved people to us so that they may be able to live a life of freedom. Send to me the flotsom and jetsam of your densely populated coast-those who have neither an abode nor a homeland of their own. See here I am at your service, standing with this torch near the Golden Gate."

Yet in this country with high sounding claims to liberty, in the biggest town and port of which stands this Statue of Liberty, the blacks are being tyrannized. This is the worst crime of the history of mankind. We would not like to say anything ourselves in this behalf. This country itself confesses that it is doing all this. And the fact of the matter is also that. And whatever is being done is deliberate and America is unabashed. A member of the Senate, Mr. James Bazanz, says :

"No black person has the right to even bring to mind the idea of political equality, as is happening in the Southern States. This country belongs to the whites and shall remain in that position."

The oppressions and tyrannies to which the Negroes are subjected are of different kinds and the crimes perpetrated in different fields. To examine the field of culture and civilization only, we find that in about twenty states of USA, the black population is barred from receiving instruction with the whites in the same school or college. In the Article 257 of the Constitution of Mississipi it has been clearly stated that

"In this field-that of education and training-it will be kept in view that the children of the white men and those of the black ones should be separate. So there will be two different types of schools for the two of them."

The state of Florida deemed it necessary to discriminate even in the matter of the syllabii, and the books taught to the whites and the blacks are quite different. In all the states of America, no white man can marry a black woman nor the other way round. In the state of Mississippi such a marriage is constitutionally void. Rather, there a white person cannot marry another with even one eighth of his or her blood out of the black stock.

The discrimination in the field of the work of labour is so much that far from a black person sitting on the same table with a white person, the former cannot enter even through the gates reserved for the white men.

Socially, the racial discrimination is that in fourteen states of USA in a railway train the black persons have to sit segregated from the white men. There are separate arrangements for the Negroes in railway trains, buses, telephone booths. In the hospitals too there are separate rooms for the Negroes, so much so that even in mental hospitals white mad men are kept segregated from the black mad persons, and the former enjoy special privileges even here. And still more amazing is that proclamation made by the officer in charge of the Burial ground of dogs in Washington. He said in it that he would not allow the dogs of black men to be buried in the graveyard of white men's dogs. The owner of that graveyard admits that the dead dogs have no "objection" to the burial of their own brethren, however belonging to black men, even if they were to be buried in the same pit. But how can their civilized masters tolerate that their honourable dogs be buried beside one belonging to some black person. How could they be guilty of the "heinous sin" of equality even at this lower level?

Sometimes the American politicians explain this shameful state of affairs by asserting that racial discrimination exists only in the Southern states, and they are not so civilized even now as those in the northern states. But apart from the fact that this is a case of adding injury to insult, the facts also give a lie to such assertions, and the true situation of the country in this respect falsifies all claims of things being any better in the northern states. In all the northern towns of America, the Negro population lives in such filthy areas in houses built with reeds and planks, abounding in filth, stinking, swarming with flies and mosquito-infested. The wooden shacks often catch fire and are completely gutted. In Harlem, the Negro locality in New York, about nineteen persons live in one room. One of their papers writes: "If we were to settle the Americans at the rate of the density of population of Harlem, the entire population of America could be accommodated in half the existing New York city." Just opposite to the White House in Washington and under the shadow of the famous beautiful statue of Abraham Lincoln, is situated the Negro quarters holding a quarter million men, about one fourth of the total population of the capital. And they are existing at the animal level - like cattle in their enclosures. And in this capital they are not allowed to enter those schools, hospitals, recreation grounds, hotels and restaurants reserved for the white men, so much so that they cannot enter the churches for the white men only. Once a Negro from the republic of Panama entered a Catholic Church in Washington and just as he was praying with due concentration, some one from the churchmen handed over to him a slip giving the address of a Catholic Church reserved for the black men. And when that priest was asked the reason for that uncivil act, he said in reply that there were Churches in that town for the Negro Catholics and this black man could worship his God there. This is the attitude and behaviour of those who give humanity the glad tidings that Christ is the saviour of mankind as a whole.

In such a disdainful atmosphere afflicted with poverty and wretchedness and prey to various maladies, about fifteen million Negroes are doing bitter existence in the United States of America, about one tenth of the total population of that country. But in spite of all that America asserts in the UNO that it is the standard-bearer of liberty and freedom and well-being and freedom of all nations.

Here we are going to give extracts from *'The Freedom of the Negroes'* a book by an American:

"Undoubtedly, nowhere except South Africa, no people has been so much abased as slaves, as the Negroes in our country. Although slavery in its popular sense has been abolished and people do not own other men and women like they own chattel. But due to a system based on classes being at work, slavery persists. And today slavery has taken a shape in which there are all sorts of provisions for a happy and prosperous life for the white people and the populations of black people may be kept under conditions of extreme lowness and humility. And for strengthening this policy, various means are adopted. So this policy is something enforced in the form of orders for murder and destruction, issued by the world armed with power and authority or in the form of tyrannical and unjust legal orders, and at yet other times in the form of such usages for which God has revealed no authority."

The famous American economist, Mr. Factor Barlow says:

"There is no doubt about the fact that the industrialists of the northern states, who had, during the American civil war, taken possession of the Federal government, had in reality no intention of emancipating the Negroes. Rather, they wanted that the southern states, that were in possession of the black slaves whom they were exploiting to their utmost advantage, should not be allowed to do so all by themselves, but they too should share this cheap labour with them. The fact is that the democratic party and the army resorted to the stratagem in the southern states that in league with the former masters of the slaves, the Negroes should be enslaved a new."

The same author says:

"The venom of the racial discrimination has spread in the length and the breadth of the country, and has seeped into the American life to such an extent that the common people have now become used to it that no opportunity should be lost of debasing and humiliating the Negroes and other minorities. And they design new interpretations and suggestions for such humiliation and vilification."

Jack Leet and Lee Mortimer say:

"America is renowned among the nations of the world in this respect that its distinctive mark is the "Statue of Liberty" which signifies that 'we welcome every visitor to our country and anyone seeking asylum irrespective of whether he has run away from the hardships of oppression and tyranny or wants to get out of the reach of the oppression and afflictions.' But it is a great pity that since this statue of liberty has been erected, the words liberty and equality have lost their meaning in America."

And lastly this incident which is so disgusting in its nature. In Columbia city in 1946, a Negro and his mother went to a repair shop to get their radio set repaired. 'When they had paid the shopkeeper the repair charges, they found on trial that the defect in their set persisted. It had not been repaired. The mother of the Negro said to the shopkeeper that he had charged them thirteen dollars and the radio set was dumb as before. This `audacity' infuriated the shopkeeper and he ordered his assistant to bundle her out of the shop. The assistant kicked the poor woman out and she fell on her face. This enraged her son who beat the servant and floored him. That raised the alarm and the white men around raised a hue and cry that the miscreant must be put to death. A crowd soon gathered that was insistent on revenge. It must be borne in mind that American's revenge against the Negro signifies nothing short of beheading him without trial. Anyway, the poor Negroes were rescued from the crazy mob and were entrusted to the police lock-up. But the fury of the mob did not abate. They fell on a Negro locality so that they might avenge themselves on some Negro woman and her son. And the Police cordoned off this quarter of the town and did not let the Negroes run to safety, with the result that the enraged mob fell on them with ravage, destruction and loot and arson. The houses were set on fire and the inmates shot at, leaving many dead and wounded. And all this oppression and tyranny and the crimes of loot, arson and murder were perpetrated because of the very much justified complaint of the Negroes that repair charges were realized without repairing her defective radio set. This is that golden example presented by the enlightened western civilization of the twentieth century.

SEVEN

People's Well-being Supreme

The greatest argument in favour of a nation being called a living nation and its rapid progress on the road to evolution, is this that the hearts of its individuals are full of the lofty sentiments of philanthropy, and it is these sentiments of that nation that furnish the strongest argument in favour of its becoming the leader of the world.

Such sentiments which not only shower blessings and mercy on the society but all the human beings and animals living on this sphere are benefited by them. They present the norms according to which the civilizations of the nations are blessed with permanence, and the superiority of one over the other or all the rest is also determined by the traces and traditions which they leave behind in this field.

High Ranks

The Muslim Ummah attained a height in this field not attained by any other nation in the history of the world, before it or even after it. The nations of the past kept the field of virtue and goodness limited to the places of worship and the seats of learning. As for the present period, undoubtedly the western nations have attained great heights in the matter of meeting collective needs through collective institutions. But they have failed to attain this high position of sympathy for human beings purely for seeking the countenance of God, which had been accomplished by the Muslim Ummah in its hey-day. Rather, the western nations have failed to attain even that position of human sympathy which was the share of the Muslim ummah in its period of degradation and degeneration.

The sentiments at work behind the good deeds of the western nations have always been a desire for fame, propaganda and pomp and show which prompted them to various public welfare works. But the Muslim ummah has kept in view only one thing in all the works of benevolence and welfare and that was seeking the countenance of God, whether their efforts became known to the people or not. In this behalf, a very good pattern is Salahuddin Ayyubi who spent all his wealth in public welfare works and filled the existing lands of Syria and Egypt with the institutions of public welfare like mosques, schools, inns and such other places. But he never named any one of those institutions after himself. Rather, he used the names of his military officers, ministers, helpers and friends for this purpose. In connection, with the welfare works it is this high norm of seeking the pleasure of God which is free from even a shadow of self-aggrandisement.

Significant Feature

There is another aspect too which is worthy of consideration. Only those people can be benefited by the institutions established there, who are the citizens of those countries or putting up there temporarily. But the doors of the institutions, established by the Muslims, were open to everyone without distinction of nationality, language or religion. Moreover, we had established these collective institutions for those reasons of well-being and collective support of people which are unknown to the western nations even today. And these reasons too are such as amaze a person even after such a long time, and one learns from them that the concept of philanthropy of the Muslim ummah is broader, better defined and more all-embracing in its scope than those of other nations.

Fundamental Conceptions

Before we take up discussion of the various forms of public welfare works, it appears in the fitness of things that the basic concepts and principles of the Islamic civilization about the public welfare may be explained. In fact, it was these concepts and principles that had such a profound influence on the individuals of the Muslim ummah and as a result these institutions came into existence, unparalleled in the history of mankind.

Islam calls man to goodness in such a way that the fear of the Satanic whispering like stinginess, illiberality and poverty and indigence cannot find their way to the human psyche. So we find that after prompting the believers to spend their substance in the way of God, the Quran goes on to say:

> The Evil One threatens you with poverty and bids you to conduct unseemly. God promiseth you his forgiveness and bounties. (Al Quran II: 268)

Islam calls every person with means and power, rather every human being, to goodness, he may be poor or rich. The rich person can do good with the power of his wealth, position and influence. As the poor or even indigent person, he ought to do it with his hands, His will and his tongue. Under the Islamic order, there can be no person who cannot do good one way or the other. During the period of the Prophet, some men with very limited means complained to him that the monied people had gone far ahead of them in the field of goodness on the strength of their wealth spent in virtuous deeds to individuals and contributions to welfare works benefiting the society. But the indigent and the needy have nothing to spend as Sadaqah. The Prophet explained to them that wealth was not the only means of doing good, but every thing that can benefit humanity in any way is a good deed and a Sadaqah. He went on to say, "Your praise and sanctification of God is also a Sadaqah. Enjoining good is a Sadaqah and so is forbidding evil. To remove thorns, stones or anything else from the path, troublesome for the wayfarers, is also a Sadaqah. And helping a person on to his mount is a Sadaqah. In this way Islam opens the doors of goodness to every body, and a common worker, trader, farmer, disciple, teacher, woman, helpless, old, blind and infirm, all can, in their own way, do good, and their economic condition does not deter them from doing a good turn to the society within their limits. Islam takes him even further and brings him to such a high position of philanthropy where the benefits of good and righteousness become common for the entire humanity, however different their languages, their countries and their nationalities may be. The Prophet has said:

"People are as if they were the children of God. So the person most loved by God is he who is of utmost beneficence to His children."

After that Islam drawing man's psyche towards good and righteousness addresses it saying that in righteousness and good lies his own benefit, and the doer of good shall be the first to be benefited by it. He will be the beloved of the people, shall be praised everywhere and shall be the topic of people's talk. And in the Hereafter he shall be rewarded for it.

> Whatever good ye give, shall be rendered back to you.
> (Al Quran II: 272)

> Whoever works righteousness benefits his own soul.
> (Al Quran XLI: 46)

Effects of Teaching

So long as man is dominated by the sentiment of individualism he must naturally look to his own benefit. But this mode of thinking had a peculiar effect on the human psyche. The miser became generous and the niggardly started giving away liberally, and his wealth was now being freely spent on other people; the thought for the morrow and the well-being of the offspring and the relatives did not trouble him now as it had done earlier, when the following verse of the Quran was revealed:

> Who is he that will loan to God a beautiful loan, which God will double unto his credit and multiply many times? (Al Quran 11: 245)

A companion, Abu-al-Dahdah, on hearing it asked the Prophet, "O Prophet of God! Does God Almighty too ask His slaves to give Him a loan ?" The Prophet replied in the affirmative. On this the companion asked the Prophet to extend his hand and to stand witness that he gave away such and such of his date-palm grove in the way of God. He went on to say, "I am its sole proprietor and there is nobody else having any claims to it." Let it be known that there were seven hundred date-palm trees in that grove. After this, the companion went home and informed his wife of his action. The family lived in this grove and the two started shifting from there at once. His wife's comment while vacating the grove was, "Abu-al-Dahdah! This bargain of yours has been extremely beneficial to you."

Establishing a Trust

When the Quranic verse was revealed:

> By no means shall ye attain righteousness unless ye give (freely; Of that which ye love; (Al Quran III;92)

Abu Talhah Ansari said to the Prophet, "O Prophet of God "Bairaha" is the most beloved of all my properties. I give it away in the way of God and look to Him for my reward. You may do what you like with it.," The Prophet said in reply, "No, it is a property that is beneficial to you. This is of great benefit to you. Keep the property itself (the grove with the well) in your own charge and give away only its produce in the way of God." This sadaqah was the first Islamic trust. And then it became catching and a whole series of trusts started and proved that major means on which the collective institutions were fed and performed their functions effectively. Rather, the trust proved a milestone in our civilization, which paved the way for all the collective institutions of public welfare.

In this connection the Prophet set a lofty example for the Ummah. He gave away as trust two groves about which some Mujahid had made out a will that the Prophet could do with them what he liked. He devoted them to help the indigent and the needy, those fighting in the way of God but in want, and such other needy persons. After that 'Umar Ibn-e-Khattab endowed his landed property of Khyber, and other companions, Abu Bakr, 'Uthman, 'Ali, Zubair and many other endowed their properties as trusts, until every companion who could give something, gave it away in the way of God. This movement started afresh during the period of 'Umar's caliphate when he himself endowed a piece of land of his in the way of God. On this occasion he called the selected individuals from both the Muhajirs (migrants) and Ansars (helpers) and made them witnesses to this testacy. Jabir bin-e-Abdullah Ansari says, "Every one of the companions of the Prophet, I know, did endow something from his belongings as *sadaqah*, which could neither be sold nor bestowed on any one nor passed on to the heirs as legacy. After that the Muslims continued this practice of endowments, generation after generation, and lands, groves, houses and the produce of the fields kept coming for the public welfare works which were needed by the Islamic society. In this connection so many institutions came into existence which appear beyond the means (apparently) at their disposal."

People's Welfare

It is not possible for us to mention here all kinds of public welfare institutions. However, some important items are being given below:

1. The first item among the public welfare institutions is the mosque. People vied with one another in building mosques to seek the countenance of God. Even the kings competed with one another in building grand mosques and in their extension and addition to their beauty and grandeur. Waleed bin-e-Abd-al Malik spent such a big fortune on the construction of the Jami' Umvi and such a large number of men participated in its construction that the facts and figures appear almost incredible at first sight.

2. Next to the mosques in importance came the welfare institutions of schools and hospitals, which, God willing, we shall take up as a separate topic later on.

3. Construction of inns and kitchens for the travellers somehow left behind by their caravan. Other persons coming that way, and in need of shelter and food could also be benefited by these guesthouses.

4. Abodes of the recluses and secluded cells meant for those devoted entirely to the worship of God and communion with him.

5. Building of houses for those indigent and needy persons who could neither build nor rent houses for themselves.

6. To provide a regular supply of drinking water on the way for way-farers.

7. To build free kitchens and eating houses for the unemployed, where bread, meat, soup and a sweet dish (halwa) were distributed. In Damascus, the patterns of the eating places

of Takya-e-Sultan Saleem and Tkyah-e-Sheikh Mohayyuddin have come down to our own days.

8. To build houses for the Hajj pilgrims in Makkah where they could stay for the duration of the Hajj. Such houses were built in such large numbers that they had covered almost the entire land of Makkah. That is why some legists issued verdicts against letting out houses in Makkah since in their opinion all the houses in Makkah were originally meant as trusts for the Hajj pilgrims.

9. To dig wells in ravines and mountain valleys so that they may serve the cattle, agricultural needs and the travellers. There were many such wells between Baghdad and Makkah, and also between Damascus and Madina they were in super-abundance. Besides they were in abundance in the headquarters of the Islamic states and also between other towns and shrines, so that in those days, there was no question of any traveller going thirsty anywhere on his journey.

10. To build outposts for frontier guards so that some unknown enemy may not attack the colonies standing on the periphery of the state. There were several such institutions exclusively meant for the frontier guards, where they lived in comfort and got all the necessities of life without any difficulty, for example, food, clothes, arms and ammunition dumps and other necessities of life. It was due to the establishment of such institutions that during the period of the Abbasids the skirmishes with the Romans came to an end. Similarly, the crusades of the western countries against Syria and Egypt came to an end.

11. After that it comes to the trusts of horses, swords, spears and other weapons of war, which provided the Mujahids with all the military hardware. This had the effect of promoting the war-industries in the Muslim countries to a very large extent and large factories of arms were established in our cities. The war-mongers of the days of crusades also went about freely in our countries during the period of armistice and made purchases of arms. It was for this reason that our 'Ulama had to pass a religious verdict against sale of arms to the enemy.

Here we must pause to see how things have taken a turn in our days. We have to beg the western countries for arms and they offer them to us only at the cost of our self-respect and independence.

12. There were also trusts whose income was meant exclusively for those venturing out to fight in the way of God, and for those men engaged in fighting and the government was not in a position to meet all these expenses. As a result of it whoever came out with the intention of fighting in the way of Allah, was not at all worried on this score and was provided with all that he needed, and in this way in return for this world he came to deserve that heaven with an expanse greater than the heavens and the earth. But now we have degraded ourselves to the position of celebrating the Arms Week and collecting funds for arming our fighting forces. If we had the collective understanding and insight and true faith, we would be donating something every day for this purpose instead of celebrating a particular week, and would have established huge arms factories to keep our fighting forces supplied with up-to-date arms adequately, so that they might be counted among the most powerful armies for the defence of the country and keep away the invaders from our frontiers.

13. Trusts whose income was meant for the protection and construction and repair of roads, bridges and pathways.

14. There were trust lands to serve as burial grounds. People endowed large tracts of lands for graveyards.

15. And there were trusts for the burial of the indigent.

16. In spite of the superabundance of trusts for the collective support, there were exclusive trusts for the children without support and orphans, as also for their circumcision and protection.

17. Institutions for the upkeep of the disabled, blind and helpless persons, where all their necessities like food, clothes, shelter and education and training were provided and where they could spend a life of honour and dignity.

18. Establishing institutions for improving the condition of prisoners, raising their standard of living, provision of food for and protection of their health.

19. Establishment of institutions whose income was to be spent on those looking after the blind and the disabled.

20. Trusts to look after the marriage of young boys and girls whose guardians could not pay for their expenses such as Mahr (dower). How compassionate to think of such people and how much we stand in need of this sentiment today.

21. Institutions established to help mothers. These institutions supplied milk and sugar to mothers long before the modern ogranizations like Milk-Supply Centres in our country. Our own (Islamic) institutions were working for the welfare of mothers. And they were based on the passion of getting closer to God. One of the philanthropic deeds of Salahuddin Ayyubi was to establish two reservoirs, one of milk and the other of fresh drinking water close to the gate of his fort which still stand in Damascus. Twice a week, mothers of young babies used to come and take away milk and sugar for the needs of their children.

22. You may be surprised to learn that some institutions were maintained to replace the broken earthen wares of those children and slaves who accidentally broke theirs in transit from the market to their homes. In case of such accidents they came to these institutions, and taking intact vessels in place of the broken ones to their parents or masters who were unaware of those breakages.

23. The last category of institutions and Trust was that established for the treatment of sick animals, their feed, and providing pastures for the permanently disabled animals. The area of Maraj-al-Akhzar, where stands the Municipal playground of Damascus, was one of such trusts. This was essential for horses and other old and infirm (discarded) animals so that they might live here and feed in peace till the end of their days. In short, the institutions established for the public welfare, in our civilization, fell under more or less thirty categories, and those mentioned here are symbolic only. Can you find any parallel in the civilization of any of the peoples of the past ? Rather, some of them are such as cannot be traced even in the western civilization of our own days, which is so much noised about.

God is our witness that this is the path of life abiding which we were treading alone while the rest of the world was wandering aimlessly in a state of unawareness, ignorance and backwardness and groping in the dark. By God! This is that path of life eternal by treading which we had rid badly tormented humanity of its miseries and grief.

But alas! Which path is that we have ourselves taken? Where are those hands that wiped and dried the tears of the orphans, put balm on the wounded hearts, and which had made our society one in which one and all lived happily in peace and security with honour and safety.

Educational Institutions

While talking of the institutions of public welfare in the Islamic civilization and their amazing and multifarious activities and how the philanthropy of the Muslim Ummah inspired it to attain great heights in this field, we had just mentioned schools and hospitals under that head, with promise to take them up in detail in their proper place. So in this connection we are here taking up schools of the Islamic civilization first.

Islamic schools were established with the income of large properties of Muslim endowments. These trusts had been instituted at different times by different nobles, leaders, 'Ulama, traders and kings. So numerous were these schools that there was hardly any town or village worth the name that went without one, where many teachers were employed for public instruction.

In our civilization the mosque was that centre which developed the school. At that time the mosque was not only a place of worship, but its extensive open space served as a school where young children learnt recital of the Quran, calligraphy, the Quranic disciplines, Fiqh and the Shariah, language and literature.

Then gradually Maktabs, separate from the mosque but attached to them, came into existence, where besides recital of the Quran, calligraphy and the Quranic disciplines, the Arabic disciplines and Mathematics were also taught. These maktabs resembled our present day primary schools and were in such large numbers that according to Ibn-e-Hauqal's count in a small town of Sicily there were about six hundred maktabs. And so spacious were they that at times in a single maktab hundreds and thousands of students received instruction. Abu; Qasim

Balakhi in his history writes about his own maktab that three thousand students were on its rolls, and this maktab was so spacious that in its big compound a mount had to be used for supervision of and remaining informed about the circumstances and needs of the students.

Again, as an advancement over the maktabs, schools attached to the mosque were established. And these schools resembled our present day institutions of secondary and higher education. Education imparted here was totally free of cost and people of all classes of society sent their children to these schools, and unlike our existing secondary and higher educational institutions the students were not charged any educational fees. There the education was not exclusively meant for any particular group. They all had the same opportunities without any discrimination. Whoever came to its portals, was granted entry and no distinction was made between the poor and the rich. They all sat together, shoulder to shoulder, nobles, traders, peasants and craftsmen were in the same row. Two types of instructions were imparted in these schools, one for boarders and another for day-scholars. Boarders were mostly those students whose parents or guardians were not economically in a position to meet the expenses of their wards. The other category was that of the day-scholars who attended school during the day but left for their own homes or those of their relatives for the night. Education was free for all of them, but the boarders received all the amenities of life free of charge, board, lodging and the rest. That is why attached to almost every mosque was a school with the classrooms, residential quarters for the students, libraries, kitchens and bathrooms. Some of these schools had vast open spaces too, that served as playgrounds for the students where they had facilities for physical exercises and sports. Some of them have survived to this day in the Muslim world, which once existed in large numbers throughout the Islamic world.

The Past Glory

Madrasah-e-Nooriyah stands in Damascus to this day. It was instituted by Imam Nooruddin Shaheed. Standing in Suq-al-

Yhayyatin, even today it speaks of the glory of the past and gives us a glimpse of the general features of the Madrasahs during the hey-day of the Islamic civilization. The well-known traveller, Ibn-e-Habib, who visited this school, was amazed and has written about it:

"The madrasah established by Nooruddin is counted among the most beautiful schools of the world. It is difficult to believe it to be a school, standing as it does in a beautiful palatial building. For its water-supply a canal has been constructed upto the school building, in the centre of which stands a fountain, dividing the fallicid water into two small streams which further on join to fill a big reservoir situated in the centre of this palace. The beauty of the scene is fascinating."

In spite of the fact that the vicissitudes of time played havoc with this institution and several segments of it have been snatched from it, even then, its building, class rooms, the mosque and the residential quarters of the teachers, as also their retiring rooms have survived. These retiring rooms served the purpose of the staff rooms of our modern schools and colleges. A special house too stands there which was the residence of the head-master or principal of the school with his family. The residence of the students and the servants of the school stand to this day. Presently the neighbours of the school have taken possession of the school-kitchen, the spacious dining hall and the kitchen store for the storage of grains, vegetables and other food materials. This building of the school is a living pattern of the Muslim schools of olden days.

Similarly the Qaumi, Shahi and 'Uthmani madrasahs of Halab (Allepo) stand as monuments of the past glory, where the students' hostel rooms and class rooms stand out separately to this day. Earlier these schools catered food to the students. But later on the students were paid their expenses including food at the end of every month.'

And Jami'ah Azhar too is a living specimen of these schools which is, really speaking, a mosque, in whose different sections students gather to pursue their studies under the guidance of a teacher. Around the mosque stand rooms where these students reside. These rooms are known as "Rawaqs", in which students of different countries live in their own groups. For example, there were separate rawaqs for the Syrian, Turkish, Sudanese and Iraqi students. Even today the students of the Azhar (University) along with free of charge education get also monthly stipends regularly from the income of the properties endowed for Azhar.

It would be just the proper thing for us to say something about the teachers and their remunerations also under the account of Muslim schools of the past. The principal used to be some great learned man renowned in his own discipline. The biographies of famous 'Ulama tell us where and at what centres of learning they had been spreading the light of learning. For example Imam Navavi, Ibn-al-Salah, Abu Shammah Taqi-ud-din Subuki and Imaduddin taught at the School of Hadith in Damascus. Ghazali, Shirazi, Imam-al-Haramain Allamah Shasabi, Khateeb Tabrezi, Qazwini and Firozabadi, and so many other luminaries taught at Madrasah-e-Nizamiyah, Baghdad. In the early period, these teachers never accepted any remuneration for their services. But at the height of the Islamic civilization, great seats of learning came into existence, large endowments were made for them and monthly salaries were allocated in the budgets for the teachers also.

It would be proper to mention here the incident speaking of the insight and far-sightedness of the 'Ulama of Mawara-al-Nahr. When Nizam-ul-Mulk (Toosi) instituted his famous schools in Mawara-ul-Nahr region, and definite monthly salaries were allocated to the teachers, the 'Ulama gathered together and reproved him much for this innovation, and mourned over the intended change that, according to them, was commercialization of a noble profession which would take away the value and blessing of knowledge, undertaken solely for its nobility and grandeur as also to attain perfection in learning. But now that material gain is being attached to learning, those avaricious in the matter of material benefits and personal interest shall throng to the centres of learning with the result that knowledge and learning themselves shall no longer be of value. They will become poor in quality and suffer degradation also. But this point of view was not accepted because of the consideration of the changing times and the growing fresh needs of the society, and finally the salaries of the teachers were allocated, which differed from place to place in keeping with the region, the status of the school and the endowments supporting it. Still these salaries were adequate for a clean and decent living for the teachers. The remuneration paid to the teachers for the job of teaching was over and above the subsistence allowance for all their economic needs, normally granted to the teachers. Sheikh Najm-uddin Habooshani, who had been appointed the principal of his Madrasah-e-Salahiyah by Sultan Salahuddin, was paid forty pounds for his services of teaching, ten pounds for the supervision of the trusts of the school, and a daily ration of sixty Egyptian Ratals of bread and two leather bags full of water from Nile. The Sheikh-e-Azhar had among other allowances his conveyance allowance also, charged to the particular endowment of Azhar to which the maintenance of the horse was to be charged. This amounted to about hundred pounds in later periods, nearer ours, and which was finally merged with the pay of Sheikh-al-Azhar.

Only those people discharged the duties of teaching who were certified by the experts in this field that they were perfectly fit for the job. During the early days of Islam, the teachers themselves permitted their bright and capable students to detach themselves from the teacher and start their own circles of teaching. Or in case of the death of the teacher, the brightest student of his circle was elected to take the seat of the teacher. And if he did not comply, he was reproved and severely criticised. A well known incident is that of the life of Qazi Abu Yusuf, a pet disciple of Imam Abu Hanifah, who later became the Qazi-al-Quzzat (Lord Chief Justice) during the period of Harun Rasheed. He fell seriously ill during the life time of Imam Abu Hanifah. The teacher came to ask after the health of his favourite pupil and said that he was very much worried with his illness since it was he whom he expected to come up to the expectations of the Muslims after he (Abu Hanifah) had left the world. Abu Yusuf got over that illness by the Grace of God and came round. But he had found the very encouraging remark of this affectionate teacher too much to digest and started his own circle of teaching. Abu Hanifah knew only too well that he had not attained maturity. So he sent him a set of five problematic questions, demanding much thought and great detail to be answered satisfactorily, to show him his true position. When Abu Yusuf blundered in answering those questions, he realized that he had also blundered in deserting the circle of teaching of his master Abu Hanifah, and at once atoned by returning to that circle. Abu Hanifah told him that he had become dried like a fruit before it was ripe. And also that whoever laboured under the erroneous notion that he had become independent of acquiring knowledge should mourn this crooked mentality of his. That was in the early period of development of the educational system. But when schools were established, they started awarding degrees, diplomas and certificates for the various prescribed courses of studies and written testimonials to this effect were given to the successful candidates. The physicians, in particular. were not allowed to establish their practice until they had formally obtained a testimonial to the effect that they had successfully completed their prescribed courses and were now fully competent to treat the sick. And these testimonials were issued by the great learned men in the discipline or the trade concerned.

The teachers used to put on a particular type of dress which distinguished them from. other professions. The dress in vogue at the time of Abu Yusuf was a black turban and sheet. During the Fatimid dynasty a green turban, a golden dress comprising six pieces, important among which was a cap and a sheet. As for the gown which was exclusive to the 'ulama and the teachers, had come into vogue during the period of Ummayyids. In Andalusia the dress of the teachers and the 'ulama was a bit different from those of the East. The more marked difference lay in the turban which was very small in their case. Some even went without a turban. So when a renowned man of letters, Imam Abu Ali, went to Andalusia and the local 'ulama came to greet him, they were surprised at his big turban. And the silly people and children even chided him and threw pebbles at him. The western countries took the pattern of their dress from the Muslims of Andalusia, and the dress of the learned people of the universities of Europe in the form of a hood and gown to this day, owes its source to the Muslim teachers.

During this period there was a regular independent association of the teachers, just as we have unions of students, citizens and different types of workmen in our own society. The teachers elected their representatives and the president, and they were totally independent in this matter. The state interfered in these matters only when any dissension arose among them. Abu Shammah in his Rauzatain has reported from Muqallid Daulai, "When Hafiz Muradi died, there were two groups among the legists, Arabs and Kurds. And we fell out among ourselves. Some of us were inclined towards Fiqh and therefore wanted that to fill the vacancy, Sheikh Sharfuddin Abul Hazroon should be brought here. But some others had a bias for Logical Sciences and Ethics, so they were in favour of Qutub Neshapuri, being called for this job. There was lot of hubbub and noise due to this dissension and it came to the knowledge of Nooruddin. He called all the learned men and his deputy, Majadduddin bin-al-Dayah, talked to them. He informed them that the Sultan said that he had founded the Madrasah Nooriyah for the propagation of faith and knowledge, as also for the eradication of innovations introduced into the faith, and not for quarrels and brawls. Their mutual discord was most unhappy. So to bring accord between the two opposing sections he would call both the persons favoured by either party. So both were called and Sharfuddin was appointed the principal of the Madrasah Nooriyah and Qutubuddin was detailed for the principalship of "Madrasah Nafari."

There was such a super abundance of schools and, particularly institutions of higher education, that the entire Islamic world was full of these higher institutions. The Islamic history presents with pride the names of some such sons of Islam who played an important role in building big schools in every city of the Islamic world. The name of Salahuddin Ayyubi tops the list, who had spread a network of schools in every part of Egypt, Damascus, Mosul and Bait-al-Maqdis. Nooruddin, the martyr, is also among those people. He established fourteen big schools in Syria alone, out of which six were established in Damascus, four in Halab, two in Hamat and Hamas and one in Ba'lbak. And Nizam-al-Mulk Toosi, the Chief Minister of the Suljuqis is also one of those men. He had packed Iraq and Khorasan with madrasahs. The historians tell us that he established an educational institution for higher studies in every city of Iraq and Khorasan, and founded schools in places far off from the principal cities and towns. For example, he established a magnificent madrasah in Jazeerrah Ibne-'Umar which was very beautiful and imposing. Whenever he heard of a learned man of extraordinary worth, he instituted a madrasah for him there with adequate endowments to support and maintain it, and a fairly big library was also established there for the benefit of the school.

Nizamiah of Baghdad was the most important and well organized madrasah. Between the fifth and the ninth century of the Hijrah, great learned men came out of this institution. The number of students on its rolls touched six thousand. And among them were the children of the rich nobility and also those of the most indigent persons, studying side by side, neither paying any educational fees. But for the poor boys in addition to free education there were stipends to meet all their needs, paid to them from the income of lands endowed for this purpose.

Along with these great men with high rank and position, there were other wealthy persons and traders also who vied with one another in establishing schools and arranging endowments for their support and maintenance so that with these endowments at their back the economic condition of the schools might be sound and their students might turn to them in perfect security about the continuity of the school. There have also been many other bountiful persons who had converted their own houses into madrasahs and whatever stock of books they had or the properties in their possession were endowed for the benefit of the students.

For these reasons in the entire Islamic world in general and in the 'Eastern Muslim countries in particular, the madrasahs were in great abundance. Ibn-e-Jubair, the well known traveller of Andalusia was amazed to see the abundance of these madrasahs, their vast endowments, their plentiful yields and unlimited income, and had induced the people of Andalusia to go to East to acquire knowledge. He says:

"In the Eastern countries there are countless endowments for. the students of the madrasahs, particularly in Damascus. Our western (Andalusian) students desirous of security, ease and affluence should go there. There they will come by so many advantages helpful in their quest for knowledge and particularly in economic matters they will be free from want and anxiety "

Ibn-e-Jubair's evidence has a special significance, for he enjoys a position of a truthful and honest traveller in the matter of his statement of facts. And he has made particular mention of Damascus with regard to the abundance of trusts and the number of madrasahs, since there were at that time more than four hundred fully functioning madrasahs in Damascus to which came students from far off places. And in this connection the historical evidence too is of great interest that the superabundance of madrasahs in Damascus made it impossible for a student coming to this town for one year's sojourn, to stay more than one night at any one of these schools, and his sojourn came to an end.

Ibn-e-Asakir has quoted an eulogy of Sultan bin-e-Ali bin-eManqaz Al-Katani exalting Damascus, in his history. In this poem he has mentioned the madrasahs of Damascus in these words:

"There you will find such teachers, before whom you may present any problem, some young man must come forward to solve it for you immediately. Whoever goes there in perplexity will get over it there, and will be guided to the right path. And one who is poor in thought will become rich at once. With the produce of the trust properties of these schools the prisoners obtain their release and the poor become rich and contented. There are imams (authorities in learning) who impart knowledge and there are such masters of the system of self purification who can prove a cure for all the ills of the psyche, although these ills are very complicated."

Now we shall put forth some examples which can give an idea of the abundance of endowments. The endowments of Madrasah-e-Nooriyah Kubra, according to the document at its entrance, were the following:

All the new bagnios or Turkish baths of the wheat market, two new baths of waraqah outside Bab-al-Salam and their annexe, the factory of "Auniah-e-Hima" and the small grove of Aaraq and Wazir, three fourth of the "Jauza grove" of Arzah, the eleven shops outside Bab-e-Jabiyah and nine fields of Daria.*People's Well Being Supreme*

The endowments for the Noorie Hospital of Halab were as follows:

The entire village of Mi'rata, half the cultivated land of the 'Asl valley of Sam'an mountain, five fiddan out of the land of Kufr Taba (Land enough to be conveniently tilled by five pairs of bullocks), and one third of the Khalidi field, a flour mill of Malakh as also the entire income of the flour mill in front of Bab-al-Jinan, and three fiddan from the field of Abu Miraya (land enough to be tilled by three pairs of bullocks), and eight pairs of bullocks worth land from the "Humairah" field of Matakh, land worth eleven pairs of bullocks from the Farzal field of Mu'arrah, one third of the income of Bait-e-Ra'eel village of Gharbiyat, ten shops of Hawa market, the general stores and shops outside Bab-e-Intakiah, Bab-e-Faraj and Bab-e-Jinan.

To give an idea of the abundance of endowments for the mosque and madrasahs of Damascus, it would be enough to say that Imam Navawi (d.676 A.H) never tasted a fruit grown in Damascus all his life, since the greater part of 'Ghotah' and most other gardens of Damascus were endowed properties which had been misappropriated by tyrants.

Special Schools

There were many schools meant for various purposes. Some of them imparted the knowledge of the Quran only, its exegesis, recital and committing it to memory. There were others where Hadith and relevant disciplines were taught. There were yet others exclusively imparting knowledge of Fiqh, and were in large numbers. Again, there was a separate madrasah for every school of Fiqh. Similarly, there were separate madrasahs for the education of medical science. And there were schools only for the orphans.

Na'eemi, who is the most outstanding among the 'ulama of the tenth century, has given a complete list of the schools of Damascus and their endowments in his *Kitab 'Al -Daramin-fii-Tarikh-al-Madaris'*. It tells us that there were seven madrasahs meant exclusively for the education of the Quran and relevant disciplines, sixteen for the teaching of Hadith, three for the Quran and Hadith combined, sixty-three madrasahs for the Shafi'i Fiqh, fifty-two for Hanafi Fiqh, four for the Maliki school of Fiqh and eleven for the Hanbali Fiqh. There were entirely separate schools for the education of medical sciences. And houses of seclusion (monasteries), inns and the great congregation mosques were over and above these institutions. It must be kept in view that at all these places too, pursuit of teaching and learning were in full swing.

Example of Europe

Comparing these conditions with those prevailing in the west would be advisable. You may be surprised to learn that they were totally ignorant and unmannerly. Knowledge was confined to the monasteries of the monks and hermits, and exclusive to the soothsayers and priests. From this comparison it becomes easily known that during the period when our civilization was at its height, what heights the Muslim ummah had touched. From the point of view of the history of the social institutions and the centres of learning how magnificent are the feats of our civilization. And also how Islam spared no pains in the propagation of knowledge and raising the standard of human civilization and providing these facilities for all the individuals of every religion and community.

Ibn-e-Kathir, in his book *Al-Badayah wa-al-Nihayah,* writes under the events of 631 A.H.:

"This year the building of Madrasah-e-Mustansarryah was completed. No such madrasah was ever built before that. This was dedicated to all the four schools of Fiqh. Sixty-two legists of every school of Fiqh worked at this madrasah. Four out of them were experts, one teacher of every school, one Shaikh-al-Hadith, two Qaris (well versed in the recital of the Quran with proper intonation), ten Sami's (listeners who guard against the Qari making any lapses and correcting him on the spot), one Sheikh-e-Tibb (Chief medical expert) and ten Muslim Physicians who ran the clinics. There was also a maktab of orphans. For every student there was a fixed quantity of bread, meat and sweets and a particular amount of money for other expenses which was far in excess of his needs."

He goes further to say:

"And for this school a library was endowed, unparalleled in our knowledge. There were large number of books which were the nicest specimens of the art of calligraphy. And the best books of every discipline were collected here."

Health Amenities

One of the bases on which the edifice of our civilization has been raised, is that herein both physical and spiritual needs have been safeguarded. The Islamic civilization paid due attention to the development and care of the physique so that along with a resplendent soul man may attain the highest position in advancement. In this connection the words of the founder of the Islamic civilization, Muhammad, Sal'aam, are worthy of attention:

"Assuredly thy body too has a claim over thee."

(Bukhari and Muslim)

If all the forms of the Islamic worship are carefully examined, principles of public health and hygiene, which is the most important objective of medical science, have been kept in view with attention to the minutest details.' So it is observed that all the conditions laid down for prayer, fasting and Hajj, and in whatever manner the body has to exert itself during their performance, is extremely useful for the hygiene, maintenance of health and keeping the body fresh and active. And along with that when we see how the Islamic civilization combated diseases and their spread, and how people have been induced to take up treatment of every disease, we come to know that in the field of medicine too it has been founded on solid and very strong principles, and its feats have attained great heights in this field too. It established large hospitals and other medical institutions which benefited the entire humanity, and produced such medical men of extraordinary worth, of whose accomplishments in the field of learning and technical work, the world is proud to this day.

The Arabs were acquainted with the medical college at Chandesapur established by the emperor of Iran in the later half of the sixth century of the Christian era. Some of the Arab physicians had been trained there, for example, Harith bin-e-Kaldah who lived during the time of the Prophet and was the medical advisor to some of his companions, and used to look after them when they fell ill.

Experiments in Health

The Muslims established their first ever hospital during the period of Waleed bin-e-Abd-al Malik, which was meant exclusively for the leprosy patients. The physicians appointed to this hospital were granted large properties and salaries. And those undergoing treatment at this hospital had orders to stay permanently at the hospital (as indoor patients, Tr.), and were granted stipends, just as they had been granted to the blind. Then after this hospital followed a whole series of them called 'Bimaristans' (the asylums of the sick).

Hospitals were of two kinds:

1) Mobile Dispensaries And

2) Regular Hospitals Lodged In Permanent Buildings.

One such mobile dispensary is traceable to the period of the Prophet himself, that was established during the Ghazwah Khandaq (the battle of the Ditch). In this battle a separate tent was erected for the wounded. When Sa'd bin-e-Mu'az was wounded and one of the blood vessels of his arm was injured, the Prophet ordered that he should be kept in the tent for the wounded so that he might personally look after him. And that would be possible only when Mu'az was close to him. It was the first mobile dispensary. Later on the caliphs and the kings developed and extended them, until in a mobile hospital all those facilities were provided which the patients need — medical care, diet, medicines, clothes, doctors and compounders. These mobile hospitals moved from village to village where there were no permanent hospitals.

Wazir 'Isa-bin-e-'All bin-e-Jarah wrote to Sinan Ibn-e-Thabit who was then in charge of the hospitals in Baghdad and those around and affiliated to it:

"I have been thinking of the people living in Savad-e-`Aini village where people must be falling ill but fail to receive medical attention, there being no doctor around. You please bring together a group of doctors and provide also a fairly large stock of medicines and decoctions, for their use. They should go to the villages and stay as long as it may be necessary. And after they have treated all the patients there, should move on to another village:"

During the reign of Sultan Muhammad Saljuqi the mobile hospital had become so cumbersome that its equipment needed forty camels for transport.

As for the permanent hospitals, they were in such large numbers that every big and small town benefited by them. Even the smallest town boasted of more than one hospital. For example there was a time when Qurtobah (Cordoba) alone had fifty major hospitals.

The nature of these hospitals too had changed. Some of them were reserved for the army men, and had their own special doctors. These doctors were in addition to the Special doctors attending to the caliphs, the military commanders, and the nobles. There were separate hospitals for the prisoners. The doctor examined the prisoners every day and they were provided the necessary facilities of treatment. Wazir 'All-bin-Isa bin-e-Jarah bin-e-Thabit writes to the Chief medical officer, Baghdad:

"I am very much worried about the prisoners. Their large numbers and the condition of prisons makes it certain that there must be many ailing persons among them. Therefore I am of the opinion that they must have their own doctors who should examine them every day and give them, where necessary, medicines and decoctions. Such doctors should visit all prisons and treat the sick prisoners there."

There were also centres to provide first (medical) aid, which were usually located at busy public places like the big congregation mosques and such other places. Maqrizi writes:

"Ibn-e-Tulun when he built his world famous mosque in Egypt, at one end of it there was a place for ablutions and a dispensary also as annexe. The dispensary was well-equipped with medicines and attendants. On Friday there used to be a doctor on duty there so that he might attend immediately to any casualties on the occasion of this mammoth gathering."

Some hospitals were of a general nature open to all at all hours of the day and the night. They had two categories:

1. All-male hospitals

2. Secluded female hospitals

They were far removed from one another. Either category had several departments dealing with different diseases. For example:

1. Department of systemic diseases

2. Opthalmic department
3. Surgicai department
4. Orthopaedic department
5. Department of mental diseases

The department of Systemic diseases was further divided into sub-sections:

1. Section dealing with fevers
2. Section dealing with digestive troubles

Every department had an officer-in-charge and a presiding officer. And each one of them had a specialist of its own. And there was a superintendent, supervising the working and management of the entire institution. He was known as Sa'ur.

There were fixed working hours for the physicians during which they attended to the patients coming to their departments.

Every hospital had its own junior staff of compounders and nurses. There were others to assist them. Their salaries were definitely fixed and reasonably lucrative also. Every hospital had a pharmacy known as the store of beverages (decoctions). They comprised many kinds of fluid medicines, fine electuaries and high quality medicinally preserved fruit. Moreover there were some very refined preparations and juices, essences and distilled decoctions, available only at the hospitals and nowhere else. They also had in these hospitals fine surgical instruments, glass containers and other vessels which formerly were to be had in the king's palaces only.

These hospitals served also as institutions for the training of medical students. Every hospital had a big lecture theatre for the teaching of the students. The Chief medical officer, other medical men and medical students gathered there. And all sorts of medical books and surgical instruments were also available. After the patients had been attended to, the students used to sit before the teachers and they started discussing medical problems. These discussions were of practical importance and very useful. The text books were of a high standard. So often the teachers took the students with them to the hospital wards and they participated in the practical work, just as students are given a chance to see patients and other hospital work in our own day hospitals attached to the medical colleges. Ibn-e-Abi-'Usaiba'ah, who had received his medical education at the Noorie hospital of Damascus, writes:

"When Hakeem Muhazabuddin and Hakeem `Imran became free from examination and treatment of patients in the hospital, I would be with them and sat with Shaikh Raziuddin Rahabi and marked the way of their arguments in arriving at the diagnosis of diseases. Whatever statements they made about the patients and whatever they prescribed for them, I discussed with them most of those diseases and their prescriptions."

Every body could not be allowed to practice on his own. Any one who wished to establish a practice had to appear before the Chief medical officer appointed by the government to prove his worth. He had to write a treatise on the subject in which he wanted to obtain a certificate of proficiency. This treatise was either his own writing or somebody else's in which case he had to write his notes and comments. The Chief medical officer interviewed him at length and questioned him on all the relevant problems of his subject. If he succeeded in giving satisfactory answers to all his questions, only then he would permit the candidate to practice. An incident of the period of Muqtadir Billah about 319 A.H. has been reported. Some doctor treated a patient on the wrong lines culminating in the patient's death. The caliph ordered that all the doctors be examined afresh. So the Chief medical officer, Sinan bin-e-Thabit tested the capabilities of all the doctors afresh. On this occasion the number of such doctors was found to be more than 860, and this was over and above those who had been practising since long and well-known in their profession, and those who attended to the nobility and the caliphs as their personal physicians, and as such did not stand in need of any tests.

It should also be kept in mind that every big hospital had a big library for the benefit of both the students and the doctors. It is said that the Ibn-e-Tulun Hospital of Egypt had a library comprising a hundred thousand books on various branches of medical science.

The portals of these hospitals were open to everybody and no fees of any kind were charged. No distinction was made between the poor and the rich, related and alien, local and foreign and a common man and a distinguished person. In the out-door department the patient was carefully examined and in case of those in need of casual attention were given the prescribed medicines to be taken at home. But those that were serious cases requiring regular attention and supervision were registered as indoor patients. They were sent to the bathroom and were provided a clean change of hospital uniform while their own clothes were kept in the hospital store. He was taken to the hospital ward where a bed was ready for him with clean sheets. The course of treatment prescribed by the doctor was started forthwith. He was given nourishing diet, helpful in his recovery and improving his health. The quality of diet was also fixed. The patients received the following items of diet .... mutton, beef, meat of poultry and other birds. The criterion of sound health (on recovery from illness) was that he would take the amount of bread, normally taken by a perfectly healthy person, with the roasted meat of a whole bird at a time. And if he could easily digest it, he was considered perfectly recovered and healthy. The patients that were cured of their malady but were weak, were transferred to the ward for convalescents until their return to robust health. Before discharge they were given a new dress and along with that enough monetary aid to establish some means of their livelihood. The hospital rooms and wards were neat and tidy with regular supply of water in abundance. These rooms were furnished with clean carpets. Every hospital had a sanitary inspector and accountants and other executive staff. The caliph in office would visit these hospitals, meet the patients and take interest in their problems.

That was the excellent system at work in all the hospitals of the Islamic world, be they of the East or the West. This was the uniform system in vogue in all the hospitals of Baghdad, Damascus, Cairo, Bait-al-Maqdis, Makkah, Madinah and Andalusia.

Now we would like to take up in some detail the conditions existing in the four major hospitals of the four big cities of the Islamic world.

It was built by 'Azd-al-daulah bin-e-Buwaih in 371 A.H. The site for this hospital was selected by the then most renowned medical man Razi (Rhazes of Europc) by keeping a piece of fresh meat at each of the four different proposed sites for it, in the city of Baghdad, at night. On examination in the morning the place where the piece was found least affected by degenerative changes, was considered suitable for the hospital and construction was undertaken. A magnificent building was constructed at a tremendous cost and twenty-four most capable doctors were selected for the staff. A library, pharmacy, a store and kitchen were provided for the hospital and were well-equipped. In 449 A. H. the caliph Qa'im-be-Amrillah organized the hospital afresh and equipped it with liquid medicines (infusious, decoctions, distilled extracts and syrups), herbs and roots and other medicines, which were of a rare type. The patients were provided with sheets and blankets. Moreover arrangements were made for perfumes, ice, attendants, peons, sentinels, watchmen and doctors who were available all the time (resident doctors. Tr.). A big hammam (complex of bath rooms with supply of hot and cold water), was constructed and a garden and orchard were provided with flowers and fruits of all kinds in them. The patients who were too weak to move and did not have access to any other conveyance, were regularly ferried from various places to this hospital, and the doctors attended to them morning and evening during their duty hours.

The just Sultan, Malik Nooruddin, the martyr, constructed this hospital with the ransom paid to him by one of the Christian monarchs. At the time of its construction this was the most excellent and beautiful hospital in the entire Islamic world. He had put a ban on the entry of the moneyed and the resourceful to this hospital, been devoted entirely to the service of the poor and the resourceless. The rich persons were however, allowed to be benefited by it only in case of an emergency when there was no way out. The patients attending this hospital were given medicines only in the morning session. A traveller, Ibn-e-Jubair visited this hospital in 580 A.H. He has praised the kind treatment of the doctors and their almost devotional care in the administration of medicines and offering them other facilities. There was a special department set apart for the management of the mental cases. Those cases that were found to be dangerous had to be chained for security of others and their own safety. However, they were properly fed and looked after in the matter of treatment. The historians have recorded that in 831 A.H. some non-Arab visitor came to Damascus. He was not only a great learned person but had fine tastes too. He happened to visit the hospital also. He was simply amazed to see the large number of doctors and their interest in patients and devoted service to them, and the food and other facilities provided for the patients. What was still more surprising was that over and above the normal amenities, the patients had decoration and luxury articles too supplied to them. He took it into his head to test the skill of the physicians of that hospital and feigning to be ill, managed to be hospitalised for three days for diagnosis and treatment. For three days the chief medical officer noted his pulse and appeared to be diagnosing his trouble. But they had discovered the very first day that he was hale and hearty and had come only to test their skill. Therefore they prescribed for him rich diet, good poultry meat, sweet dishes and refreshing and stimulating drinks and various kinds of fruits. For three days he was given this diet at the hospital. After three days, the chief medical officer left a note for him which read: "Hospitality here is for a limited period of three days." That suggested to the non-Arab visitor that they had seen through his game and had entertained him only as a guest for three days.

This hospital was functioning upto 1317 A.H. After that it was converted into the foreigner's hospital. It is the same hospital where the Tibbiyah College, run under the university of Syria, is functioning. Winding up the hospital, a medical college and local school were established there.

This hospital has been known as the "Bimaristan-e-Qalawoon." It used to be the palace of some noble. Malik Mansoor Saifuddin Qalawoon converted it into a hospital in 683 A.H. (1284 A.D), and endowed a particular estate for it, bringing annually one thousand dirhems. A mosque, a madrasah and a maktab for the orphans were also established along with it. The historians say about the reasons behind the establishment of this hospital that when in 1275 A.D. Amir Qalawoon, during the period of Zahir Babyrus, came out as the army general, to oppose the advancing Roman armies, he was suddenly taken ill at Damascus. The doctors there treated him and the medicines were supplied from the Noorie hospital. When he was completely cured he personally visited and inspected the Noorie hospital. He was very much impressed by it and vowed that if God brought him to rule, he would build a hospital like that. When he came to the throne, he selected this palace and purchasing it he converted it into a hospital. This hospital from the point of view of organization and disposition was the only hospital of its kind. In the morning hours master and the slave, the king and the subject, men and women all alike, benefited by it. The patient discharged cured from this hospital was given clothes to wear and those dead were buried at the hospital's cost. There were separate doctors in charge of each branch of the medical sciences. There were attendants and nurses to wash the clothes of the patient, to help them in taking bath (or sponging their bodies), cleaning and tidying the rooms and the beddings and for such other facilities provided to the patients. There were two attendants for every patient who did everything for his convenience and comfort. Every patient had his separate bed and bedding, and there were separate wards for patients of one type. There were fixed spots for discussions on medical themes and for lectures, where the principal used to teach the students. This hospital had this peculiarity also that it did not only treat in-patients at the hospital but also those that came as outdoor patients. But they were supplied medicines and nutrient food even under these conditions. In this way it continued functioning. One of the opthalmologists at this hospital is reported to have said that more than four thousand cases, both indoor and outdoor were treated at this hospital daily. Whoever was cured and discharged, before leaving the portals of the hospital was offered clothes and cash to help him start some petty business or industry for his subsistence so that he may not starve on coming out of the hospital.

The documents relating to the endowments of these hospitals tell us that a patient in the hospital was given his food in a vessel reserved for his exclusive use and no other patient could use it, and the food was always served covered. Another peculiarity of this hospital was that patients suffering from insomnia had a place set apart for them where they were entertained with fascinating music and interesting stories. An expert story teller held charge of this work. Very weak patients. were treated to acting of pleasantries and jokes, and rural dances were also presented which the rustics appreciated so much. The mu'azzins of the neighbourhood were ordered to make calls for the early morning prayer two hours ahead of the scheduled time, and recite verses with proper intonation so that the patients may be cheered and their distress may be reduced, since lack of sleep and long nights were painful for them. It was under these conditions of the hospitals that the French entered Egypt in 1795 and the French learned men saw these things with their own eyes, and stated them in their books in detail.

By God! This is that lofty standard of humanity which the modern world has attained in our own time with great difficulty. In this connection something came to my mind that I had heard in Tripoli: There is a trust in that city whose income is reserved exclusively for those persons who must go to hospitals every day and approaching the patients, whisper in such a way that the patients may overhear and receive the impression that they are improving, the glow of health on their faces and the brightness of their eyes being evidence of that improvement.

We deem it necessary here that the Trust deed of this magnificent hospital be placed before the reader in its entirety, as reported by the author of "*Tarikh-al-Bimaristanat fil-Islam* (History of the hospitals of the Islamic world)".

"The opportunities of the reward of the highest acts of righteousness afforded to lofty aims, and the feats and virtuous acts which are regarded very very beneficial, and for the unlimited reward of which valuable good the sleeper can break his sleep, and for that excellent act of righteousness which can divert the attention of those given to turn to them, or any one who can, get up and become alert, they are those acts of goodness which have a reward everlasting, bringing people happiness, and the ancestors may regularly be getting their share of reward, and that they are based on the firm foundation of Taqwa (piety) with aspirations of a farreaching nature apparently such acts of goodness are Trusts only, whose beneficence is general, whose reward is abiding, whose benefits are unlimited and the reward of the Hereafter is very valuable. So in fact these acts of goodness are the real heaven, and this is the one sacrifice that takes one to the Good Will and pleasure of God. This is the Sadaqah which is the mahr (dower) of the *hoors* in heaven. The reward of this charitable act is not only pearls and coral but the oceans bearing them in plenty .....It is worthy of consideration what elation a helpless patient feels, how much support is afforded tô a broken heart and how, through treatment of his malady and offering him refuge, he comes to feel independent. In short its reward is so great that it cannot be expressed in words. Fortunate indeed is that person who has had such a deal with his Lord, the Forgiving and Most Merciful God. And in his income and expenditure he had such a deal with God, Who knows his apparent and hidden acts both And he offered a goodly loan to Allah according to his capacity, and he valued the opportunity of surpassing others in the field of virtue. And he helped a sick Muslim brother in his treatment, and took away his grief, as a reward of which Tomorrow in the Court of Divine Justice he will have deliverance from the torment of hell. And over and above that there is also hope of being the recipient of further exaltation in his rank and position from God. He will be endowed with the good fortune of closeness to God, where he will have no fear of any oppression or tyranny. In short, this is such a virtuous act that will become a means of the forgiveness of all his sins, and he will be free from all grief."

So under the urge of the attainment of these high ranks, Malike-Adil Mansoor ordered the endowment of the Mansoori Hospital (Here the deed of this Trust mentions the endowment, their situation and particulars).

"This hospital is dedicated to the treatment of the rich, the poor, men and women alike, irrespective of their place of residence, Cairo or the Egyptian lands around it, local inhabitants (Egyptian nationals) or foreign nationals regardless of colour or race from whatever malady or trouble they are tormented, whether they are physical ailments or spiritual and nervous, and those maladies may be mild or sufficiently aggravated and whether they are similar or dissimilar, apparent or concealed, or they may be victims of mental aberration whose correction is one of the important objectives, and whose treatment is most imperative and of great importance, and which can neither be overlooked nor slighted and discarded. Or they may be suffering from any other disorder whose removal and correction is so necessary for man (Here treatment will be undertaken with roots and herbs that are well known to the doctors and popular with them, and employed here, busy with their pursuit of medical sciences and their medical practice which are both expected to be beneficial to the patients.

"Here common people individually and collectively, old and young and minor boys and girls will all be eligible for treatment. Indigent patients, male or female, shall stay at the hospital as inpatients for the duration of their treatment (until completely cured). There they shall receive all the facilities of treatment available at the hospital and the necessities shall be distributed among all those in need of them, irrespective of their being strangers or relatives, local or aliens on a journey here, strong or weak, from the masses or the classes, high or low, rich or poor, officer or subordinate, blind or seeing, superior or inferior, renowned or unknown, glorious or worthless and unimportant, affluent or poverty-stricken, master or slave, this `treatment shall be free of charge, and nobody shall have any objection to it. This treatment shall be undertaken for the pleasure of God alone, attainment of the reward of the Hereafter and His General Beneficence, since Allah has ordained spending on those for the welfare of the patient and those things that are necessary for the patient and those who take care of the patients, such as doctors, opthalmologists, surgeons, compounders, those cooking tasty and appetising meals those preparing electuaries, collyria men, those preparing simple and compound purgatives, peons, treasurers, Amins (guardians or trustees), Mutawalli (superintendent), and besides them all those workers who are employed in hospitals for various jobs. Also those things that are necessary for the treatment of the patients. Also things needed for the food and the dress of the patients, things needed for the eyes, cauldrons and the like. And electuaries, various kinds of ointments, oils, drinks (decoctions, infusions, arqs or distilled decoctions), simple and compound drugs, carpets and beddings, vessels and implements needed in this work. The manager shall have the authority to append on the daily needs of the patients for example, the daily expenses of incense burnt by them (to keep the place wholesome Tr.), the plates to eat food from, glass tumblers to drink water and other drinks from, earthenware tumblers and goblets, the earthen lamps and the oil to burn in them, to procure drinking water from Nile used for drinking and cooking food, to purchase covers for the food offered to the patients; during the summer season the date-palm leaf fans must be purchased. The superintendent or manager of the Trusts shall spend on all these things from the income of the Trust, but this expenditure shall not be extravagant, nor ought to waste anything wilfully, there ought to be no excess over what is sufficient, all the expenses must be within the limits of genuine needs, so that as much as possible reward may be had (expected, Tr.).

The controller of the Trusts shall appoint two persons paid from the income of this trust who must be Muslims, trustworthy and honest. One of them shall hold charge of the distribution of various commodities and articles — liquid medicines, collyria, roots and herbs, Ciectuaries, oils and wicks, and issue only those things sanctioned by the officer concerned. The other person shall distribute their particular cups to the patients, male or female, every morning and evening and give them the dose prescribed for them. It will also be his duty to supervise the working of the kitchen where nourishing food for the patients, poultry meat, chicken and other kinds of meat, shall be prepared. It will be his duty to give every patient the food prescribed for him on a platter exclusively set apart for his use. No other patient shall partake of at food with him. It will also be his duty to distribute food properly covered among the patients, and shall supervise the distribution until every patient has received his prescribed food. He will be responsible for such distribution in a proper manner every morning and evening . The controller shall also have authority to appoint doctors (general practitioners) opthalmologists and surgeons on reasonably lucrative remuneration. These salaries shall be determined by him in keeping with the existing conditions and the needs of the patients. He is fully authorized in the matter of the fixation of pay and the number of employees, but he should not allow either excess or scantiness. An attitude of moderation should be his policy. The staff shall be duty-bound to look after the conveniences and comforts of the patients all the time. As regards duty hours they are free to either be there all at a time or take turns at it. Working hours may be fixed through mutual consultation and with the approval of the controller of endowments. It is their duty to talk to every patient and find out whether a certain patient is improving or his malady is aggravated. It should be noted properly, and with the permission of the controller of Trusts the medicines and diet of every patient should be prescribed and noted on his sheet (Redhead ticket, Tr.) and he should be given both according to that plan. The staff should stay at the hospital during the night, all of them together or by turns. The opthalmologists should sit in the out-door department daily and treat the patients that come to them. Every patient that comes in the morning any day of the week for getting his eyes tested and treated, should under no circumstances be compelled to return disappointed. They must treat him kindly and give him the necessary aid. Those with damaged eyes and poor vision should be dealt with still more courteously. If the eyes have developed wounds, the opthalmologist should consult the surgeon in his case, taking him personally to the surgeon and not leave him to fend for himself. Even after that the doctor should keep an eye on such cases until recovery. The controller of the trusts should appoint a Shaikh-al-Tibb (Superintendent of the Hospital) with the income of the trust, who will, all the time, remain engaged in the research work in the medical field, particularly the immediate problems. This expert or research officer should sit in the large consultation room that has been set apart for him in the Trust deed. It will be the duty of this expert to conduct research in various branches of the medical science and the problems cropping up from day to day. The working hours for him shall be fixed by the controller of the Trust, according to his discretion. But it must be kept in mind carefully that the staff should be within, the limits prescribed by the Trust deed. The controller of the Trusts should pay reasonably good emoluments to the predetermined staff of this hospital, and attendants, men and women. The salaries should be in keeping with the nature of their work. This remuneration is to be paid to the attendants for their services rendered to men and women that have been admitted to the hospital for treatment. They should also keep their place neat and tidy, wash their clothes and never deny them the facilities and comforts provided by the hospital. These facilities too must be in keeping with the circumstances at any-particular period . It is the duty of the controller of the Trust that he should arrange the burial of the patients, men and women, expiring at the hospital. They should be bathed and embalmed with aromatics at the cost of the hospital. The wages of digging a grave should be met by the Trust and the deceased person buried with due honours in accordance with the Sunnah of the Prophet. The

Controller of the Trust should supply a person, sick at home but helpless, at his residence whichever medicine, syrup or electuary he needs. But this should be in a manner that the in-patients at the hospital may not suffer for shortage of drugs. If such an out-patient dies at his own place the store keeper of the hospital should pay for his shroud, bath, digging of the grave and taking the dead body to the graveyard according to the status of the deceased. Those who are staying at the hospital and get cured by the grace of God, at the time of discharge, should be provided an average type of change of clothes in keeping with his status. Under this head the Controller of the Trust, in office, at any given time, should not go to such limits (of extravagance Tr.) that the internal needs of the hospital may suffer for want of funds. It is, however, left to his discretion. The Controller of this Trust should fear God and consider himself responsible to men also in the discharge of his duties and never give priority to an influential person in comparison with the common people and treat him more lavishly on the bases of discrimination between the rich and the poor. He should not give preference to a local patient over a foreign national, but must keep in view, in the matter of expenditure on them, "the reward of the Hereafter and Closeness to God Who is the Lord of all cherishers."

This was built by Sultan Mansoor Abu Yusuf, a well known ruler of the Muwahidin dynasty of the West. A spacious piece of land was selected in one of the most temperate place of Morocco for this hospital and the architects and builders were ordered to make it of the most beautiful design they could. All sorts of fruit trees and plants of most fragrant flowers were also planted on the premises. Canals of running water were passing by every room of the hospital: Four special reservoirs of water were built, one of them of pure white marble. Fine beddings were provided for the hospital beds, made out of wool, linen, silk and leather, beautiful beyond description. A pharmacy was built in the hospital in which different kinds of syrups, oils, collyria and other medicines were prepared. On being completely cured, in case of his being poor he was given sufficient amount of money which could help him start a business and earn his livelihood. Even if he was rich that amount of his share was given to him anyway. This hospital was not dedicated to the poor and the indigent only but the affluent also benefited by it. Rather, in whichever section of Morocco any stranger was found ailing, he was brought to the hospital and admitted as an in-patient. Either he was cured and discharged or died there. The Sultan went to the hospital every Friday and enquired and learnt first hand about the health of the patients, the working of the doctors and their dealings with the patients, and did all that was required by way of correction and redressal.

In short, these are the four ideal specimens out of hundreds of hospitals that were functioning at that time in the Islamic world from East to West; And they existed at the time when Europe was wandering in the wilderness of ignorance under layers of darkness, and unaware of these hospitals, their finesse, their cleanliness and the highest spirit of humanity at work in them. Let us hear in this connction what a well known German orientalist Marx Mayerhoff has to say about the European hospitals existing it that time as compared with the conditions in our hospitals narrated above. Dr. Marx says:

"The Arab hospitals and the order existing in the Islamic countries of the past is giving us a lesson which is very unpleasant and leaves a bitter taste in our mouths. We cannot fully appreciate it unless we compare and contrast, in minute detail, this system with that of the European hospitals of that period:"

About three hundred years before our time, rather even later, Europe was ignorant of the meaning of hospital. Rather it would be no exaggeration to say that upto 1710 A. D. they were living under these conditions. The patients were treated either at their own homes or at the poor-houses. The European hospitals in the past were actually poor-houses in which were kept those destitutes without any support and shelter whether they were ailing or in sound health. The best example of European hospitals or the poor-houses can be the Parisian home for the poor "Otel View" known to be the best hospital of that period. Maxi Tordo and Tanon both have given an account of this hospital in the following words:

"There are 1200 beds in this hospital. Out of these 486 beds are single, one for each patient. The remaining (714) which were not more than five paces in width, were allotted to from three to six patients. The extensive wards were damp and stinking and dark, in the absence of any windows or ventilators, in which more than eight hundred patients were lying on the ground (for want of beds). There was hardly room for them to lie down comfortably, so they were miserably huddled up there on the bare ground or on a heap of rubbish! A pitiable sight indeed for any person with human feelings! On a bed of average size, five or six patients were lying in a heap, the feet of one over the head of another, the young in the company of the old, women by the side of men. Although it violates common sense, yet it is the bare truth. On the one side there is a woman menstruating and by her side was lying a child laid down by typhoid and in a state of convulsion and burning with fever. And both these are in turn lying with a victim of skin infection and scratching his necrosed skin with his equally dirty blood stained nails, and pus is being spilled on the bed which cannot be soiled any further. The bad quality of food given to them is as bad as can be conceived, and that too in a very meagre quantity and irregularly after long intervals. The nuns supervising the working of this hospital had a preference for the rich patients, and provide wine at the cost of the poor patients. Sometimes they gave the sweet dishes and other rich foods, received as alms, to such patients for whom they were detrimental due to their peculiar maladies. So some of them died of over-eating, indigestion, even cholera, while others died of starvation. The doors of this hospital were always open and every one could find ingress and egress any time. In this way diseases could apread outside the hospital. There were heaps of human excretions and the air was heavily laden with noxious odours. Food arrangements were limited wholly to alms. If the rich people had not sent cooked food to the hospital the inmates would have died of starvation, as some of them died of overeating and drinking heavily. The beddings were teeming with insects and even vermin. The atmosphere of these wards was so foul that the nurses and attendants found it difficult to enter even after putting pieces of cloth moistened with vinegar to their noses. If a patient died there, his corpse would not be removed for at least twenty-four hours, from the hospital bed. At times such corpses got bloated and began to rot and stink, but still lay by the side of another patient on the same bed who would find himself nearer death due to this agonizingly foul atmosphere."

This is a brief comparison that brings out the difference between our hospitals and those of the Western countries. It shows to what abysmal depths of degradation due to ignorance and utter lack of knowledge of the principles and rules and regulations for the management of hospitals, the western nations had fallen. They had no knowledge of even the existence of any such thing as the principles of public health and hygiene. Rather, they were ignorant of even the most apparent principles of the maintenance of health that common sense suggests, and for which no education and training are necessary. The famous physician Usamah bin-e-Manqaz has reported two events in his book *Al-I-'tibar*, which give a correct idea of the sum of the knowledge of medical science of the Christians of the West. He says:

"Among the "marvels" (Howlers! Tr.) of the medical affairs of English men one incident is this that Sahib Munitrah wrote to his uncle that there was need of a doctor to treat his companions. The uncle sent a Christian doctor, Thabit, to them, but he came back within ten days. We asked him, "Have you been able to treat the patients in such a short period?" He said, "They had brought to me a soldier who had a boil on one of his feet. When a bandage dipped in the juice of Linjah (a plant) was applied, the abcess got burst. There was another patient, a woman whose dry and chapped skin had developed itch and was giving her trouble. I kept her on restricted diet as a preventive and tried to make her dry skin moist. But suddenly an English doctor appeared on the scene and told the people there about me, "What does he know of medical science and treatment of patients?" Then he asked the soldier with abcess on his foot whether he would like to live with one leg or die with both. The soldier said he would prefer to live with one leg only. So a sturdy soldier and a sharp axe were brought and I was a witness to this scene. The English doctor straightened his leg on a wooden board and asked the soldier (executioner? Tr.) to chop off his leg with a single stroke of his axe. He made a stroke with the axe. I was a witness to that and found that it failed to severe the leg. So he made a second attempt. The bone marrow was thrown out and the patient died immediately."

After that the author has related in great detail how he poured boiling water on the woman and she too, poor thing, passed away from this world immediately.

1. Before closing this topic, I would like to invite the attention of the readers to the results brought out by this comparison. The Islamic civilization established the highest standard in the field of the management of hospitals about nine hundred years earlier than the western civilization.

2. That our hospitals were established under such exalted human sentiments and principles of mercy and justice to humanity, which have a parallel neither in the ancient history, nor these sentiments and principles have been witnessed to this day in the western countries.

3. That Muslims is the first ummah (a party based on principles, Tr.) which discovered that melodiousness, humourous literature and giving the patient the impression psychologically that he is improving is very helpful in his speedy recovery.

4. That we have established such a high record in the matter of collective support, not attained, even in this advanced age, by the western countries. The patients were treated free of charge and their board and lodge were also arranged free. Rather after being cured, the poor and the destitute were also given enough money to help them earn their livelihood during the rest of their lives.

5. This is that high position of philanthropy which we attained when the banner of leadership was in our hands in the then civilized world. Have we ever thought over it, where we stand today, and where are the western people, compared with us?

EIGHT

The Tolerant Rulers

When the Tartars made a sudden assault on Syria and took countless men from Muslims, Jews and Christians as prisoners, Sheikh-al-Islam Ibn-e-Taimiyah talked to the Tartar Chief about the release of the prisoners. The Chief gave his assent for the release of the Muslim prisoners but refused to do so in case of the Jews and the Christians. But Sheikh-al-Islam did not agree and insisted on the release of the Jews and the Christians, who, he told him, were the Zimmis of the Islamic state and were bound to them, They could not let even one individual remain in captivity whether he belonged to their own community or from those living with them under a covenant.

Contrary to this, who does not know what the Christian 'heroes' have been doing during the crusades. During the middle ages when these wars were thrust on us, we fulfilled our contracts and they never let a chance of treachery slip by. We habitually overlooked their mischiefs but they always took revenge. We were careful to save human life as much as possible but they shed so much blood that it ran into knee-deep pools. But these merciless brutes prided in their shameful deeds, rejoiced and gloated over them.

When these heroes of the crusades in their second onslaught reached Ma'rah-al-No'man, the inmates were compelled to lay down arms. But before surrendering the town to the enemy they made the responsible leaders of the invaders guarantee the safety of their lives and property. But what actually happened ? Those ferocious wild beasts on entering the city perpetrated such crimes of cruelty, oppression and tyranny whose dreadfulness would make the children old. Some English historians who participated in this war have stated that the number of those slain was a hundred thousand souls, young and old, men and women.

After this the enemy advanced towards Bait-al-Maqdis and beseiged the civilian population. Fully convinced that they would be vanquished, they took a pledge from the supreme commander of the invading armies, Tankard, for the protection of their lives and properties. He gave the citizens a white banner to be hoisted over the Aqsa Mosque and advised them to enter that haven for their safety. And they were assured of safety of everything, in every way And then the invaders entered the town. But Ah! What horrible shambles this sacred city was converted into ! Ah, what horrid crimes were perpetrated!

The citizens of Bait-al-Maqdis took refuge in the Aqsa mosque, on which the banner given to them by Tankard was hoisted according to his instructions. This sacred mosque was packed to capacity with old men, women and children. And then came the holocaust. Those who had plighted their word to protect their lives and properties and given them the banner of peace, entered the holy mosque and slaughtered all those frail and defence less old men, children and women like goats and sheep. The place of worship was filled with human blood and touched the knees of the butchers. Thus slaughtering the citizens, they according to their own mode of thinking, sanctified the city, washed as it was with blood. The public highways and streets were littered with human skulls. Everywhere amputated limbs and other organs and deformed bodies were lying with no one to mourn or bury them. Men of our armies have stated that in the Aqsa mosque alone, seventy thousand people were slaughtered, among whom, apart from women and children, there were a large number of learned men and devout persons. The English historians too have not denied these shameful deeds of their co-religionists. Rather, they state these feats of theirs with great pride.

Ninety years after this dreadful slaughter and bloodshed, Salahuddin Ayyubi conquered Bait-al-Maqdis. Shall I tell you what he did with the inhabitants of this sanctum? About a hundred thousand western people lived there. The conqueror guaranteed security of life and property to them, and taking a small amount not from every one but only from those who could easily pay it, and allowed them to leave the town. They were also given respite for forty days for preparation before departure. In this way eighty-four thousand persons left the town in perfect safety, who went to 'Akka and other towns to their friends, relatives and co-religionists. A large number of them were exempted from payment of ransom, and his (Salahuddin's) brother Malik Adil paid the ransom for two thousand persons from his own pocket. And the treatment meted out to the women, far from expecting it from a conqueror of today, it would be unimaginable to him. And when the Christian patriarch wanted to leave the place, the Sultan permitted him to do so. He had much wealth amassed through Churches, synagogues, Sakhrah, Aqsa, and from ceremonies on the occasion of Easter whose count is known to God alone. Some counsellors advised Salahuddin to confiscate his wealth, but the Sultan told them that he could not go back upon his plighted word. He realized the same amount of ransom from him also as he had realized from an ordinary person. But what caused a fourfold increase in his honour and glory on the occasion of the conquest of Bait-al-Maqdis, was his mode of action in the process of evacuation of the Christians of the sanctum. He provided guards for the safe transit of the evacuees. The escorts had instructions to take them to the Christian habitations of Saur and Saida to their co-religionists in perfect safety. And all this in face of the entire Christian world standing in arms against the Muslims. Can any one be sure of his being awake (and not dreaming) when hearing all this? But this is not the whole story. Let us tell you the rest of it. There were several women who had paid ransom, who came to the Sultan and stated that their husbands, fathers and sons had either been killed in the battle or were in captivity. They had no one to look after them, nor was there any place where they could seek shelter. They were weeping and wailing. Seeing them tearful, the tender-hearted Sultan burst into tears himself. He ordered that after enquiry whoever of the husbands or sons or fathers of these women were in captivity should be realeased. And those whose guardians had been killed were given liberal compensation. These women wherever they went praised the Sultan loudly. And when after scrutiny the prisoners were released, they were also permitted to go to Saur, 'Akka and other places to their co-religionists.

Let us hear also what treatment was meted out to the Christian evacuees from Bait-al-Maqdis to their brethren in nearby towns. Some of them went to Antioch but the Amir (Administrator) of that city refused entry to them. And they went about wandering in search of shelter and support, and finally it was Muslims who offered them refuge. One contingent went to Tripoli (Lebanon) which was ruled by the Latin peoples. But even they did not allow them entry, and drove them away from their premises after robbing them of all their worldly goods they had been allowed to take with them by the Muslims.

Salahuddin's benevolent treatment of the western Christians during the crusades prima facie appears a tale. If the western writers had not been amazed at the noble nature and lofty morals of this great hero of Islam, the world would have certainly found room to accuse our historians of exaggeration. The westerners themselves make mention of the event that when Salahuddin learnt of the illness of Richard, the greatest and the most valiant general of the crusaders, he sent his personal physician. for his treatment and sent him also such fruits that were not easily available at that time of the year and he could not procure them. This happened while hostilities were on in full fury, and the armies of both the parties were engaged in a life and death struggle. The western writers also state that a woman approached the camp of Salahuddin, and wailing and weeping she complained to him that her child had been snatched away from her by two Abyssinian soldiers. Salahuddin himself was moved to tears by the pitiable condition of the woman, and then and there appointed a military officer for enquiry who searched out the woman's child and restored it to her. And she was escorted to her camp at his bidding. Dare any one say even in face of all this evidence that the morality of our civilization relating to the fighting forces and wars is not humane.

When Sultan Muhammad II conquered Constantinople he entered the cathedral of St. Sophia where all the priests had gathered to seek refuge, met them very courteously and assured them that he would support every reasonable request from them and they had no reason to be frightened. Those who had sought shelter there out of fear, should rest assured and return to their homes with an easy conscience. Later Muhammad II attended to the various problems of the Christians and solved them. He gave them assurance that they could follow their personal laws, religious obligations, and the customs and usages of their particular churches. Not only that; he authorised the priests to freely elect their patriarch (Bishop). And they elected Jenadeus. On this occasion the Sultan also ordered celebrations with great pomp and show which were usually made during the Byzantine rule. He said to the patriarch that in his capacity of a patriarch he was his friend at all times and at all places, and he should derive full benefit of all those rights and privileges his predecessors had enjoyed. After that the Sultan offered him a beautiful steed as a gift and detailed one of his body guards for his protection, and high-ranking government officials escorted him to his palace that the Sultan had got built for him. Then the Sultan proclaimed that he had sanctioned the laws of the orthodox church and the patriarch would protect them. All the goods of archaeological interest and abandoned articles, picked up by the people on the occasion of the conquest, he purchased from them and restored to the churches and other concerned institutions.

Sultan Muhammad, the conqueror meted out this treatment to the Christians even when there was no treaty arrived at between him and the Christians at the time of the conquest of Constantinople which he might have been obliged to fulfil. This privilege and support was kindly offered by him purely on grounds of his generosity and benevolent nature. It was due to this kind treatment of his that the people of Constantinople felt that under the new Islamic regime they were living in greater peace and religious freedom than under their former Byzantine rulers.

Similarly, the Uthmani rulers continued with kind treatment of their Christian subjects in the conquered neighbouring lands, for example, in the Bulgarian and the Greek states, such treatment was not meted out to them anywhere in Europe itself. Thus, in Hungary and Transalfania the followers of Cliffon and the unitarian Christians of Transalfania, instead of submitting themselves to the tyrannic rule of the extremely bigoted sect of Christians of the house of Habsburg, they prefered to live under the Turkish authority and rule for a long time. The Protestant sects of Silesia longed to attain religious freedom under the Muslim rule.

At the time when this kind and noble treatment was meted out to the Christians under the Turkish rule, religious prejudices were at their height. The prejudiced rulers were oppressing the sects other than their own. And the other religious sects too were at war with one another, blood was being freely shed and there was no security of life. During the seventh century, the patriarch of Antioch, Maccarios, writing about the tyrannies of the Roman Catholic sects of Poland perpetrated against the orthodox sects, says:

"We mourn bitterly the loss of those thousands of martyrs who have been murdered by the cruel Roman Catholic infidels and enemies of the faith during the last forty or fifty years and whose number approaches seventy thousand. O ye traitors! And O ye unholy sinners! O ye hard-hearted creatures! I ask you what was the fault of the nuns worshipping in the churches. Why did you put them to the sword? And how were the general run of women sinning? For what crime were the children, virgins and young girls taken? Why did you put them to the sword? Why should I not call them the accursed and damned souls of Poland when they have proved themselves more debased and cruel than the mischief-making idolators perpetrating cruelty on the Christians. In oppressing the Christians they were labouring under the erroneous notion that they would be able to efface the orthodox church altogether. God in His infinite Mercy preserve the Turkish government for all time to come, who realize their dues (Jizyah), and have no ill will against other religions-whether they are Christians, Nazerenes, Jews or Samaritans. But the Polish damned ones did not stop at realization of taxes, in spite of the fact that the Christians were willingly prepared to serve them, but they handed over the Christians to the cruel Jews who are enemies of the Christians at heart, and did not permit the Christians to build even one church, nor left alive any priest among them who could teach them their faith."

So much about the generous treatment meted out by Sultan Muhammad, the conqueror, to the Christians attached to the Cathedral of St. Sophia, and how benevolently he granted rights to the Christians of Constantinople. Now let us also hear what the European Christians did to their own brethren, the orthodox Christians when they conquered Constantinople in 1204 A.D. And instead of my telling you about it in my own words, I would like to quote the statement of Pope Innocent III (which should be more convincing, Tr.). He says:

"The duty of the followers of Jesus and the supporters of his faith was to turn the edges of their swords towards the greatest enemy of Christianity (Islam). But it is a pity they shed the blood of the Christians themselves, which was religiously forbidden to them. They did not care at all for it, and shed much blood. They neither respected the faith, nor discriminated between the sexes nor had they any regard for age, or youth in this bloodshed. They committed fornication and adultery in broad daylight. The nuns, mothers of children and virgins found themselves equally helpless before these lustful creatures and the sensual beasts of this army, so to say, devoured (ravished) them. These robbers and plunderers did not stop at robbing the king and other aristocrats of their riches, but ravaged and plundered the lands and other properties of the Churches. They desecrated the churches also, robbing them of the sacred portraits, crosses and holy relics."

And the well-known historian Chari-Dale writes:

"This army, intoxicated with power, entered the Cathedral of St. Sophia, destroyed the holy books and trampled under foot the portraits of the martyrs. A corrupt woman was occupying their chair of the patriarch, and she started singing loudly. All traces of religious knowledge were effacted from the city, and the gold and silver statues were destroyed to provide material for their gold and silver coins."

And the monks who were eye-witnesses to these painful scenes have put up their evidence thus:

"The fact is that the followers of Muhammad (Sal'am, Tr.) had never meted out the treatment to this city which it met at the hands of the monks, the votaties of Christ."

Yes. Certainly the Muslim did not do any such thing when they conquered this town (Constantinople), as evidenced by the behaviour of Sultan Muhammad Fateh. And the Muslim, so long as they were believers, could not manifest narrow-mindedness and even approach such shameful deeds of religious bigotry, as were perpetrated by the Roman Catholic followers of Christ against other followers of his, subscribing to the orthodox Catholic faith.

I would not like to take up in detail the story of the Muslim Conquerors of Andalusia and their generous treament of the minorities of that country, affectionate behaviour and extreme regard for their feelings, nor would compare it with the treatment the Muslims met at the hands of the Spaniards, when they took over the last surviving Muslim state of Granada. And they did all that in face of the treaty with Muslims comprising about sixty provisions, regarding the protection of their faith, their mosques their honour and dignity and their properties and so many other things. But they did not fulfil any of their pledges, nor met any responsibility in this behalf. Rather, they did not desist even from murder of innocent people and taking possession of their properties. Again, within thirty years of the fall of Granada, Europe declared in 1534 A. D. that all the mosques be converted into Churches. So we find that within four years of this declaration the Muslims were totally wiped out of Spain. This is how the Christians "made good their plighted word" and that was our fulfilment of pledges!

The stinging of a scorpion is nothing astonishing. It is in its nature. What amazes one is the fact they behaved in this cruel manner and were guilty of the breach of contract with their own co-religionists. And these oppressions and cruelties were no less than those perpetrated against the Muslims. Wherever they went as conquerors, they made demonstrations of the same hard-heartedness and oppression and tyranny. It may be East or West, they always appeared in their true colours as cunning and cruel wolves, no matter whether their prey was some weak Muslim or a Christian. Their writers themselves lament their national character.

The Priest Ododvalley, a courtier of Louis VII, in favour with him, and having participated in the second crusade with the king, writes in his observations:

"When the Christians were going to Bait-al- Maqdis through Asia Minor, they suffered a great defeat at the hands of the Turks in the mountainous region of Frigia. That was in 1148 A.D. With great difficulty they got to a coastal town of Italy. Here, those who could meet the heavy demands of the Greeks (they made to take the armies across the sea) reached Antioch by sea route. But they left behind their sick, wounded and ordinary people at the mercy of their perfidious Greek allies. Louis paid them (the Greeks) five hundred marks for their protection and the treatment of the disabled and the sick, so that they might be able to join their companions.

But hardly had the army left Italy when the Greeks informed the Turks of the presence of these unarmaed crusaders, and quietly waited to watch the fun of these wretched people facing starvation, disease and above all the spears of the enemy. This death and destruction came upon them when they were proceeding towards their cantonment. Four thousand individuals out of this unarmed and disabled multitude in desperation tried to escape this tragic end. The Turkish army that had returned to the cantonment, turned round with the idea of taking their victory to a conclusive end. They routed and ruined this army. Those who escaped this calamity were despairing of their lives. But the Muslims were greatly moved by their pitiable plight, and instead of enmity their hearts were now filled with affection for them. They nursed the sick and helped the hungry and the destitutes who were at the verge of death and destruction. The Muslim extended their generosity to the extent of purchasing the cash in French currency from the Greeks, who have snatched it from them, and gave it to these wretched travellers. There was a world of difference between the cruel and beastly behaviour of their own Greek Christian brethren with these travellers and the just and merciful treatment of the heathens (Muslims).

The Greeks played a dirty joke on them, beat them and whatever Louis had left for their maintenance, they robbed them of it all. This resulted in some of them entering the fold of the faith of their saviours willingly, as attested by one of our historians of yore. 'Their own cruel brothers oppressed them but the pagans (Muslims) offered them security and shelter and most benevolent treatment.'

"We learn that more than three thousand of those returning alive joined the Turks. Alas! This kindness and mercy were more disagreeable than treachery. They certainly gave them bread but snatched from them their faith and beliefs although it is true that they did not compel any one to abandon his faith, but confined their efforts to service and benevolence to them."

In New Perspective

The evidence is not far to seek. The impressions and record of the cruelties of the western nations in the two world wars and their morals and deeds in the Islamic Middle East serve clear evidence that in governance and in the battlefield their conduct has been extremely tyrannical and a model of barbarism. Their hypocritical policy is now no more any secret that in international meets they let loose loud propaganda of their civilization and culture, philanthropy and love and affection. But in their wars, in their dominions and colonies they openly demonstrate their barbarism and blood-thirstiness. Some people put up the excuse for this mode of action of the western nations that during the middle ages they were not so civilized and cultured that any other behaviour could be expected of them. But a very pertinent question is that 'now that they are civilized, rather, they claim to hold the monopoly of civilization and benefiting the whole world with sciences and arts and the new inventions, are they any better?' The real position is not that. According to our way of measuring them, the problem really is what is their true temperament which overwhelms every effort of theirs at affectation and hypocrisy. The fact of the matter is that the western nations still have those traits and habits of the days of their barbarity and idolatory in their entirety. During the middle ages these traits and habits took the shape of religious prejudice. So religion had to bear the brunt of their barbarity. And today the same cruel and barbaric habits are at work under the garb of civilization. So peace and security and civilization have to bear the burden of their hard-heartedness and inhumanity. In fact, in every period these nations have been mischief-makers, cruel, blood-thirsty, lovers of power and authority and bigoted and barbaric. How then dare they tell tales of our hard-heartedness under Islamic victories, (quite apart from the fact that it is a bundle of blatant lies) and present their despicable colonialism as a mercy and kindness. And where it comes to the bare facts, ours and their position according to some poet is this:

> "When we were in power, forgiveness was our well known habit, but when you came to rule you shed rivers of (much) blood." (F.N : 12)
>
> "This difference, between the two of us is not at all amazing since whatever are the contents of a vessel spill out of it." (F.N : 13)

NINE

A Peaceful Religion

The advent of Islam was one of those few momentous events in history which have shaped and guided the destiny of mankind for all times to come. Prophet Mohammad (P.B.U.H.) who was chosen by Allah to be His Messenger, stands out as a unique personality among the truly great men of the world. An orphan, with no claim to royalty or to riches, born in the barren sands of Arabia, which was then peopled by wild but brave and enterprising tribes, he yet, spread the splendour of Islam and made it a potent force in the world and an instrument of change of unbelievable dimensions.

His message was simple but straight, admitting of no deviation, no compromise - the message of divine unity of Godhead. Allah is both a unity and an infinity. He is what He is, admitting of no logical or metaphysical quibbling, and certainly of no teleological speculation. We know him as one and one only, and as Caliph Omar said later on, 'One cannot be two". This affirmation of unity is made by what is called `the path of negation. "There is no God, but God", proclaims the Kalima, which reminds us of the Vedantic doctrine, "Neti: Neti" - not this, by way of monastic affirmation. But Allah of Islamic conception is no mere mystical or metaphysical experience, the theme of dark silence:

"Without knowing where, I enter into Silence,

And I dwell in ignorance,

Above all knowledge: ......

A place without light, an effect without cause".

He is something more: not only the Father, Protector and Judge of the Semitic conception, but one whose presence a faithful breathes every moment of his life, a participator in his joys and sorrows, a guide and a path-finder through his Messenger, Rasool, through whom He spreads his message. Thus, a belief in the unity of divinity also entails treading the ethical path as symbolised by the Prophet. There is no scope for even a trace of anti-nomianism in Islam, the belief that faith can dispense with obligation to keep the moral law. The Prophet and his teachings symbolise the conduct of life which a faithful must keep, in order to be a follower of Islam. Therefore, in Kalima, belief in oneness of Allah must be accompanied by faith in his Rasool. Both are indispensable and they go together, the one cannot be conceived without the other. The Rasool and his teachings show the path to Allah, who is one and indivisible; this is the principal message of Islam.

Almost a thousand years before Prophet Mohammad (P.B.U.H.), Lord Buddha in India has proclaimed the revolutionary concept of man's ascent to divine state by strict obedience to moral law, but this ascent was hierarchical; if Buddhhood could not be attained without "Dharmam", it could not also be attained without "Sangham". Lord Jesus Christ also said later on that "I and Father are one", giving rise to endless argument and discussion. In Islam, however, there is no hierarchy: nothing comes between man and his maker, human or divine. All the faithful are equal; in the House of God there is neither rank nor preference. The Prophet, though the chosen of Allah, could appropriate to himself only what he had been allowed; he could not claim for himself anything, by virtue of his office, for was he not a servant of Allah as others? This innate nobility and utmost selflessness, on the part of the Prophet, was one great factor which made Islam a dynamic force. The Prophet (P.B.U.H) was over vigilant to emphasise that he was simply a human, with no other power than what God in his mercy had allowed him. He performed no miracle to spread his teachings, though his whole life in itself was a miracle. His dislike for deification of any object, human or material, except that of one supreme reality was ingrained in him so deeply that he forbade worship of any symbol, in any form, and he took good care that the followers of Islam, out of esteem and affection for him, did not deify him in any way. Perhaps, this is a singular instance in human history of self denial of this kind.

Waxing eloquent, this is what a great Christian missionary, Rev. C.F. Andrews, has to say on the message of Islam:

"One of the greatest blessings which Islam has brought to East and West alike has been the emphasis which, at a critical period in human history, it placed upon the divine unity. For, during those dark ages both in the East and the West, from 600 A.D. to 1000 A.D. this doctrine was in danger of being overlaid and obscured in Hinduism, and in Christianity itself. Islam has been, both to Europe and India, in their dark hour of aberration from sovereign truth of God's unity, an invaluable corrective and deterrent."

Now, during the period Rev. Andrews speaks of, Islam had to contend, not against Hinduism of the pure variety, which we may call as 'Advaitik' variety, which is, as the name itself suggests, pure Monism, but Mahayan Buddhism of the left Tantrik variety. The Sakas, the common name for transoxonian tribes of Central Asia, had been converted to Buddhism and assimilated in the Hindu fold. Kanishka, whose empire extended from north-west India across Kashmir to parts of China and to the Central Asian plains, was a great patron of Mahayan Buddhism, which besides drawing inspiration from Mahayan philosophers of north India, had incorporated many of the prevailing quaint tribal beliefs and rites, as well as empty rituals for propitiating gods and goddesses. As for Christianity, its basic principle was Trinity, and those days it was engulfed in the quagmire of endless sectarian quarrels. The Jews, having been dispersed from their Holy Land by the Romans, were on the run, like a hunted and persecuted race, denied not only the right to possess, but sometimes even the right to live. Among the Semitic races, they were firm believers in one God, but their God, Jehovah, was certainly not Allah of the Islamic conception.

Islam, therefore, while in comparison to these established faiths, had one inestimable advantage, unity of command and unity of execution, against the diversities on both counts, amongst its adversaries. There was but one Allah, one Rasool, and one rank of the soldiers of Allah. The equality in Islamic brotherhood generated supreme confidence in the rightness of their cause and faith in victory. The spirit of man is that splendid asset which cannot be matched. No wonder then if the march of Islam was not only spectacular but breath-taking. Opposition to Islam only steeled the will of its adherents to succeed, and with the Prophet himself at command or his example to inspire, the whole of the wild and turbulent Arabia was knit into one united Islamic brotherhood, poised for victory from Egypt and Persia to distant Spain in the West, and later on to Indonesia in the East, not to speak of Central Asia, Mongolia, China and across the Pamirs and Hindukush. Thus began the march of Islamic Arabic civilization, one of the mightiest and grandest, the original puritan Arabic Islam being tempered by the cultural influences of the races it conquered and absorbed within its fold. Arabic Islam acted as a catalyst for intellectual progress. Great centres of learning grew up in Cairo, Baghdad, Cordova, and Damascus and there was free speculation in the fields of mathematics, astronomy, alchemy (chemistry), and medicine, etc. The Arabs, like true intellectuals were not averse to borrowing freely from Alexandrian Jews or Hellenic Philosophers or Indian savants. Averros wrote his great commentaries on Plato and Aristotle in the twelfth century. AviCenna, the Philosopher, stands out as one of the world's greatest teachers of medicine. It was at Cordova in Spain that Moses Maimonides, the great physician of his age, wrote his famous Biblical commentaries. In fact, Arabic learning has been the precurser of and inspiration behind the modern European civilization and learning. The embellishment in arts and in literature was also remarkable. For early six centuries, people of Central Asia, the Mediterranean region and many other lands woke up with the call of the Muazzin to the faithful and slept when the last prayers had been said in the night. Islamic grandeur was at its best, both as a spectacle of power and as beacon of thought.

Even though the Prophet belonged ethnically to the Semitic race, the message of Islam was for mankind as a whole. The Prophet did not deny the validity of other religions but still considered it necessary to give a fresh 'message' which could save the world from distortions which had overtaken the teachings of earlier Prophets. After Arabia had been brought under the banner of Islam, the Prophet himself dispatched envoys to Emperor Heraclus of the Eastern Roman Empire, Emperor Negois of Abbyssynia, and Emperor Chorram of Persia, inviting them to embrace Islam. While urging his followers to spread Islam far and wide, the Prophet admonished them "not to differ as differed the disciples of Jesus in as much as those disciples who were dispatched a far showed reluctance to undertake the mission" (Conversation quoted at pp.229-30 of Siddique's life of Muhammad, based on *Tarikh al-Rasool wa-al Mulk*). The question may be raised, why kings and why not the commoners? In almost all countries of the world at that time, the divine right of kings prevailed. In Semitic countries, including Persia, the commoners generally followed the faith of the royalty, the king being considered the representative of God on earth, the same Judge and Father-like figure as the divine Being. This assumption is evident from the fact that wherever the royalty accepted Islam or any other religion the people of the country by and large accepted the same faith.

It would be pertinent here to examine the myth fostered by some Western writers which projects Islam being spread with the Holy Book in one hand and the sword in the other. It has to be remembered that Islam postulates Good and Evil as two separate realities, constantly at war with each other, so that man has to be ever vigilant against his evil propensities. This is represented by the word Jihad which means "striving": one's duty is to hold truth (of Islam) in face of odds and adversities. It has been said that the best of Jihad is the uttering of the word of truth in the face of a tyrant. As Bakhtiar Fateh-ul-Bari said "You can do (help the wrong-doer) by holding his hand from an act of oppression." Jihad is a positive concept in Islam which implies holding fast to the path of truth and righteousness. It has to be undertaken with the purest of motives, not for self or for worldly possessions, but to be pursued purely in the service of Allah in all humility and charity. According to another Hadith, a certain warrior had valiantly fought and died in a holy war. Followers of the Prophet hailed him as a 'Ghazi', a martyr, but the Prophet remarked that it was not so, for he had fought not for the glory of Islam, but from motives of self-aggrandisement and would not be admitted as a Ghazi before Allah. Certainly, Jihad is not Qatl, for it has been clearly laid down in the Holy Quran:

"Permitted are those who are fought against, because they have been oppressed", and further:

"And fight in the way of Allah those who fought you, and transgress not the limits; verily Allah loveth not the transgressors." Indeed, according to the tenets of Islam, it is by way of self-defence that Jihad is to be undertaken. It is not for the purpose of loot and plunder or for adding to one's riches. If that happens, it degenerates into Qatl, senseless destruction of God's creatures, which is not permissible, according to the Islamic scripture. And the greatest Jihad, according to Hadith, is victory over oneself; this is Jihad-e-Akbar.

Among the Semitic races, violence had been the rule rather than an exception; an eye for an eye and a tooth for a tooth, was the mood in these societies. In the *Old Testament* (II-kings, 18, 19 & 25) we read the blood-curdling details of the Israelites being permitted to inflict savageries on the Moalites:

"And ye shall smite every fenced city, and every choice city, and fell every good tree, and stop all wells of water and mar every good piece of land with stones". This was carried out. " And they beat down the cities, and on every good piece of land cast every man his stone, and filled it and they stopped all the wells of water, and felled all the good trees."

Wanton destruction was not alien to the Semitic temper. But the credit for softening such a temper through a heightened sense of righteousness goes to Islam. The instrument of instructions issued by Caliph Omar to the army despatched on an expedition to Syrian borders reads as follows:

"Don't commit treachery, nor depart from the right path. Don't mutilate, nor kill a child, nor aged man nor a woman .....You are likely to pass by people who have devoted their lives to monastic service; leave them to what they devoted their lives to."

The wars waged by Islamic armies were mostly thrust upon them, and it appears every effort was made by leaders so that the limits of humanity were not transgressed, since this was an obligation imposed upon the faithful by the Holy Quran. The basic human instinct of collective violence is everlasting and survives to this day, in the present age of so-called cultural advancement. We have also to take note of the ferocious and cruel practices already prevailing amongst the tribal peoples whom the Prophet had tried to lead into Islamic ethics, an action greatly in advance of the times. It would thus be an un-historical view of Islamic wars to shift the blame for the cruelties of war to Islam as such, or even to present some of the purely military or political invasions as a war intended to spread a religion.

It is interesting to note that the gospel of Lord Jesus Christ of "turning the other check" had come to be so interpreted as to justify religious wars. According to St.Thoms Acquinas:

"Jesus said that he who takes the sword shall perish by the sword. But to take means to use without warrant, and the words only prohibit unauthorized or private persons from drawing the swords". Again, "War may be the best or the only means of attaining the ends of peace."

Martin Luther had held that the gospel pre-supposed natural rights and duties and vigorously defended the Christian soldiers. Calvin argued that war was a branch of retributive justice entrusted by God to the civil magistrates, and cited the exploits of the Prophets of the Old Testament, specially of Moses and David.

Islam appears to be open and straight forward; it does not take recourse to fine arguments in order to justify "holy" wars; the only limitation being imposed is that a war to be holy must be in the path of Allah, and not for any personal or sectarian end.

It must also be understood that Islam has not sanctioned forcible conversion or even conversion by fraud or deception. Dissent is not to be visited upon with destruction, but only persuasion. The Holy Quran declares in clear terms:

"Invite (all) to the way of their Lord with wisdom and goodly exhortation, and argue with them with that which is the best.

The words to be marked are "invite", "exhortation" and "argue". All these envisage friendly discussions and the right to dissent. The teachings imply that superior ways and wisdom of Islam will win, and nothing else. Now, examine the Christian gospel:

" ..... Go out into the highways and hedges, and compel them to come in, that my house may be filled."

The word "compel" has been interpreted in St.Augustine's "Kingdom of God" as sanctioning forcible conversion. This ignores what is said further on the subject in the same gospel. "And whosoever doth not bear his cross, and come after me, cannot be my disciple." The original Christian scriptures too had not given a call for death or destruction in order to convert forcibly.

Here is another aspect of humanitarianism of our civilization. And from this aspect too the Islamic civilization is singular. Under conditions of peace and security every nation can manifest courtesy, gentleness, kindness to the weak and the infirm and tolerant attitude: towards the relatives and the neighbours when it is existing as a weak nation bereft of all power and authority But under conditions of war to be just to people, to be gentle and tolerant towards the vanquished nations, is not given to every nation nor every military general necessarily has these traits. The sight of blood makes man's blood boil, and the inimical attitude of a nation creates malice and rouses rage in him. The intoxicating effect of conquest goes to the conqueror's head, and under these conditions he is at times guilty of the manifestation of the worst hard-heartedness and revenge. This is the history of nations, be they ancient people or the modern rather it is the history of the whole world since Cain shed the blood of his brother Abel.

The Quran says:

Behold! they each presented a sacrifice (to God):

It was accepted from one, but not from the other.

Said the latter: "Be sure 1 will slay thee". "Surely", said the former, "God doth accept of the sacrifice of those who are righteous." (Al Quran V: 27)

On this occasion (of Power and glory and war) history has placed the crown of life eternal on the heads of the leaders of civilization, whether they be soldiers, or citizens, and conquerors or the rulers, since out of all civilizations ours is the only one whose great men even under the most difficult war times, manifested the highest form of humanity based on justice and affection, particularly in a situation where the circumstances rouse man to bloodshed, oppression and revenge. God is our witness that if these morals of the Muslims under conditions of war had not been proved as undeniable historical events, I, for one, would have regarded it a tale of something non-existent on this planet.

Islamic Civilization, a Boon

When Islam came to the world in its most perfect form and the last authentic version, people here were existing like wild animals in a jungle. The mighty remorselessly murdered the weak and the armed man unhesitatingly robbed the unarmed of his belongings. Fighting was something usual in the lives of all faiths and the religious laws, nations and tribes, which was not limited by any conditions nor confined to any limits. No distinction existed between the permissible and the unlawful and oppressive war. Whichever nation found itself powerful enough to snatch another nation's land, enslave its men and women and compel it to abandon its creed and thought, unhesitatingly and without any feeling of guilt did accomplish it. But our civilization could not put up with the idea that this tyrannical practice should continue in the world, which had lowered mankind to the level of beasts literally. Rather, it proclaimed to the world that in the matter of mutual relations between nations the real issue is recognition and cooperation (and not hatred and war against one another).

The Quran said:

> O mankind! We created you from a single pair) of a male and a female, and made you into nations and tribes, that ye may know each other (not that ye may despise each other). Verily the most honoured of you in the sight of God is (he who is) the most righteous of you. (Al Quran: XLIX: 13)

On this basis a state of peace and security is the natural form of relationship between one nation and another. God says:

> O ye who believe! Enter into Islam wholeheartedly;
> (Al Quran II: 208)

Now the nation that does not want to live in peace and cannot rest without war against another nation and oppressing it, and to achieve this end, is always ready to declare war on others, for the other nation too it is indispensable to be in a state of preparedness for its defence against such aggressions, since if a nation is not all the time in readiness for its defence the aggressive nation makes all possible haste to start war and aggression. The Quranic advice in such a situation is:

> Against them make ready your strength to the utmost of your power, including steeds of war, to strike terror into (the hearts of) the enemies of God and your enemies.
>
> (Al Quran VIII: 60)

Now, if the aggressive nation desists from its aggressive designs and is daunted by "armed love of peace", the first nation too must unhesitatingly extend its hand of friendship. Rather it should manifest by every gesture its desire for peace.

> But if the enemy incline towards peace, do thou also incline towards peace, and trust in God: (AI Quran VIII: 61)

But if the aggressive nations are bent on the trial of strength, only force can meet force and steel alone can confront steel. The Quran permits fighting against aggressors:

> Fight in the cause of God those who fight you,
>
> (Al Quran II: 190)

Policy on War

This is the stand on the basis of which the principles and elements of our civilisation do not allow wars for the sake of booty, pillage and debasement of nations, since its principles regard such wars totally prohibited. And in its sight only that war is permitted (Lawful) which is waged for any of the following objectives:

1. For the protection of the morals and ideology of the people.

2. For the defence of the liberty, stability and security of the nation.

> And fight them on until there is no more tumult or oppression and religion is for Allah alone.
>
> (AI Quran II: 193)

For the nation declaring war in this situation, only the liberty of its creed is not desired. Rather, it is essential for it to guarantee liberty of creed and also that of the protection of the places of worship of all religions.

> Did not God check one set of people by means of another, there would surely have been pulled down monasteries, churches, Synagogues, and mosques, in which the name of God is commemorated in abundant measure.
>
> (Al Quran XXII: 40)

Again, another very brilliant aspect of the bright principle of our civilization is that the way it has enjoined on us not to let our honour and liberty be violated in any way, it has also made it incumbent on us to support other weak and oppressed groups and stand in defence of them against their oppressors:

> And why should ye not fight in the cause of God and of those who, being weak are all treated (and oppressed)?.... Men, women and children, whose cry is.: "Our Lord Rescue us from this town, whose people are oppressors; and raise for us from Thee one who will protect; and raise for us from Thee one who will help!" (AI Quran IV: 75)

Only a war restricted by these moral restraints is one for which the believers can take the field for defence against the compulsion and violence let loose on people's creed, freedom of thought and action and their peace and security. And such a war is permitted and approved by Islam, and the fighter in this cause can get close to God and is to be rewarded with heaven. And it is about this war that the Islamic civilization has declared that it is fighting in the way of Allah, and all other wars are waged as a transgression and to create mischief in the land. The difference between the lawful war of our civilization and the wars known to other nations of the world has been excellently brought out by the following verse of the Quran:

> Those who believe fight in the cause of God and those who reject Faith fight in the cause of Evil: So fight ye against the friends of Satan: feeble indeed is the cunning of Satan.
>
> (Al Quran IV: 76)

Our civilization declares: war to exalt the word of God and to establish the way of life suggested by it. This system is the order of Truth. This is the good and this alone is the noble attitude. As against this, other people declare war to oppress others, to create mischief and to propagate wickedness. And mischief is another name for evil, rebellion and tumult. So when this is the reason behind our wars and this their objective, such a war waged in the cause of truth and for the sake of good, can never become the means of propagation of falsehood and evil. That is why one of the principles and elements of our civilization is this also that we can and shall fight only against those who fight against us and oppress us. The Quran has laid down the following principle in this behalf:

> If then anyone transgresses the prohibition against you; transgress ye likewise against him. (Al Quran II: 194)

Therefore, if we transgress these limits set by God and fight against those who do not want to fight and oppress those who are not bent on causing injury, we shall be transgressors because of perverting this war based on humanity from its high objectives, as declared by the Quran:

> Fight in the cause of God those who fight you, but do not transgress limits; for Gad loveth not transgressors.
> (AI Quran II: 190)

And at another place it has been said:

> But indeed if any do help and defend themselves after a wrong (done) to them, against such there is no cause of blame. The blame is only against those who oppress men with wrong-doing and insolently transgress beyond bounds through the land defying right and justice: for such there will be a penalty grievous. (Al Quran XLH: 41-42)

Therefore when once the war has been thrust on us, it is our duty to keep in view our principles of war all the time, lest we should become the cause of hard-heartedness, tumult and pillage and destruction. It should never be allowed to happen under any circumstances whatsoever, since the war of humanity waged in the way of God alone, even from the aspect of the means at our disposal, should remain restricted to limits of humanity, however fierce and violent that war may be.

Guidelines about War

That is why the instructions given by Islam in connection with war are not to be found in the history of any other civilization. For example, Abu Bakr the first caliph of the Prophet issued the following instructions to the army led by Usamah:

"Do not mutilate and disfigure your enemies after you have killed them. Do not kill the children and old men who cannot fight. Have nothing to do with women (do not kill them. Tr.). Do not destroy the groves (date palm and others). Do not resort to arson. Do not cut down a tree yielding fruit (for fuel. Tr.). And slaughter only as many animals as you actually need for your food. (Do not kill animals and waste their meat that can serve as food for you or for others later on Tr.). You will come upon people who have devoted themselves to churches and monasteries. Leave them alone and let them pursue the mission for which they have renounced the world."

That makes evident enough the features of the war waged in the cause of God and not for mischief, tumult and oppression. And that it adheres to the principles and elements which are a blessing to humanity and the war culminates either in victory or treaty. In case of treaty its terms are strictly adhered to which are religiously binding since (like all agreements, Tr.) it is a covenant with God.

And if they gain victory, it is the victory of a party that has strived for seeking the countenance of God alone, and its individuals become martyrs in the way of God. Such a party takes only those steps after victory which make the roots of the order of truth firmer in the land, and puts an end to all kinds of tumult and oppression among the people.

> (They are) those who, if We establish them in the land, establish regular prayer and give regular charity (Zakat), enjoin the right and forbid wrong: With God rests the end (and decision) of (all) affairs. (Al Quran XXII: 41)

These are the limits prescribed by the Islamic civilization for the activities of its conqueror ....lofty spiritualism, social justice, cooperation in deeds of righteousness and general welfare and ceaseless struggle against evil and mischief. These are the principles and 'elements of war of our civilization, and these are moral principles relating to wars which can be summed up in three words: "Justice, Mercy and fulfilment of agreements."

Practical Value

To my mind, what we have said so far is not enough for the deposition of the peace-loving policy of our civilization during the war, since presentation of principles and their general proclamation is not enough proof of the eminence and the philanthropy of a nation. Since long we have been witnessing many nations that came forward before the world with very lofty and sublime objectives, but their behaviour towards other nations was extremely disgraceful, cruel and far from human principles of mercy and justice. The game played by the colonial powers in our own country is no secret, nor the history of their shameful and cruel deeds is far removed in time. Therefore it becomes indispensable to have a close look at the practical demonstrations of these principles during the period of the zenith of our civilization. This is the point where disgrace is the portion of some nations and others are honoured. Here the Islamic *millat* becomes distinguished from all other *millats*. And in the matter of philanthropy neither any nation comes close to it nor any civilization can touch it.

Holy Prophet's Example

We shall first of all present some events from the life of the Prophet, since he is (under injunctions from God, Tr.) the originator of our civilization, its founder and responsible for the formulation of its rules and regulations. And it was he who was competent to correctly interpret the aims and objects of the Islamic civilization. The history of the prophets and the reformers bears out the fact that no other prophet had to face such torments and hardships in the way of his call to the truth in quantity or quality as confronted and patiently gone through by the Prophet. His Meccan life, spread over thirteen long years of suffering is before us all. During this whole period, both he and his party of believers had to face the malice, enmity, torments and reproach and revilement of the opponents, so much so that attempts were made on his own life and those of his companions. After that even a cursory glance at his ten years of life at Madinah, reveals that this entire period is occupied by untiring struggle and constant Jehad and Maghazi (religious wars in which the Prophet took part in person). He could not discard completely the armour until, a short while before his passing away, the entire Arabian peninsula had been dominated by him. It has been generally observed that one who has constantly been a prey to enmities, oppression and tyranny and conspiracies, becomes revengeful and when he enters the battlefield and lifts the sword and comes to grips with the enemy, his nature becomes ferocious and cruel. But look at the moral behaviour of the Prophet in all those wars that were actually forced on him, and how he practically demonstrated the principles of war of the Islamic civilization proclaimed by him.

During the battle of Uhad, when, due to violation of the instructions of the Prophet, the believers were confronted with a set-back and the enemies surrounded him and to put an end to his life they fell upon him from all sides and he was wounded, and one of his teeth was lost, his face was injured and one of the rings of his helmet got embedded in his cheek, his companions imperilled their own lives to defend him against the enemies and rescued him from their circle. At this juncture some of his companions requested him to curse the enemies. He said in reply, "God did not send me to reproach (and curse) people but as a mercy to them and as one calling them to the truth." This is that love of truth that at times compels a Believer to take up arms against the opponents, but he does not wage wars to quench the thirst for blood. Rather, in the battle field itself and under such dire circumstances, the words uttered by the Prophet bear testimony to the fact that blood-shed and conquests are not the aim of war but an intense desire to lead humanity to the right path (of guidance).

And it was in the battle of Uhad that the prime martyr Hamzah met his martyrdom. Hamzah was the Prophet's uncle and one of the most outstanding horsemen of Arabia. He was murdered by a slave, Wahshi by name. And this murder was not accidental but pre-planned and at the behest of Hind, the wife of Abu-Sufyan. And when he fell a martyr in the battle-field, Hind searched his dead body out and taking out his heart and liver, tried to chew them, thus establishing a world record of malice and hard-heartedness. Strange as it may appear, the change of circumstances brought both Hind and Wahshi to the fold of Islam and they appeared before the Prophet, who not only gave them asylum under the canopy of Islam, but prayed to God for the forgiveness of Hind. To Wahshi he said only this, "It would be better for you to live far away from us (to keep out of our sight so as not to remind us of the murder of Hamzah. Tr.). This is the treatment that 'the Prophet (a Mercy for mankind, QXXI: 107 Tr.) meted out to his uncle's murderer and also the one who chewed his liver and heart.

In one of the battles, the Prophet found a woman who had been killed. He was very angry and strictly warning the fighters in the way of God said to them. "Did I not prohibit killing of women in battle? She was not fighting against you?" This is the Prophet of God (Peace and Blessings of God on him) who is giving a lesson in humanity even in the battle field, thus making a practical demonstration of his instructions (teachings) relating to war, when he himself is the Supreme commander of the Islamic army and personally participates in the battles.

He conquers Makkah, and enters the city in pomp and glory at the head of , ten thousand venturesome companions. And the scene is totally different from the usual. The malicious and spiteful enemies of twenty one years standing, the Quraish of Makkah, who had crossed all limits in tormenting him and his companions, were standing before him vanquished, humiliated and with bowed heads, waiting for his decision against themselves. Looking at them in this plight, he put to them just one question, "O ye people of Quraish ! What do you think I am going to do with you ?" They said in reply to his query, "We expect extremely benevolent treatment from you. You are a noble brother and the son of a noble brother." To this he replied, "I will say the same to you that Joseph had said to his brothers that 'This day let no reproach be (cast) on you; God will forgive you, and he is the Most Merciful of those who show Mercy!' Go, ye are all free (from blame and punishment)". This is the person, the Chief of the created beings, the holy Prophet, who taught all goodness to mankind, and not a blood-thirsty general who wages wars for self-aggrandisement and authority and becomes intoxicated with his military successes.

Companions' Follow-up

After the Prophet the attitude and behaviour of his caliphs and companions was the same in all their wars and victories. "They lighted their lamps borrowing heat and light from this lamp spreading light," (Al Quran XXXIII: 46), followed the same course that he had taken and kept on demonstrating practically the principles and elements of the Islamic civilization, under the most difficult conditions and at the most critical stages, they kept themselves under control and even after the greatest victories they did not forget their principles.

Nobody above Law

Some miscreants of Lebanon rose in revolt against the governor Ali bin-e-Abdullah bin-e-Abbas. He fought against them and defeated them. He deemed it in the fitness of things not to allow the rebels another chance to join forces and rise in tumult and insurrection against him, and decided to disperse them, and deport some of them. This was the minimum punishment that in our own times also the rulers of even the most 'civilized' countries resort to and execute also. But a contemporary, Imam Auza'i, a great learned man, held in great esteem, wrote to him that his action would go against the Islamic Shari'ah. To punish other Zimmist along with those that took part in rebellion and their deportation could not be permitted. Only those whose guilt was proved could be punished. In the letter he had written to the governor of Lebanon, this particular part is noteworthy

"It has come to my knowledge that you have executed some Zimmis of the Lebanon mountains and others you have deported. Some of the exiled are those who did not co-operate with the rebels. Let me know under which principle you are punishing the people in general for the sins of a particular person or a group. You are turning them out of their homes and sending them away from their properties, whereas God had ordained

No bearer of burdens can bear the burden of another.

(AI Quran XVI: 15)

"This is the best stand and worth pursuing." And also the following injunction of the Prophet must always be kept in view :

> "Whoever oppressed a person living under guarantee of protection by the Islamic state (Zimmi) or burdened him with a burden beyond his capacity, I shall uphold his cause on the Day of Reckoning."

And the governor had no option but to repatriate the deported people to their homes and hearths honourably.

I have no intention of commenting on the incident itself. However, it would suffice for the purpose of this book to remind people of the behaviour of the French with us during our struggle for freedom, when they were surprisingly occupying our country. And presently they are meting out the same treatment to the Arab people of North Africa. They have murdered millions of people and razed so many cities and towns to the ground that they present an appearance of wilderness where it seems no body ever lived. Also the barbaric treatment of the Britishers with the Arabs during their struggle for freedom of Palestine is very much before us. I believe, to have an idea of the merciful treatment of our civilization during the wars and after the victories it would be enough to point out this practice of the most civilized nations of the modern age.

No Parallels

When 'Umar bin-e-Abd-al-Aziz came to the office of caliphate, a delegation of men from Samarqand saw him and represented that the general of the Islamic armies, Qutaibah, had unjustifiably stationed his army men in the town in their midst. Umar bin-e-Abd-al-Aziz wrote to the governor of Samarqand that he should appoint a tribunal to judge and settle the dispute between Qutaibah and the people of Samarqand. If the judgement of the tribunal goes against the army chief and his men are asked to vacate they must do so at once. The governor appointed Jami' bin-e-Hadhir Albaji as judge for enquiry. After the enquiry was over, he, though himself a Muslim, passed the judgement that the Muslim army must vacate the town. He also remarked that the commander of the Muslim forces ought to have served an ultimatum of war to the city, and according to the Islamic Law relating to war, he ought to have cancelled all the treaties with them so that the people of Samarqand could get time to prepare for the war. "Sudden attack on them without warning was unlawful."

When the people of Samarqand witnessed this state of affairs, they were convinced that this was an unparalleld case in the history of mankind the state keeping its Commander-in-Chief and the armies under such strict discipline and control, bound by lofty moral principles. And consequently they decided that fighting against such a people would be futile. Rather, they came to regard it as mercy and a blessing from God. Therefore they agreed to live with the Islamic army in Samarqand.

Just imagine. An army conquers a city and enters it. The inhabitants of that city complain to the victorious government and the judges of that government decide the case against the victorious army, and order its externment, saying that they could not live there without the consent of the people of that city. Can either the ancient or modern history of mankind point out any war in which the fighting men kept themselves so strictly bound by the moral code, and followed such lofty principles of truth and justice, as demonstrated by the sons of our civilization? In so far as my own knowledge is concerned, not one among the nations of the world can be pointed out which demonstrated such lofty morals.

True to Words

Our victorious armies conquer Damascus, Hams and the remaining towns of Syria and according to the terms of the treaty they realize some amount of tax for the protection of the life and property of the citizens and the defence of the country. But later the Muslim leaders received news that Heraclitus had brought a big army which he was anxious to bring against the Muslims. Therefore they decided to bring together their own scattered armies in various conquered towns to concentrate at one point to face the hordes of Heraclitus with joint effort. So in keeping with this decision our armies started leaving the towns of Hams, Damascus and other towns. Khalid in Hams, Abu 'Ubaidah in Damascus and other generals in other towns addressed the citizens thus:

"The money or monies we had realized from you were meant for the protection of your lives and properties, and also to defend your lands from outside aggression. But we are sorry to inform you that we are parting with you and since we would not be able to protect and defend you, we are returning the amounts of taxes collected from you."

To this the citizens said in reply:

"God be with you and bring you back victorious. Your governance and your justice and equity have enamoured us, since the Romans in spite of being our co-religionists, we have bitter experience of their oppression and tyranny. By God! If they had been in your position they would not have returned a copper out of the taxes collected from us. Rather, they would have taken away everything they could from here belonging to us."

Even in our so-called civilized period it is like that. If an army has to vacate a station, it does not leave there anything that the enemy could utilize to advantage. But is there a single example of the practice of the victorious armies of our civilization, in the entire history of mankind. By God! If I had no faith in lofty values, and did not believe in their success or like the politicians of the modern age, considered it necessary to keep morals and principles dominated by the political interests, I would have said that the leaders of our armies stuck to lofty values and love of principles due to their unawareness and simplicity. But it is a fact that they were really true Believers and did not like to say things they could not'put into practice.

TEN

Treatment with Animals

This is really a strange topic of discourse of the series of the charming aspects of our civilization. Although in our own age it may not have much novelty, the reason lies in the fact that until recently the world could not even imagine that animals too could be deserving of mercy and justice. And with some peoples even today it is the usual practice to kill animals as a recreation on the occasion of sports, celebrations and national festivals. But here too our civilization, with regard to its principles and mode of action, came forward as a messenger of human consciousness and in such a merciful form which was neither given to any civilization of the past nor any civilization following the Islamic civilization, came to give kind treatment to the animals. And this has been so outstanding that it cannot be over looked. Rather, it is fascinating and amazing for every one. Let us tell you something about it.

The World of Animals

The principles and elements of our civilization declared, to begin with, that the animal world too was one in its own right, just like that of the human world. It has some characteristics and peculiarities of its own, and a temperament. And it has a consciousness of a peculiar type. The Quran says:

> There is not an animal (that lives) on earth, nor a being that flies on its wings, but (forms part) of communities like you.
> (Al Quran VI: 38)

Mercy on Animals

Since they are a community like man, they too deserve mercy and affection. The Prophet has said:

"Our Most Merciful God showers His Mercy on those who are themselves merciful. One who has been endowed with a gentle nature, has received a portion of the goodness of this world and the next."

Kindness to animals may at times become the means of his being rewarded with an abode in heaven. The Prophet is reported to have said:

"A person was going his way when he felt very thirsty. He came upon a well. He went down into the well and quenched his thirst. On coming up he saw a dog panting and urged by its extreme thirst licking the moist earth around the well, He thought to himself that the dog too was restless with thirst just as he had been ill at ease for want of water in his system. So he got down the well once again and filling one of his leather stockings with water and holding it with his teeth came up and offered that water to the dog to slake its thirst. God looked with favour on this-act of kindness of his and forgave him his sins."

> Some one from the audience asked him, "O Prophet of God! Shall we be rewarded for kindness to animals also?" The Prophet said in reply, "You will be rewarded for kind treatment of all those having a liver (living)and subsisting on fodder (feed of some sort).
>
> (Bukhari, Muslim, Malik Ahmad Abu Da'ood)

And contrariwise cruelty to animals may at times land a person in hell.

> "A certain woman came to deserve an abode in hell due to a cat that she kept tied in her house, neither feeding her, nor freeing her to seek her food among the reptiles and rodents of the earth." (Bukhari)

And it was not limited to inducement and instilling fear in men, but legislation has been resorted to in connection with prevention of cruelty to animals. So we find that it has been forbidden that a person mounted on its beast of burden should make it stand so long (that it gets restless due to distress, Tr.) while he himself is engaged in talking to somebody on his way. The Prophet has said

"Do not make the backs of your animals your chairs."
(Ahmad, Hakim)

Similarly it has been prohibited to men to keep their animals hungry and keeping them in poor condition (weak, lean and thin). Once the Prophet happened to pass by a camel whose empty stomach was touching its back. At this he said:

"Do fear God in the matter of these dumb creatures. Use them for riding only when they are in a fit condition and leave them (to rest) from work while they have yet some energy left in them."

Similarly, it is not permitted to us to work the animals beyond their capacity. The Prophet of God once went to the grove of an Ansari gentleman. There he saw a camel. On looking at the Prophet, the camel began to moan piteously and tears welled up in its eyes. The Prophet approached the camel and wiped its tears and then asked, "Who is the owner of this camel?" The owner came up to him and said, "I am the owner, O Prophet of God!" Turning to him the Prophet said, "Do you have any fear of God in relation to this animal ? That which God has given to thee as thy possession, has complained to me that thou takest work from. it but dost not feed him." (Ahmad)

Similarly wanton killing of animals for fun and sport has been strictly prohibited. The Prophet has said:

"Whoever, killed even one bird wantonly, it will complain to God on the day of Reckoning, "O My Lord and Cherisher ! This person had killed me sportively and not for benefit."
(Nasal, Ibn-e-Habban)

Likewise, using animals as targets for practice is also prohibited. The Prophet has said:

"Cursed be the person who uses a living object as a target (for practice only)." (Bukhari, Muslim)

The Prophet has prohibited making the animals fight (for sport and gambling as practised all over the world). And branding with hot irons for the sake of distinction. Tr.) is also prohibited. The Prophet passed by a donkey that had been branded on the face, and said, "Cursed be the person who has done it." If an animal is to be slaughtered for food, kindness demands that a very sharp knife should be used for slaughter, the animal should be offered water to drink, and after slaughter, the carcass should be allowed to cool down before skinning. The Prophet is reported to have said:

> "God has made it binding on us to do acts of kindness to every thing. Therefore if slaughter has to be done, it must be in the best way possible .....the person slaughtering it should use a very sharp knife and the carcass of the slaughtered animal should be allowed time to cool down."
>
> (Muslim)

Unparalleled Teachings

Rather, so much care has been exercised in this matter that felling of animals before sharpening the knife has been termed cruelty and hard-heartedness. The Prophet saw somebody sharpening his knife after felling the goat he was going to slaughter, and said to him, "Do you want to change it into carrion before slaughtering it?" And then added, "Why did you not sharpen your knife beforehand?" The following incident is very touching in connection with kindness to animals, and brings out the spirit of our civilization. Abdullah-ibn-e-Mas'ood says:

> "We were on a journey with the Prophet. We saw at one place on the way a small bird like sparrow, called Hamrah, which had two nestlings also with it. We caught both of them. The mother bird hovered over our heads. 1n the meanwhile it attracted the Prophet's notice and he came to us asking, "Who has troubled this bird by snatching from it its young ones ? Please restore them to the vexed mother:" And on the same journey the Prophet observed that an ant-hill had been destroyed by setting fire to it, and said, "Who has burnt it ?" Ibn-e-Mas'ood says that we owned it, to which the Prophet said, "No other but Allah has the right to inflict the torment of fire on any creature."
>
> (Abu Da'ood)

In the light of these teachings the legists of the Islamic order have made such laws relating to the kind treatment of animals which could never have been conceived. For example they say it is imperative for the owner of animals that he should provide all the needs of these creatures. But if he does not do so he will be forced to dispose them off or let them loose in wilderness where they can find food and shelter. If that animal is permitted as food, it should be slaughtered. Some people have gone even further and have said. "If a blind cat enters somebody's house and is unable to move about to seek its food, it becomes incumbent on the house-holders to feed it." The legists have also prohibited people from putting greater burden on the beasts than they can easily bear. And from this principle they have deduced several legal rights. One of them is that if somebody hires a beast and loads it with a burden heavier than its capacity which causes its death he becomes liable to pay damages for it.

Similarly, the legists have also determined the amount of weight (burden) which can be loaded on the mule and the donkey. An interesting fact about it is that a certain legist determined the quantity that can be loaded on the donkey and the mule, but another legist did not agree with him saying, "In prescribing this amount justice has been done to the mule but great injustice has been done to the donkey."

However, if an animal oppresses another, it is nonsensical to think of it and judge it in human terms, and so no 'criminal' beast shall be punished for this 'crime'. However, its owner can be brought to account and compensate for it, if it can be proved that he has been careless in keeping his animal properly secured and restraining it from doing harm. These are some of those golden principles that have been formulated by our civilization and our Shari'ah about the beasts. The question, however, remains what was the practical shape of their enforcement and practice in general?

Kind Treatment

While the Prophet of God was on a journey an Ansari woman said to her mount, a she-camel, "cursed be thou" while she was on its back. When the cursing of that woman came to the ears of the Prophet, he was very much displeased and ordered those around him. "Take whatever is on the she-camel and let her be released, since she is `accursed'." So the she-camel was left to roam about freely among the people and nobody troubled her. (Muslim)

'Umar, the second caliph, saw a person dragging a goat by its leg to slaughter it. He said to him, "Ruin overtake thee, if thou wouldst take it to its death, let it be in the proper manner."

This was the kind treatment and tender-heartedness which was meted out to the animals by the Islamic state and other social institutions in the Islamic civilization.

State Responsible

What better proof of the importance the Islamic state attached to the kind treatment of the animals, can be furnished than the fact that the caliph issued instructions to the common people to the effect that the animals should not be put to hardship and given trouble and they should be treated kindly. 'Umar bin-e-Abd-al-Aziz, in a letter of his, instructs the governors to stop people from whipping their horses and goading with pricks. He wrote to the officer in charge of the Traffic Police and Patrolling body that he should not allow anybody to put a painful bit of heavy reins in his horses' mouth nor use whips with an iron piece at its end. The duties of the Muhtasib in this period also included prohibition of putting heavy loads on the beasts of burden, also of inflicting injuries on animals unnecessarily and during a journey goading them on beyond their capacity. The Muhtasib who finds people indulging in any of these vicious practices, is duty-bound to bring him to the right path and punish him also. The law in this connection is as follows:

"The Muhtasib has the right to use his authority to compel people to comply with the rules and regulations in this behalf, since they imply general expediency. People cannot be allowed to load their animals with loads heavier than their capacity, nor can they be permitted to goad them to great speed when they are carrying heavy loads. They should be made to desist from beating them mercilessly. They should not tie their animals in public parks either. All these (evil) practices are against the Islamic Shariah. It is the duty of the owners of the animals to be God-fearing in the matter of their feed. The fodder should be enough to fully satisfy animals's hunger. It should neither be of a poor quality nor meagre in quantity.

Trusts for Animals

As for the collective institutions for the animals, they too were not lacking. The best proof of this is furnished by those documents of the trusts of the past which were concerned only with the treatment of sick animals. There were also land trusts that were meant solely for the arrangement of the grazing of old disabled animals. One of these is the "Maraj-e-Akhzar" of Damascus which has been converted into a playground by the Municipal Corporation. This pasture was meant for the horses abandoned by their owners as useless (no more serviceable Tr.). Such steeds grazed there till their end. One of the trusts of Damascus was meant exclusively for the cats. These cats were provided with food and shelter there. In this way hundreds of well-fed cats had gathered there in the cat house and since they received their daily food without any effort, they did not move away from there except for jumping, frisking and merry-making.

Acts of Kindness

A very charming example of kind treatment to animals is that presented by a high-ranking companion Abu Darda'. At the time of his death he said to his camel, "O my camel! Do not quarrel with me before Our Lord and Cherisher, for I never took work from thee beyond thy capacity." Also there was another companion Adi bin-eHatim who crushed the bread into fine powder for the ants and said, "These are our neighbours, therefore they have a claim on our hospitality." Imam Kabeer Abu Ishaq Shirazi was one day going along with his friends, when a dog confronted him. Its master tried to drive it away from his path, when the Imam prevented him from doing that saying "Do you not know that the roads are common between us (humans) and the dogs."

Past Examples

We cannot fully appreciate the value of this most outstanding aspect of the Islamic civilization and its mode of action in the matter of kind treatment of animals, unless we know how these poor creatures, were treated in olden times and during the middle ages, and what was the behaviour of other nations concerning torment of animals and causing pain to them.

In this connection what is worthy of consideration, first of all, is the fact that in the (moral or religious) teachings of other nations there are no such instructions in which kindness to animals might have been stressed or mercy to them must have been made binding on them. That is why there is no trace of any obligations relating to the feeding and care of animals by their owners.

After that we come across that amazing situation which existed during the middle ages and continued even upto the nineteenth century, in which an animal was made liable to punishment for its own crime or that of its owner. It was treated in a manner they would have treated a rational being like man. Judgments were passed against animals just as they would have been passed against men. It was imprisoned, exiled, so much so that the sentence of capital punishment was pronounced against these dumb creatures just as a criminal person would be sentenced.

The following articles are met within the Jewish Law:

"If a bullock gores a man or a woman with its horns and he or she dies as a consequence of it, the bullock must, in that case, be stoned to death." If, however, the animal was not habitually aggressive and accidentally gored somebody and caused his or her death, the owner of the animal in such a case would not be called to account or compensate for the damage done by his beast. But in case it was known to be a habitual offender and the owner in spite of being warned that the animal was a potential danger, did not even then care to keep it in check in proper manner. If this resulted in somebody's death, the offending beast would be stoned to death and the owner would also be put to death. There was another situation too where the beast was punished. For example, if a person was found guilty of bestiality, the person guilty of such an unnatural heinous crime and the animal, the object of this crime, both would be put to death.

The ancient Greeks had an exclusive department to try and punish animals found guilty of the death of man or a woman, so much so that even lifeless objects were tried that became the cause of the death of a person. This department was called "Berteoneon". This was the place where these "criminals" were tried and sessions held for such trials. Plato has also written in his book, *Laws*, that if a beast killed a person, the members of the family of the person thus killed had the right to sue the animal in the court, and the guardians of the person killed were also entitled to select the judge from amongst the landlords. In case of the guilt being proved, killing of that animal became obligatory, and the carcass was thrown outside the country. But in case of those animals that were reared for combats with men, on the occassion of festivals and sports, if a person was killed in combat against the animal, the latter was not considered guilty of murder. If an inanimate object fell on a person causing his death, the closest from among the neighbouring relatives of the deceased was appointed the judge, who would give the decision of throwing that object beyond the bounds of the country. The animals were convicted not only in case of causing loss of life but for all other crimes less serious than murder too they were convicted. For example, in case of a dog biting a person, the owner of the dog was bound to bring that dog securely held with ropes and present it to the bitten person, who had a right to take revenge on it as he was pleased, killing it, inflicting corporal punishment on it or any other treatment that he deemed fit.

Similarly, animals belonging to a person also came for punishment in case of any member of the family of the owner being found guilty of any crime. For example the person who was guilty of a serious crime against religion or the state, not only he was put to death but his animals, properties and slaves were also killed, burnt or banished.

One of the articles of the ancient Roman Law was that if a farmer's bullock, during the period of cultivation crossed the field of its owner and beyond the fence went to the field of the neighbour, the bullock and its owner both were put to death. The least punishment for a dog biting a person was that it was handed over to the person bitten so that he might do with it what he liked. Similarly, if an animal browsed on the bramble of another person, not owned by its master, it too was handed over to the master of the pasture land.

These Greek and Roman Laws relating to animals were also in vogue in ancient Germany.

And in Persia of Yore, the Laws relating to animals were still more amazing. If a rabid dog bit a kid causing its death, or in case of biting a man wounded him, the right ear of that rabid dog would be cut off. If it had the audacity to repeat the offence, the left ear was chopped off. Repetition of it for the third time would make it liable to lose its right leg and a fourth offence deprived it of the left leg also. (And if it survived these operations, Tr.) and repeated the offence for the fifth time, its tail was removed wholly.

During the middle ages France was the first country among the European nations that deemed the animals also responsible for their doings, in the thirteenth century, and tried them in organized courts, just as human beings were tried. And the charges against them were brought under the same law that was framed for men. After that about the close of the fourteenth century Sardinia too promulgated the same laws. During the last part of the fifteenth century Belgium enforced this law. About the middle of the sixteenth century Holland, Germany, Italy and Sweden too followed suit. In some parts of Sicily this law persisted upto the nineteenth century.

A case was taken up against an animal either at the request of the person affected or the government brought up cases against the offenders. Then advocates upholding the convicted animal, appeared at the court and tried to defend it. At times the court committed the animal to the police lock-up as a matter of precaution. After that the judgement was pronounced as in case of human criminals, and was executed in the presence of the public as it was the custom in case of men. At times the animal was stoned to death, beheaded or burnt. Or even its limbs and various organs were amputated before killing it. The reader should not misapprehend that these cases were brought against the animals for fun's sake or as mere consolation to the injured party. Rather, they were taken up in all earnestness. The diction of the decisions and the legal orders indicate that they were very serious about it. For example this sentence of the decision "The animal is sentenced to death so that the demands of justice may be met;" or "It is being crucified since it has been guilty of the most barbaric and heinous crimes."

The most amazing traditions are those in which it has been said that these people instituted cases against animals for this reason also that these animals, according to their mode of thinking, had meddled with the law of Nature or the physical laws. They charged the animals with sorcery. Sorcery was such a crime, in their code of justice, whose perpetrator deserved nothing short of the punishment of being burnt. On the occasions of the enforcement of the punishments on animals they held ceremonial gatherings. The executioners came with chips of wood which were placed in the centre of the open ground. The cats convicted and sentenced were brought in icon cages. When it came to the execution, some monks visited the scene and with them came some officials of the state. One of them held two burning brands to light the wood of the pyre. When it was lighted the officials ordered that the cats should be thrown into the flames so that they might be burnt to ashes, since they were guilty of a heinous crime like sorcery.

At this stage it appears in the fitness of things to place before the reader the accounts of some of those cases brought up against the animals during the middle ages. A famous case among these is that brought against the rats in the city of Octave in France. This is an incident of the fifteenth century. The charge levelled against the rats was that they gather in large numbers in horrible form in the streets of the town which disturbs the peace of the people. For their defence the famous advocate of France of that period, Shasania took the field. He asked the Court for time since the rats could not present themselves at the court when summoned, some of the very young and old rats being sick at the time. They could attend the court only after some time. So the court allowed them respite. But when it came to attending the court next, the rats still could not present themselves. But their advocate put up the excuse in their defence that they were mighty afraid of the cats in case of coming to the court. At this the Chief Justice said that in that case it was the responsibility of the Court to provide their safe arrival at the court. And the advocate requested that the court should issue orders for the confinement of all cats when the rats came to attend the court, so that they might not be in danger of losing their lives. The court granted the prayer. And orders were accordingly issued that the cats and dogs should not come to the public roads to ensure safety of the rats. But the citizens did not comply with the orders to this effect. At this the court was constrained to acquit the rats, since justice demanded that every one (convicted) should have the facilities of explaining his position, and since the rats were deprived of such facilities, they were declared free of the charges brought against them. The advocate earned great renown through this novel defence in this case. We cannot, however, say whether he was able to realize his fee for his pains from the clients, the rats. It is just possible they might have stopped gnawing at his books on law.

Still more amazing is the case of the egg-laying cock. This too is an event of the middle ages. This case was presented in the city of Bal in Switzerland in 1474 A.D. The charge against the cock was that it had laid an egg. And this was a crime for the reason that, according to them, the sorcerers were looking for the egg laid by a cock., which they used in their sorcery for evil purposes. The cock was brought to the court. The advocate for defence pleaded that the cock was helpless in this matter. It had no means at its disposal to escape from this crime. But this explanation of the cock's position failed to move the court; and the cock was sentenced to death. They laid down in their decision that this should be an eye-opener to other cocks.

Among the amazing cases brought against the animals one was that in France in 1494. In the province, San Julian, the owners of vineyards filed a case against the insects that they have done untold damage to the grapes and vines, causing them great monetary loss. In this case two expert lawyers took up the defence. The case lingered on for forty years. Since the complainants were sick due to delay in decision of their case, they were in agreement with'the decision that a piece of vineyard be left exclusively for the ravages of the insects where they might do what they liked and eat as much of the fruit and vines as they could.

Comments

I have presented before you the subtle comparisons between the points of view of the Islamic civilization and those of others relating to the animals. It has clearly brought out the fact that the Muslim Ummah stands out among the ancient peoples and the modern nations in two things which are conspicuous by their absence elsewhere.

Firstly, the Muslims established collective institutions made arrangements for the infirmity, old age and sickness of the animals.

Secondly, about fourteen hundred years earlier Islam put a stop to the animals being called to account for their doings, credit for which the modern civilization is seeking today for itself. That is why the history of our civilization and culture is totally free from the nonsensical cases brought up against dumb animals. Moreover, the Islamic civilization strictly put an end to the cruel practice of animal combats cock, ram and bullfights whereas the Greeks and the Romans regarded it lawful and a source of great pleasure. And in Hispanolia (Spain) it is lawful and a favourite sport and recreation even today and great ceremonials accompany their traditional bull fights. Undoubtedly it is a vestige of the barbaric pursuit of the Europeans of the Middle Ages, from which our civilization has ever been free.

ELEVEN

The Great Heritage

By the fifteenth century, Islam in India had taken, by and large, an Indian garb, socially and culturally, and assumed a character peculiarly Indian in texture and in spirit, distinguishable from those of the faithful of other lands, such as Iraq, Egypt, Central Asia or Iran. As with other great movements, Islam also, in course of the centuries, had come to be plagued by schisms, often leading to bloody conflicts and internal strife. Their echoes were no doubt heard in India also but these were distant and, might have caused ripples, but no waves. For the problem Islam faced in India was peculiarly different. Here was a land where social status and economic occupation with all consequent opportunities and handicaps were determined by the accident of birth, this accident being neither tribal nor regional like in other lands; here there was a predetermined mould of social hierarchy and economic status. The doctrine of absolute equality and democratic functioning of social institutions which Islam so ardently preached got garbled under conditions into one of graded equality and social hierarchy.

Earlier, we have discussed at some length the emergence of 'Muslim castes' in India. However, the point to be noted is that the Muslim social structure became a counterpart of the 'Hindu' or the Indian social structure and was more Indian in content and character than alien in anyway. This is what enabled it to become a part and parcel of general Indian psyche to produce a composite culture. The higher classes, Saiyads and Pathans, conformed to the higher varna of the Hindus, Brahmins and Kshatriyas, while the Shaikh was the general mass, the Vaisya of the Hindus. Not to speak of the indigenous Indian converts, even those who came from outside like Central Asia, Iraq and Iran, tried to preserve their ethnic and other peculiarities and formed distinct groups in course of time, petrifying into rigid social structures. For example, Ibrahim bin Abu Bakar, a migrant Sufi and a redoubtable fighter for his faith, also called Malik Baiya, left a legacy of his own among his followers and descendants who bonded themselves together and came to be known as Maliks. They are to be found chiefly in Central Bihar. In spite of the holy character and fighting qualities of their ancestor, Malik Balya, the Maliks of Bihar distance and distinguish themselves from both the Saiyads and Pathans and claim a distinct identity, almost like a caste, for themselves. Then again, descendants of divines and Mema calling themselves Shahs claimed for themselves a higher status than that of Saiyads even, something like the Agnihotri Brahmins, and, like them, depended for their livelihood on the profession of dispensing spiritual solace and religious instructions to Muslim masses, and even to those Hindus who were inclined to receive them. Thus several of the castes in northern India came to have their Muslim counterparts. The Hindu Tatwa, for example had a Muslim counterpart in Dolaha, Kalwar in Kalal, Dangi in Kunjra, and so on. While the Muslims had Islam as their religion, the social structure they created for themselves was purely Indian, What mattered most in the Indian polity, essentially secular, was the social structure than ecclesiastical beliefs. Faiths or beliefs could be different and many and could be changed at will but the social mould was pre-determined and rigid, as in India one had little control over the choice of occupation. Thus Islam, despite its egalitarian philosophy, came in India to be divided into at least two broad social orders, the higher and lower; the higher order calling themselves Shorafa or Ashraf, consisting mostly of foreign Muslim nobles and soldiery and of Hindu converts of higher castes and the lower order or Ajlaf comprising Hindu converts of lower castes or even of artisans and workmen of foreign extraction who had settled in India in their professions. The extent to which Islam in India got 'Indianised' could be judged by the fact that the Census of 1911 enumerated 292 Muslim castes, including the Muslim Bohras who got themselves enumerated as Hussaini Brahmins. In moods and mores, in observances and prohibitions, the two classes of Muslims, the commoners became, in course of time, permeated with the Indian psyche and made easy the growth of an integrated Indian society by the sixteenth-seventeenth centuries. During this period, religious conflicts between Hindus and Muslims in India were almost unknown, while such conflicts were the order of the day on the continent of Europe right upto the eighteenth century.

This is not to say, however, that Islam was overwhelmed by and submerged under the perennial Indian social stream of caste system. The distinct identity of Islam was still maintained, with its unity of command as exemplified by firm faith in one God, one Prophet and one Book, as the supreme arbiter, whatever the diffusion and differentiation in social or personal behaviour. All the channels of thought and behaviour had to conform to these cardinal principles of faith. During the course of its acceptance in different lands and among different groups of people, Islam had, no doubt, acquired native variations and distinctions, but these never proved so strong as to obliterate the core of its teachings to the faithful. Whatever the intellectual quibblings and differences in interpretations of the Islamic law and jurisprudence, or howsoever bitter the sectarian quarrels, it is due to the unity of command in respect of fundamental Islamic teachings that Islam has been able to maintain its identity. Another factor which helped the mass of Indian Muslims to keep themselves distinguished from the mass of Indian Hindus was the egalitarian spirit of Islam with its near-about lack of taboos. In Hindu society, after all, there was no single line of control: the diffusion of intellectual dialectics, and the toleration with which different schools of philosophical speculations were nurtured left ordinary persons confused and bemused making it virtually impossible to provide for any unifying or universal principles of life. In this welter of conflicting prescriptions it is the rigid code of social behaviour binding individuals into groups or castes of distinct sociological and economic character which has kept the Hindu society as a well-recognised entity. There is however one immutable, fixed central idea which has run like a line of fate in the Indian psyche, making the whole purpose of life coherent and its institutional framework meaningful; that is the all-embracing theory of the Law of Karma or retributive justice which is believed to operate the processes of creation, conservation and destruction, in the endless chain of births and deaths. Progression and regression, according to this law, is the result of one's own Karma, which includes not only concrete actions, but even the thought-processes of individuals. The fruits of one's action have to be gathered and one's destiny and station in life, the result of past Karmas, accepted, while striving all the time to excel such destiny by appropriate action, the fruits of which could be available in this life or in life hereafter. This is the line of command in Hindu ethos to which everyone has to submit.

This accounts for the typical accommodative spirit of Hinduism, or better, of the "Indianism" of this subcontinent. To this was added the spirit of Islam with its own scheme of retributive justice, not believing in the succession of births and deaths but in life fully lived in this very existence. However, death still had its own fascination irrespective of religious theories. Keats had said, "death is life's high need;" the vision of a succession of life, death being only an interlude, was alluring to imaginative minds, whether Muslim or Hindu. This could also be termed as an echo of the Christian conception of "life eternal". Islam does not believe in this, but reverberation of such thoughts are heard in the works of early Muslim poets such as Malik Mohammad *Jayasi,* whose story of "Padamavat" is a beautiful synthesis of Hindu and Muslim views of life. Similar in intent are Manjhan's *Madhmalati,* Usman's *Chitravali,* Kasim Shah's *Hams Jawahar,* Nur Mohammad's *Anurag Bharthi* and many others.

However, for an enduring fusion of Hindu and Muslim ideas, we have to go to the common mass of people, their mores and attitudes. Lucretius, the Greek philosopher, had thought that it was fear which first made the gods, but the fact remains that it is both a lurking fear and an ever rising hope which make one burn incense at the shrine of deities, for banishment of evil which we fear and for fulfilment of the hope we cherish. Rationally, monism, holding one system of law for the universe may appear to be the correct view, but even then, the naughty charms of polytheism have always proved irresistible to the common mind. William James says "Perhaps the ancients were wiser than we and polytheism may be truer than monotheism to the astonishing diversity of the world. Such polytheism has always been the real religion of common people and is so still today." There is a kernal of truth in what he says.

It is a fact, Indian Muslims, both of native origin and of foreign extraction, in course of time, began to take their hopes and fears to the shrines of Sufi saints and Aulias, 'Khankahs as well 'Dargahs' which became seats of veneration and in many cases arbiter of their conduct, both religious and worldly. A broad humanitarian approach to life, sense of tolerance, and amity not only amongst themselves but in relation to their Hindu brethren also, with whom social and economic ties were many and indissoluble in the circumstances, emerged in the social relationship among the various communities and castes of India. Thus there were common occasions of joy and sorrow for both the communities. Holi, the festival of spring, with sprinkling of colour on each other and a joyous abandon, had fascinated even those of foreign origin. Tughra's Persian poem on Holi reflects the sense of joy that the occasion provided to even those inclined to be serious in life. Similarly, Muharrum was an occasion of universal sorrow for the Hindus too. The Hindus drew their ethical inspirations from the war heroes celebrated in the epics, the *Ramayana* and the *Mahabharata*, which exemplified the victory of righteousness over evil. The trials and tribulations the heroes of the Hindu epics had had to undergo to uphold dharma were already an ever-abiding inspiration to the common people. The story of the martyrdom of Hazrat Imam Husain, his exemplary courage and fortitude in face of adversity, his sacrifices for the cause he represented made him, even in the eyes of the Hindus, an embodiment of truth and righteousness; he was venerated, if not exactly worshipped. The Hindus were not concerned with the right or wrong of the battle of Karbala, but Hazrat Imam Husain and his companions were to them those great figures of history, whom the Hindu mind associated with a halo bordering on divinity on account of their superhuman character. The difference of religion was no obstacle to this. The observance of Muharrum in the Indian context had become national in character. Inevitably, Muharrum came to assume certain Indian characteristics, not to be found elsewhere in the Muslim world. Most of the Hindus considered it a privilege to play the role of 'Paik' or foot soldier of Hazrat Imam Husain and it was commonly believed that he was really alive and could grant boons, and ward off evils, if sincerely approached in prayers. The orthodox fretted and fumed but could do little to influence the mind and attitude of the common mass of people which is the cultural bond superseding all chauvinisms in every society.

Not only Hazrat Imam Husain, but even 'Allah' of Islamic conception took hold of the common Hindu mind. In Islamic thought, Allah is *lasharik*, an absolute categorical imperative, beyond time and space since both are relative; beyond perception of senses, as otherwise, it would involve duality. He is, in the words of Upanishads, achintiya; that is, beyond sensuous contemplation. His realization is a gift of the Divine rather than a product of the mind. The common mass of people, however, had nothing to do with such subtleties; it was enough for them that God, of the Islamic conception was to be propitiated and supplicated. Moreover, when in the Hindu mind all phenomena of nature were so many manifestations of God's Majesty, how could it allow the Islamic conception of God as its very own exclusively? Hence in many Hindu homes, even of the so called higher castes, at least in northern India Mian Saheb, a general name for Allah or God of the Muslims, came to be included in the pantheon to be worshipped by the Hindus. In many a Hindu household, a room or a portion of a room or a niche in the wall without any figure or emblem in deference to Muslim tenets was reserved for the worship of Mian Saheb, where incense was burnt, and sweetmeats offered. On special occasions, the Maulvi of the village would be called to offer *namaz* and tender *neyaz* and *fateha* for the well-being of the worshippers. For these services the Maulvi was paid the customary fees. The ordinary Hindu did not see any contradiction in worshipping idols of his own gods, as well as the formless Allah. He saw in both the same divine power. No amount of logic or metaphysical hair-splitting could convince him that what he was doing went against his dharma; what mattered to him was that it ensured his well-being if he worshipped God in as many ways as possible. Similarly, many Hindus converted to Islam continued their old attitude towards religion. For example, sun-worship was noticed among Muslim women at several places in Bihar according to Gaya Gazeteer. Many pious and devout Muslims, in deference to the sentiments of their Hindu brethren would give them material and financial help in constructing their temples. If there were marauders who destroyed temples and idols in their blind fanaticism, there were others who were catholic enough to help in constructing temples, specially in the rural areas.

The influence of Sufi saints and other Muslim divines kept growing with the passage of time; the Hindus were as ardent followers and admirers of the Muslim Mirs and Auryas as the Muslims themselves. They were in no way behind their Muslim brethren in paying homage at Muslim shrines and dargahs and mausoleums of Muslim saints and fakirs. Being more numerous than the Muslims, they simply outnumbered them on the occasions of Urs held in the memory of such Muslims. Some Muslim kings had frowned upon this practice and done their best to suppress such congregations, but they were overwhelmed ultimately, since this was becoming a regular feature in an Indian's life. The orthodox among the Hindus also would look at the practice with disdain. In one of the *dohas* No.49640 (Gita press Edition), Tulsidas deprecates the practice of visiting the tomb of Salar Masud, the celebrated saint killed by Raja Sahadeo and Hardeo in 1033 A.D. at Bahraich (UP), for grant of boons such as restoration of lost sight or limb, or birth of a son to a barren women which Tulsidas says, he never heard realized actually. However, in spite of the chagrin of orthodox elements among both Hindus and Muslims and occasional sectarian quarrels, mostly in terms of verbal darts against each other, the common mass of people of both religions came to develop a common religious outlook, while still adhering strictly to the tenets of their own faith,

Both Hindus and Muslims were using the same language and dress, and similar manners and customs; the diversity existed only on a regional or linguistic or cultural basis; religion was not a cause of division. Muslim poets had taken to *brajbhasa* and *awadh*, the languages of the Ganga-Jamuna tracts, in a big way, and their poetic gifts were finding expression in these languages. The allusions and images they used were largely from Hindu scriptures, specially the Puranas; and this sometimes offended the puritans among the Muslims. For example, Noor Mohammad, a poet of the people, when needled for disloyalty to his faith, asserts in *Auraq Bansart* "My Maker knows what is in my heart. How so much I may express myself in the language of the Hindus, I can never set my foot on their path. My heart is ever with Islam and the tenets of my religion. Nobody else can take the place of Rasul Allah, redeemer of the brotherhood, just as `Asur' (tyrant) cannot take the place of 'Sur' (brave)."

What is remarkable in this passage is not the protest of the poet against unjust accusation of disloyalty to his faith, for that is understandable, but the fact that the similies he uses for making known his firmness of faith in Islam are still of Hindu origin. This shows the extent to which emotional integration of the religious groups had been achieved on a wide scale.

The place of women in society is one of the indices of civilizing processes of human mind and behaviour. In an essentially patriarchical society, where the male is the dominant partner who takes advantage of physical weakness of females, the women are automatically relegated to a secondary position, if not made victims of oppression and discrimination. In pre-Islamic tribal Arabia, women were a possession to be used by the males, abused, and even inherited, as appears from the Quranic prohibition. "O Ye who believe ! It is not allowed unto thee that you may heir the woman." There was no clear-cut idea of incest, and sexual abuse of women was frequent, sexual liaison outside the tribe only was considered adultery. Women did not possess any rights whatsoever, and did not function either socially, economically or juridically. They were considered instruments of pleasure and procreation and in pre-Islamic Arabic society, an individual child was a child of the tribe, juridically. This attitude to women was not peculiar to pre-Islamic Arabia, but was common, more or less, in other semitic societies, in the Mediterranean countries and in the Hellas. We know about the communion of wives advocated by Plato, but the views of Aristotle, the prime mentor of western civilization, are more definite in regard to the place of women in human society. In his works, "*De Gen Animalium* (if. 3) *Hist. Animalium* (viv.1) *and Politics* (1. 5) Aristotle considers that a woman is to man as the slave to the master, the manual to the mental worker, the barbarian to the Greek. His definite view is that woman is an unfinished man, left standing on a lower step in the scale of development. The male is by nature superior; the one rules and the other is ruled and this principle extends, of necessity, to all mankind. Woman is weak of will, and, therefore, incapable of independence of character or position; her best condition is a quiet home life in which, while ruled by the men in her external relations, she may be allowed to be supreme on domestic affairs. Women should not be made more like men, as in Plato's republic, rather the dissimilarity should be promoted; whatever is different is also attractive. To quote him "The courage of a man and that of a woman are not, as Socrates supposed, the same: the courage of a man is shown in commanding: that of a woman in obeying ... as the poet says 'silence is a woman's glory." This has been the attitude of male dominated society in almost all civilized countries, more so in the western: world, which Aristotle faithfully expressed, giving it a seal of approval. The attitude has been at best one of levity and at worst one of superciliousness One may recall Meredith's remark: "Women will be the last thing civilized by man" and, opposed to it, Voltaire's words: "God created women only to tame mankind."

Before we come to Islamic concept in this regard, let us consider the Indian view of the question. India has been an admixture of different racial groups in various stages of development. However, there are some common streaks which impart characteristics of "Indianness" to the various aspects of life in India. In regard to women, an average Indian view, echoing the usual male chauvinism, is that she is *bhogya*, i.e., a vehicle to impart pleasure to man, an attitude in keeping with man's atavistic mind. This has been responsible for the brutalities inflicted on womankind in war and peace in all countries and in all ages. But then differentiation comes when one considers domestic life; for a Hindu a woman becomes *bharyya* that is a companion. She becomes a civilizing factor, a partner in life, and as the Aryans put it, *sahdharmini*, an equal participant in the religious and spiritual life of man, a real helpmate in the battle of life; "united in life and thereafter", as the marriage vow says. As Silappadigram, a Tamilian classic, as well as Sanskrit works life *Mrichchhakatika* show, woman in ancient India had wit, intelligence, grace and poise; she was not merely a housewife or a domesticated being, but had a public character of her own. But, then she basked in a reflected glory in what was essentially a man's world; "a joint and an aid, sometimes a playmate but more often than not a plaything" as the poet Bharatrihari says. It should also be remembered that no nation has excelled the Indians in producing erotic literature. *Anang-Rang* and *Kamasutra* are manuals for the art of love which for sensuous details, and for a psychological insight in the erogenous zones of the body of both men and women remain unparalleled. These works do not show the ancient Indians exactly as ascetics or abstemious, as the common supposition is, but rather as men and women bent upon drinking the cup of sensual pleasures to the last drop. The Indian womanhood, however, had another character, that of a *pujyya*, one to be worshipped as "Mother" for, after all, she was the procreater of the race, at once the cause and effect of the continuity of mankind. The Tantras say that a woman's feet are to be worshipped as those of a guru or preceptor. In short, the Indians interpreted womanhood in three forms, as a beloved, as a wife and as a mother; the treatment to be given to them differed according to the character they lived.

Islam, on the other hand, true to its characteristic straightforwardness and clarity, has no use for such sophistry. It does not view woman in conjunction with man: She is considered an independent entity, with her own rights and obligations defined both as an individual as well as in reciprocal relationship with man. Such a view was really revolutionary, and a precurser to modern ideas about women's place in society. The advent of Islam brought a great deal of emancipation of woman from the bondage of man. At earlier civilization, she was considered 'an enchantress, and a sorceress' as in the classical Greece; 'a temptress' as in semitic writings; 'an instrument of pleasure and procreation' as in the old Aryan view; and a 'mere chattel and possession' as in the pre-Islamic Arabic society. Islam tried to change all that. No matrimonial alliance was valid in Muslim law without express consent of the bride. No father had the right to dispose her off as he liked, as she was considered to have a will of her own recognised and sanctioned by Islamic injunctions. This may be contrasted with the old Hindu view in regard to the fate of daughters. The basic assumption here is that a daughter never belongs to the family of the father, as Yaska's *Nirukta* (11-4, Anand Ashram Edition, p.208) declares: "they give away to other the female children. There exists *dana, utkraya,* and *atisaraga* of the female but not of the male." In other words, a daughter was to be given in gift (*dana*), or in sale (*utkraya*) or simply abandoned (*atisaraga*). The Vedic Indians who formulated such ideas for social organisation appear or have been excessively obsessed with notions of purity of the race as well as with the fertility syndrome. Purity of race was the prime consideration but then they appear to have been aware of the principle of eugenics that cross fertilization is necessary for healthy and abundant procreation; constant fertilization within the same social group results in dwindling of numbers as well as lop-sided development of the progeny. Hence the conception of *dana*, gifting of the daughter for purpose of marriage outsides the clan, (*gotra*), but within the racial group (*varna*). Thus, Vedic marriages were both endogamous as well as exogamous, ensuring purity of the race and cross-fertilization. Vikraya, sale, was a less reputable device, but was still recognised if it became necessary for both sides. Giving of daughter by the king to another king as part of diplomatic alliance was also a form of *vikrau*. Diplomatic marriage alliances between Rajput kings and Mughal Emperors are well known. What is, perhaps, not so well known is the fact that Feruz Bahmani was given a Vijyanagar princess in marriage even though Vijyanagar was comparatively the stronger party whose splendour, according to Abdur Razzaque, the Timurid Envoy, `eyes had not seen nor ears heard'. Atisarga (abandonment) was of course, the most despicable mode of disposal, and was rarely practised. Kalidas, the great Sanskrit poet, has risen to great heights in depicting the situation when Sakuntala, having come from the ashram, where she had been brought up and where she had got married to the king Dushayant after a romance with him, is disowned by him. Her dignified disdain of the king as *anarya*, Aryan, a term of contemptuous abuse is illustrative of the wounded pride of a forlorn and abandoned woman. It is, therefore, clear that irrespective of the sanctity attached to *'dana'* of a daughter as a part of sacramental form of marriage in Hindu conception and practice, the personal feelings of women as an individual is of much less importance than her position or utility on the social plane.

The stand of Islam, on the contrary, is one of equality of sexes. Marriage is a contract between two contracting parties of opposite sex, entered into willingly, to live together according to Islamic injunctions, the right of dissolution of the contract inhering in both the parties. The .contract is also subject to payment of a fixed amount of dower by the male to the female, fixed at the time of the contract. Contractual marriage is not peculiar to Islam, but is common among other semitic races; what is special about Islamic form of marriage is the payment of dower by the male to the female, a kind of jointure, enforceable under law and custom.

Lord Buddha had advocated equality of sexes, and admitted women to the ascetic order; so had the Jains. But then, with no clear-cut social formulations, equality of sexes both among the Buddhists and the Jains had remained pious wishes. The admission of women into ascetic order only provides the equality of abstinence and austerities, and does not extend to equality of life and comfort. It was a kind of *atisarg*, abandonment, than the conferring of any privilege on womanhood, similar to the admission of Catholic girls in convents and nunneries. Islam does not admit of any ascetic order, male or female. It, as a matter of fact, does not admit any special class among the faithful and inequality, in any form, is repugnant to Islamic teachings. Even then, complete equality between the sexes could not be achieved even in such egalitarianism. For example, in case of adultery (all extra marital relationship are fornication in the eyes of Islamic law), the dice is heavily loaded against the females as compared to males in respect of proof of guilt as well as punishment for guilt. This could not be the fault of Islamic teachings; the drawbacks, if any, are the result of human infirmities, and the them semitic ideas and practices which Islam, in spite of itself, could not eschew completely.

Islam, most of all, ensured economic independence for women by giving to daughters, along with sons, a share in the inheritance of the property of the father, and to widows, a share in the estate of her husband along with her sons and daughters. Dower was actually a promised share to the wife in the estate of her husband, and could be collected, whenever required. She is, above all, a person with legal status in the eyes of Islamic laws. In Christian societies, a daughter could get bequests and gifts but a wife's property became her husband's at marriage. In England, the Married Women Property Acts put an end to this unjust law only late in the Victorian period. It was then said, that a wife could resist surrendering her virginity to her husband, but not her property. However, in old Hindu law, rights of women to inherit property either as daughter or as widow was denied, but not her right to possess property, called as *stridhan* consisting of gifts and bequests received at the time of marriage, and property acquired either from the income of stridhan or out of savings from the maintenance allowance to which she was entitled as a widow out of her husband's property. She was, therefore, not such a helpless creature as in some Christian countries. It must also be emphasised that in Hindu polity, from the king to the commoner, the right to possess or inherity property was not absolute even for the Hindu males; it was limited to possession, and to enjoying the fruits of the property, but not to the property itself which was considered to be in the nature of trust. It would be interesting in this context to note the views of a modern philosopher like Schophenhaur. For him the will to reproduce is an extension of the will to live, and in his scheme of things he assigns definitely a lower position to women in relation to men. He thinks it absurd to give property rights to women who are inclined to extravagance because they live only in the present. He says, "women think that it is men's business to earn money, and theirs to spend it. I am, therefore, of opinion that women should never be allowed altogether to manage their own concerns, but should always stand under male supervision, be it of father, of husband, of son or of the state, as in the case in Hindusthani and that consequently they should never be given full power to dispose of any property they have not themselves acquired."

One common charge against Islamic law in regard to women is that Islam sanctions and practices polygamy, and, therefore, cannot be called such a champion of women's rights as it is made out to be. However, let us examine the position according to Quranic injunctions. A careful reading of the relevant Quranic precepts would show that though possession of more than one wife in special circumstances was allowed, polygamy by itself does not appear to have had a general sanction. The Holy Quran says:

"And if you are apprehensive that you shall not deal fairly with orphans, then of other women who seem good in your eyes marry but two, three or four, and if you still fear that you shall not act equitably then one only." We have already said that in pre-Islamic society, the child was a charge of the whole tribe. Now, at the time of advent of Islam, wars had raged between the believers and the non-believers, involving large killings, and many children of the tribe were left orphaned. It was to provide for such orphans that the Holy Quran allowed marriages - two, three, four so that the orphans might get fatherly affection. This was the special circumstance in which marrying more than one wife was allowed; but then again, the rider was a difficult, if not an impossible one. All the wives were to be treated equally. If one was not sure that he would have equal affection for all his wives, he was debarred from marrying more than one wife even to meet the special situation. Polygamy is allowed in Islam only to meet an exigency and to fulfil a social duty, not for satisfaction of lust. A plain reading of these injunctions would also show that marriage a second, third or fourth time was to be with widows and mature women, as the prime consideration was welfare of orphans. The principle of Islamic equality prevails here, in the care and consideration Islam had for women.

Lest the personal example of the Prophet (PBUH) be perniciously appropriated by the faithful, the Holy Quran makes the position very clear:

"O Prophet ! We allow thee thy wives whom thou hast dowered, and the slaves whom thy right hand possesseth out of the booty which hath granted thee, and the daughters of thy uncle, and of thy paternal aunts who migrated with thee to Madina, and any believing woman who hath given herself up to the Prophet, if the Prophet desired to wed her - a privilege to thee above the rest of the faithfuls."

Thus, the privilege granted to the Prophet (PBUH) applies to him only and to no others. There is a Persian saying "*khuda ra khuda danad*' "God only knows God's ways" and this applies appropriately to such special privilege.

It is true that constant interpretation, re-interpretation and codification of the Quran and the Hadith by the various Muslim jurists and divines, coloured by their personal inclinations and pre-possessions, as also the customs and usage of the different countries and the changing times they lived in, did produce a great deal of variations not contemplated originally. This situation occurs in all great movements. The eighth and ninth centuries were periods of consolidation and expansion of Islam in various countries. Abu Abd Allah Malik Ibn Anas (716-795 A.D.), founder of the Malik School of law favoured the historical approach to Shariat, but being a practical jurist, he often went beyond Quran, and strove for agreed solutions based on common sense and exigencies of circumstances. However, Abu Hanifa Al-Numan Ibn Thabit (700-767 A.D.), who was among the earliest of the jurists, and founder of the Hanifi School of law was more acceptable. Ahmad Ibn Hanal (780-855 A.D.) was a stickler for form. Imam Bukhari (Abu Abdullah Ibn Ismail) (810-870 A.D.) collected 70,000 Hadith, but applying stricter rules of reliability, actually accepted only 7000 of them. It was, however, Abul Hassan Ashiruddin Muslim (817-825 A.D.) better known as Imam Muslim who sub-divided the Hadith under different heads. However, Muslims of Shiat persuasion do not accept all the 7000 Hadith, and are said to believe in only about 6000 of them arranged in four books, known as Kutub-i-Arbna. In such circumstances, there was bound to be clash and confusion of views. It was left to Abu Hamid Md. Al-Ghazzali (1058-1111. A.D.) to reconcile many of these conflicting views and interpretations. His method and approach was intuitive: he went more by faith than reason, and prayed to God to send him just thoughts in His wisdom. "Inner light is a surer guide than the outer, physical light", he says. No wonder, he has been called Hijjatul Islam, the Proof of Islam. If, therefore, we find any deviation from the original Islamic position in regard to women, it is due to subsequent Juristic interpretations and applications, owing to the fact that, both semitic and customary laws, as the case may be, were allowed to operate in many of the countries where Islam was adopted as a religion.

In India, the position, to say the least, was curious. We have already said that Muslim invaders came to this country in waves not to proselytize - not like the Ansars of the old -but to found home, hearth and fief. Most of the conversions they effected were born of military, political or social necessity. It was, however, the Sufi saints who generally spread the light of Islam on an extensive and almost country wide scale, laying stress more on the substance of faith than its form. Foreign dignitaries who came from many lands of Central Asia and the Middle East brought with them their own local variations. Finally, added to these was the mental make up of the Indian converts. As habit to an individual is on the personal plane, so is custom on the collective plane. 'Custom is the king,' or as Bacon puts it: "Custom is the principal magistrate of man's life". In regard to chastity and fidelity of women, Indians had had very strong views; this persisted with the Muslims too. Divorce though sanctioned, was rarely resorted to. Again, in regard to incestuous liason, the prohibited degrees were wider and more extensive in India than those in the Islamic laws, and generally the Indian Muslims observed their old taboos in this regard customarily, and marriages among first-cousins were rare among Indian converts. The practice in Islam had grown to keep up to four wives; there was no such limit in Indian society. But, generally, the common mass of people could not normally afford more than one wife, and polygamy, if at all, was practised mostly among the rich and princely classes, both Muslims and Hindus.

One pernicious practice which the Muslim rulers, in imitation of the Persian court, brought with them was the keeping of a seraglio or harem which the Rajput and other Hindu princes sometimes copied. The Muslim rulers could, however keep only four wives according to the Shariat law, as against the old Iranian rulers of pre-Islamic days who had no such restriction. However, the seraglio was not only a habitat of wives of the ruler; it was in the nature of an inner court, just like the court of the king, presided over by the chief queen with her own retinue of female officials, eunuchs, peace keepers, and female hangerson. It was a female kingdom where her writ ran, and the king but seldom interfered. There were intrigues galore, and dramas of passion and profligacy, kindness and compassion, were enacted frequently. Sometimes the inner court also interfered and exercised undue influence in affairs of the state. The Muslim nobles and Amirs, in imitation, also kept harems on a smaller scale. However, it must be clearly stated that far from being only a social phenomenon, this practice had farreaching and disastrous consequences for the abilities and character of the people in positions of power. For one thing, a rival seat of power of the court did not allow a polity of nobles to emerge who could take independent and healthy decisions in moments of crisis and advise and act accordingly; secondly, it sapped the energies of the ruler to manage two kingdoms one real and the other, pseudo. The harem most of all, exercised a deleterious effect on the upbringing of the princes of the realm, and with exceptions, made them unfit, by training and inclination, to be efficient administrators. This was indeed one of the potent causes of the decline of the Mughal Empire in India, and later on, of the Turkish Empire in Europe. As Stanley Lanepool said, "the Muslims in India had grown effete; a race of conquerors had become a jostling crowd."

Islam prescribes 'hejab' or modesty in dress and manners. The Hindu also considered modesty to be an ornament for the women. However, due to historical reasons, as also the fact that in a male dominated society beautiful women were considered a possession and were likely to be carried away by enemies, if unguarded, in those turbulent days of unsettled conditions in Middle East, Central Asia, and Northern India, the practice of wearing a veil or purdah came in vogue. The nobility did not allow unfamiliar males to gaze upon their ladies; the portraits of royal ladies are more a product of imagination than of reality. This also resulted in cloistering the ladies of noble birth, stunting their growth intellectually and spiritually, even though there were some remarkable exceptions and a few of them became historical figures. However, this was not the case with women of working classes, either Hindus or Muslims, but then, certain social evils, like child-marriage, and female infanticide in some Hindu communities crept in. The tribals were mostly unaffected by these social changes, and in some tribal communities of Central India, Kamrup, and hilly regions, it was mostly the women who dominated socially and economically, the males being generally wastrels.

The real difficulty in regard to inheritance by women arose from the law of inheritance in an agricultural country, like India where all social institutions, customs, and economic activities were woven around an agricultural almanac. Islam enjoins a well-defined scheme of proportionate share in property of the deceased, for sons, daughters, widows etc. Now, the main property in India consisted of agricultural lands with rights of tillage and possession and could be inherited. Mere title to land was of no great consequence, as the utility of land consisted in its tillage and not in its mere possession, and agricultural operations were the joint effort of the entire family. Parcelling of land resulted in uneconomic holdings. Daughters married elsewhere without a habitat in the village itself, could not be expected to carry on the agricultural operations properly, at least in small holdings. These were the practical difficulties in ensuring strict observance of the Islamic law of inheritance, and Indian converts, generally, chose to follow their old customary law of inheritance. Since Urfi law or customary law is also recognised in Muslim law, the Muslim divines chose to ignore these deviations from Islamic practice, and the rulers, on demand, enforced the customary law in respect of Indian converts. Then again, many of the Hindu chieftains who turned Muslim continued to observe the law of primogeniture, and chose to claim the right to impartible estate to themselves. However, the nobles of foreign extraction generally followed the Islamic inheritance law, though, in their case too, deviations were not rare. This state of affairs continued right through the British rule. It was only in 1937 that, in the heat of communal passions, enactment was made for uniform application of Shariat law to all Muslims irrespective of any customary law to the contrary. An opportunity was thus lost to maintain a common code of inheritance for all Indians, Hindus, Muslims and others in the light of these historical developments.

Art and Architecture

The place of worship is the place where man turns to seek communion with moments of eternity in his ephemeral existence, and, as such, in building this place he gives expression to his inner most convictions of faith and hope. Islam's religious consciousness was moulded in Arabia, and in the building of mosques - embodiments of reverence and worship in stone the history, traditions, and environment of Arabia got expressed. For the Arab, the universe is a great expanse peopled scantily at intervals but otherwise a void. He looks upwards and the heavens spread to infinity and the sky is cloudless. But when he looks below, the earth as far as the eye can reach is a plain with a few scattered plain trees breathing the vast immensity of glittering particles of sand. God dwells in this universe and beyond. So if a tabernacle is to be built to express the exaltation and majesty of the Lord of creation, surely, a dome "whose circular surface is boundless and whose curves represent the limitless value of heavens" is the most appropriate form. Thus, the dome is basic to the Islamic architecture of mosques. However, the architectural design got mixed up with minds formed under different conditions as Islam spread far and wide in different countries. For example, in Turkey, in the sixteenth century. Siman Ibu Abdulmenan, an Albanian by birth, and employed as the chief court architect, introduced and perfected a new architectural design in building the Mosque of Shahzade in Istambul, commissioned by Sultan Sulaiman in the memory of his favourite son who died at an early age. Sinan reversed the principle of interiority fundamental to Islamic buildings, by employing the outer skin as well, enriching it by ornamental hexagonal forms, and this integrated the precepts of Islamic interiority with Greco-Roman exteriority. The Muslims brought to India architectural ideas from pre and post Islamization periods in Asia, Africa and the Mediterranean lands, and architectural ideas got mixed up in the process.

In India, the architectural design for places of worship is founded upon the Hindu attitude towards the cosmic principle. For the Hindus, the human soul is the Absolute. He seeks to identify his soul with the cosmic principle of the Supreme soul, and must commune with God in isolation. He is alone with his Master, and, therefore, in the temple, he creates a *garbha grih* into which light does not penetrate and all forms, suggestive of multiplicity, are blotted out. In this isolation of splendour, he tries to feel the veritable presence of the Absolute and must meditate upon Him. Surrounding this inner sanctum is the exterior representing the universe with its multiplicity, and hence the "temple outside revels in multitudinous forms; the platform, the walls, the pillars, the doors and the spires are a riot of sculpture and moulding, a veritable forest crowded with life."

Architecture was a well developed art in ancient India, and the Indians were great temple builders. With the expansion of Buddhism and Brahminism , overseas, the Indian architectural ideas travelled to South East Asia, China, and Middle East. The Mongols who came to rule over China, Central Asia, Iran, and Mesopotamia imbibed many of these ideas. The Indian builders were in great demand. Timur's architects and masons were mostly Indians impressed or invited into his service to build the capital city of Samarkand after his Jamuna valley campaign. Babar, like Timur, employed Indian masons and stone-cutters along with disciples of Sinan, the Turkish master builder. It is, therefore no wonder that in India, the simple Islamic mosque, at the hands of Indian builders came to reflect their consciousness and the result was the "Indian mosque with roofs provided with bunches of domes and cupolas, pairs of turrets and towers, gates within recessed gates, rows of niches in the walls, multicusped arches, statacties and squinches, stately pillars and capitals, and the effusion of colour through white, black and multicoloured marble, and red stone, and flowing inscriptions engraved on walls and doorways." There were regional variations too, reflecting local conditions. In Bengal, the Adina Mosque of 400 domes built at Padua in 1368 A.D. adopted, what is called, the Gaur style i.e., traditional Hindu temple style of curvilinear cornices copied from bamboo structures and symbolic decoration like the lotus. In Gujarat, in building mosques, the old "frozen lace" style was adopted in keeping with older traditions. The Gulbarga mosque built by Feruz Bahmani, who had married a Vijyanagar princess, is perhaps the only large mosque in India completely roofed (as against the open courtyard in the traditional Islamic style symbolising the vastness of universe in open sky), and owed this peculiarity to the example of capacious temples of Vijyanagar. In Moti Mahal Masjid of Agra, we have arches, and pillars repetition of Hindu symbolism and forms fittingly adapted for Muslim religious purposes. The Rajput architectural form has been called a specimen of 'Rajput monumental dignity', and this style of building got reflected in the court buildings of Fatehpur Sikri and elsewhere, and also in many of the mosques, built during the period of Mughal-Rajput-collaboration. An example of this type of architecture can be seen in what is called, 'Man Singh's Mosque' at Rajmahal (Bihar) built at the instance of Raja Man Singh, while Governor of Bengal and Bihar.

If the Hindu style of architecture influenced the building of Islamic mosques in India, so did Islamic ideas influence the subsequent Hindu style of temple structures. While the Hindu commune individually, Islam provide for congregational prayers. We have already seen that the Sufi saints popularised congregational chanting of God's name, and active participation in devotional singing. Chaitanya, the celebrated Bengali saint, introduced mass devotional singing and chanting of God's name as the best form of worship. Thus spacious 'Jagmohan' came to be built in India to accommodate devotees collectively. Examples of this are found now everywhere, but the temples of Govind and Madan Mohan at Vrindaban, the temple of Hamirdeva at Govardhan, the Jain temple of Sonagarh in Bundelkhand are perhaps, some of the best examples of the influence of Islamic forms on construction of temples. In building houses, palaces, and pavilions a distinct

Indo-Islamic style of architecture also emerged, and became India's very own. The pavillions and palaces in Vijayanagar, Chandrapuri, Madura, Tanjore and Rajputana built by Hindu rulers and chieftains are some of the illustrations of such a composite style. Raja Jai Singh built a new city of Jaipur in 1728 A.D. according to strict Hindu traditions and the art of Hindu town-planning and architecture under the guidance of a Bengali Brahmin architect and town-planner, Vidyadhar, but even here, the peculiar Indo-Islamic style of architecture predominates. It has been truly said that stones are not mute spectators, but speak eloquently the minds of the people to whom they provide shelter to live, pray, and die.

In the sphere of painting, the contribution of Muslims towards the emergence of a composite style of painting was immense. Islam is against idealisation of form, and there could not be and never was an Islamic school of painting. What happened was that the Mongols came to conquer and rule over a large part of China, Mesopotamia and Iran and all these countries had been under some sort of Indian cultural influence in the past during pre-Islamic days. This influence persisted in China, particularly, which had turned Buddhist, and wall frescoes, and colour painting according to Indian Buddhist traditions which became widely prevalent there since seventh-eighth centuries. The Mongols introduced this kind of painting in Persia, a country itself of noble cultural traditions. The result was a fusion of Chinese-Persian style of painting on paper and with Bihzad of Herat, the celebrated painter, a distinct school of Persian painting emerged. Humayun, after his return to India from his forced sojourn in Persia, brought two of the disciples of Bihzad, who studied the Indian style of painting, and soon a corps of painters under the patronage of the imperial court at Delhi and of the nobles and chieftains, both Muslims and Hindus, came to be formed. This had turned a full circle: the Indian style of painting travelled to many lands, acquiring some of the peculiarities and characteristics of each of them, and finally came back to India. Akbar was a great patron of painting, and granted *'mansabs'* to many of the painters. Jahangir was a connoisseur of this art which flourished during his reign. Shahjahan was indifferent, and Aurangzeb definitely hostile. But a new style of painting had already come into vogue, expressing the cultural renaissance of the period. The painters were mostly employed in illustrating pages of celebrated books. The illustrations of Dastan-i-Amir Hamzah, done by Persian painters, Mir Sayyid Ali, "The Raphael of the East", and Khwaja Abdus Samad, are mostly influenced by the Persian style with more colour and vivacity. However, the Indian influence soon predominated and the line and colour got integrated. There was greater restraint and more of realism, and the whole picture was a unity rather than a multiplicity. This can be seen clearly in the paintings in the copies of the *Khandan-i-Timuria*, and *Padshahnama*, both of which are happily preserved in the Khuda Bakhsh Oriental Library of Patna. Since the Indian mind is essentially egocentric, there being no conflict between intuition and intellect, in Indian painting the technique implies a combination of realism and abstraction. The art of painting is one of the highest manifestations of creative power: man seeking to bring into existence a world of imagination, beauty and truth which rivals the world of everyday experience and seeks to transform it near to his heart's desire. Thus, the paintings of this age exhibit a style of wondrous beauty scenes of everyday life, pageantry and simplicity, splendour and penury, heroism and cowardice; but behind all the scenes is the totality of expression of an integrated approach to life of unity in multiplicity. Mona Lisa's smile might appear intriguing to a European mind, but perhaps, at the hands of an Indian painter, her smile would have been either one of self-satisfaction or of self-abrasion.

So, also in the field of music, one of the highest forms of self-expression. India has had one of the most developed techniques of creating harmony and consonance of sound, at once pleasing to the ears, and satisfying to the soul, a kind of a spiritual experience. The Sufi saints, employing music as a form of intimate soulful communion with the Creator, added new dimensions to the Indian music. Man Singh Tomar vernacularised the ancient Dhrupad compositions. This was music in the classic mould, in which the form and structure were unalterable. As the art came closer to the lives of the people, the Kheyal style developed, allowing untrammelled expression to the lyrical and emotional content. A European critic may characterize this as the majestic Dionysus giving way to beauteous Apollo, but the differences, if any, were more apparent than real for both Dhrupad and Kheyal styles were pure Indian in conception; both had an air of submissiveness, serenity and total dedication to the particular mood. For example, both Beethoven's Fifth and Ninth Symphonies and the Indian Raga "Mian ki Todi", said to have been composed by the musician son-in-law of Mian Tansen, at the funeral of the latter are melancholy strains of music. In listening to Beethoven we feel as if marching in measured steps irresistibly towards a vault of extinction with a strange exhilarating feeling of ultimate hope and cheer. Mian-ki-Todi in Dhrupad builds up, no doubt, an air of gentle pensiveness, bit. There is an undercurrent of feeling of fulfilment - of a life having come to rest at its moorings. Both Dhrupad and Kheyal are great music in their own way, in as much as both show us the eternal and universal behind the transitory and the individual. Spinoza has said, "so far as the mind sees things in their eternal aspect it participates in eternity." Muslim composers, singers and instrumentalists were the chief architects of the grand traditions of what is termed as Hindustani music of North India. These masters left legacies of their own styles now called gharanas, which continues to enrich Indian music till today through the continuity of the teacher-disciple system unique in the world.

Search for Knowledge

In the field of education, the position was comparable to prevalent world conditions. The peculiarity in India was that certain castes had a monopoly of education and learning. Among the Hindus, the Brahmins, deemed it a sacred duty to pursue education and to make it an avocation of life. However, this was personality-based rather than institution-based. As soon as a person attained eminence as a scholar in any field, he attracted students from far and wide. All seekers to learn at his feet. Students underwent rigorous discipline of both body and mind, and had to prove their probity, character and love for learning by exemplary conduct. Generally, they were fed and clothed at the expense of their teacher and his patrons. Benares, Nawadip, Puri, in the north, Madurai, Conjivaram (both Vishnu Kanchi and Siva Kanchi). Tanjore, Sringeri and Ulepi in the South and Nasik, Girnar, Dwarka in the west were great seats of learning. The Muslim rulers allowed these centres to grow and some of them made endowments towards the upkeep of these establishments. In Bengal was founded a new system of Indian logic and metaphysics, called Nava-Nayaya, which took Indian dialectics to new heights. Madhusudan Saraswati, originally from Bengal, settled down at Benares, which was already attracting scholars of all-India standing. There was virtually a cluster of names in learning at Benares at that time. Madhusudan Saraswati lived to a ripe old age of more than hundred years. He was contemporary of both Chaitanyadeo, and of Tulsidas, and is said to have come to the rescue of Tulsidas when he was being berated by the Pandits for having written *Ramayan* in vernacular rather than in Sanskrit. "Nectar served either in golden bowl or in wooden cup is nevertheless nectar", he is reported to have opined, effectively silencing the obscurantist Pandits. Madhusudan Saraswati is remembered for his monumental work *Advait Siddhi,* supposed to be a commentary on Sankar's philosophy of monism. In fact this is more of an original work on the theory and practice of monism, with traces of arguments of a *shirkat* as in Islamic theology as well. Respected by Muslim rulers for his learning and character he is said to have been responsible for abolition of many of irksome tolls and duties which the Hindus only had to pay at Benares, said to have been imposed by Sikandar Lodi.

The Muslims had almost the same system of education as far as theology was concerned, but the Muslim rulers established Islamic seminaries at Agra, Delhi, Bijapur, Golcunda and Burahanpur where great many subjects other than theology were taught under eminent teachers, many of whom were from Persia and Arabia. It is true, that Indian Muslim rulers failed to cultivate such universities of learning as Cairo, Baghdad or Cordova. This could be due to the fact that in India, education was teacher-based, and the Muslim rulers had followed this system.

So far as the common people were concerned, certain castes, again, monopolised liberal education i.e., language, literature, mathematics with moral and religious instructions being thrown in between. It is they who provided the lower echelon of bureaucracy. Every town and village, wherever they resided in good numbers, had educational institutions. Others, who had not had the privilege of going to school, nevertheless, received instructions and training in character building and ethical conduct by example of family elders, the precepts of spiritual and religious teachers and itinerant monks and holymen. This applied to both Hindu and Muslim masses. Every mosque of note had had a Madarsa attached to it where many learnt to recite Holy Quran and imbibe the teachings of Hadith. Similarly attached to the temple of repute, specially in the south, there was a system of imparting religious instructions in the intricacies of rituals and the philosophy relating to the particular deity to which the temple was dedicated, such as Vishnu, Siva, Mahabir (Jain) etc. Small girls could receive education along with boys in such schools, but once they attained puberty, they were withdrawn from the school. In the case of nobles and the rich people, elderly teachers were engaged for their education and many women of noble families not only got educated but also participated in social affairs.

There are no reliable statistics for the rate of literacy in India during these periods. The classical languages which attracted the maximum number of scholars were Sanskrit and Persian. Unfortunately, the study of Arabic - may be due to the difficulty of the language - was not promoted and except for Islamic theologians, Arabic sciences and its literature in original did not acquire any large readership. For full five centuries since the advent of Islam, Arabic scholarship had been noted for its spirit of enquiry and a limitless thirst for expanding human knowledge garnered from classical writings in Sanskrit, Hebrew, Greek and Latin. Astronomy, Chemistry (Al Chemia) and Medicine had made great strides in Islamic seats of learning like Cairo, Baghdad, and Cordova, and the Islamic world continued to be the leading light in these fields. The Europeans advance of science is traced from Copernicus (1473-1543) and Galileo (1584-1642) but what they claimed to have discovered was largely known to the Indians and had been formulated by Aryabhat (5th century A.D.) and Varahmihir (6th century A.D.). On the basis of these the Arabs had already developed their theories. Raja Jai Singh II, got the Arabic *Al-Majesti,* a compendium on Astronomy, translated into Sanskrit which greatly facilitated his astronomical studies and in building up and running his astronomical observatories. Similarly, the researches of Vasalius (1514-1564) in Anatomy or of Harvey (1578-1657) on the circulation of blood had been anticipated by Sushrut (Fourth century A.D.) in India and Abu-Cina and Jal-e-Noos, (8th-9th centuries), famous Arab physicians. Medical science appears to have been well advanced in India and in the Islamic world, when compared to Europe, However, one great drawback has to be noticed; there was little co-relation between theoretical knowledge as propounded by original writers and the practitioners of the traditional skill. For example, Bhaskaracharya (born in 1114 A.D.) appears to have propounded the theory of Gravity, some five hundred years before Newton, but we do not know what use was made of this by practising professionals. Highly developed skills in the fields of architecture, town-planning, production of finished metals etc, remained confined to certain traditional castes, and even among them within certain families. Some of the skills so acquired were thus lost to subsequent generations due to these being family secrets. Cases of such lost skills have been noticed in respect of steel-making for example. The making of rustless steel, as in Kutub Minar, was lost to Indian skill for ever. However, this was not peculiar to India only. For example, in medieval England, the Churches were filled with stained glass, through which light not only crept in but flooded the whole structure. The skill of making such glass is now lost as it had remained a guarded secret. So was the secret of the "Greek Fire" - a composition burning in either or in water, kept guarded by the Byzantine Greeks. With all the modern engineering skill and advanced technology, it would, perhaps, be difficult to rival the grandeur, and the indescribable elegance of Taj Mahal, a product of that fine, delicate expression of beauty combined with majesty which had come to be characterised as Indo-Iranian style of architecture. The comment of Vincent Smith describing the Taj Mahal as: "the product of a combination of European and Asiatic genius", goes against all historical evidence. There is nothing "European" in the design and execution of the Taj Mahal. The "Victoria Memorial", planned to rival the Taj Mahal in beauty and elegance as a tribute to the superiority of European skill has not achieved the status of even a poor second in the world of architecture. The only building to have come up to the level of excellence of the Taj is the mausoleum of Mohammad of Bijapur (1626-56) with the second largest dome in the world built contemporaneously with the Taj. This mausoleum is a marvel of skill, influenced by Vijayanagar style of architecture which did combine in itself Mediterranean and Indian Oceanic influences, with traces of European art intermixed with its Indian features.

Persian had come to be accepted widely as the language of culture and of higher administration. The Muslim rulers, though natives of different Central Asian regions, had adopted Persian as the language of learning and common medium of communication amongst themselves and of their Governments. A branch of the Indo-Aryan group of Languages, Persian, "simple, sweet and sonorous" had come to captivate and charm the Indians, and it became a mark of refinement to write and compose poetry in Persian. Hafiz, Rumi, Attar and other eminent Persian poets had their admirers in India, and to copy them both in thought and in diction became a fashion. Eventually, galaxy of eminent Hindu writers were using Persian as their medium. Mention may be made, amongst others, of Mirza Manohar Tansini, Chandrabhan Brahaman, Mathuradas Hindu, Banwalidas Walt, "Wamiq", "Di was", "Begham", "Amanat" and "Bedar" who were poets; Bhagwan Dass, Hiraman, Bindraban Das, Sujan Bir, Narayan Shafaq, Birbal Kachru, Khushal Chand, and Rai Chatarman who were historians; Har Karan, Madho Ram, Malikzada Munshi and Munshi Uderaj who were letter writers; and Ravi Anand Ram Mukhlis, Sialkoti Mal Warsta, and Tek Chand Bahar who were lexicographers.

Most of the modern Indian vernacular languages reached their full form and enriched their contents during the period. These regional languages were spoken and written both by the Hindus and the Muslims and could be called their mother tongues. It is to be particularly noted that the writings of Muslims in prose and verse, were racy: the scenes they depicted unfolded broad sweeping rivers, the flora and fauna of their region and the common aspirations, love and hate of the people; the imageries were typically Indian in character, and the hero and heroines they sang of were Indians. Ram and Sita, Krishna and Radha, and hosts of traditional 'Hindu' figures appeared in their writings. This was particularly true of Bengal where the Muslim writers chose typically Hindu themes as in *Gorakh Vyay* of Faizullah and in *Gopichand Sanyas* of Abdush Shakoor Mahmud on the pattern of Maladhar Basu's *Shree Krishna Vyay*. The Bengali language is, undoubtedly, a common heritage of both Hindus and Muslims. This is now well-proved when, in modern times, the legacy of great Bengali poets such as Rabindra Nath Tagore and Qazi Na Tul Islam is being cherished and promoted equally in West Bengal and Bangladesh, In the central region, around Delhi, UP and Bihar, Khari Boli had emerged as the language of the people which ultimately developed into a literary style of the region; the contribution of Muslim scholars towards its growth and development is noteworthy. For example, Rahim Khan-e-Khana, who wrote in Hindi was a versatile genius-soldier, poet and statesman he translated the Life of Babur from Turkish into Persian and is known for his 'Dohas', epigrams, in Hindi, said to have been composed instantaneously as a situation demanded exact, polished and vivacious. For his poetical prowess in Hindi he has been justly compared with the great Sanskrit poet, Bharatrihari. However, there was one great difficulty with the Muslim nobles and elite who were mostly settled in and around Delhi, Agra and towards west in the Jamuna-Ganga valley. Their native tongues were dialects of the Central Asian regions from where they came originally; their language of culture and elegance was Persian; and they had to converse with the native population in Khari Boli. In the circumstances, and for convenience, a new mixed language evolved in which the grammar, phonetical system, and idiom were those of Khari Boli or Hindi while the fountain of words and expressions, the literary flashes and literary devices were those of Persian. In course of time, a new Persianised version of Khari Boli originated, developed and perfected into a distinct Urdu language. The literate Hindus who had already adopted Persian as the medium of their literary expression took also to Urdu in a big way. The Sufi saints also found Urdu a convenient tool to propagate their ideas and teachings. Specially in the Deccan, Urdu language and literature had an early flowering. The early Urdu writers of repute were mostly from the Deccan. The output of Sufi poetry in Urdu by Khawja Banda Nawaz Gesudaraz, Shah Aligmdhani, Shah Miranji, Shamshul Ushaq, Shah Burhanuddin Janam was impressive. Muhammad Quli Qutub Shah of Qutub Shahi dynasty was a master of the Urdu language in which he composed Ghazals, Qasidas, Masnawis, Rubai's and Marsias. Another noted prose writer in Urdu who came from the south was Aminuddin Ala (died 1675), who wrote the treatise, Risala Mazhabul Salikin on comparative religions demonstrating the unity of Godhead in all religions. With the extinction of the Muslim Sultanate in Deccan, Urdu writers and poets took refuge in Delhi, Agra, Lucknow and Patna, in search of patronage and livelihood, and the scene of literary activities in Urdu literature shifted to north. Both Hindus and Muslims made great contribution to it. Stars of magnitude were Mir Taqi Mir, Rafi Sauda, Mir Dard, Chandrabhan Brahaman, Nawab Rai Wafa, Saraf Singh, Divana, amongst many others of repute.

By the eighteenth century, however, Urdu poetry as also Hindi and other vernacular literatures of the country were sliding down to decadence, Their thought processes had fallen into a rut. Forms of expression and imagery, already used to great effect by old masters, were repeated, without the underlying inspiration. The cultural and literary decline was only a symptom of the socio-political stagnation which was to overtake the Indian society eighteenth century onwards. The ancient glory had become a monument of ruins rather than a foundation for future. It will be our endeavour to trace its causes and courses in the subsequent pages.

TWELVE

Love for Books

Along with our talks on the topic of public welfare institutions in the Islamic civilization it will not be out of place to discuss the libraries as well. There were numerous madrasahs and many other educational institutions besides, on which 'Ulama, nobles and influential people spent their resources, particularly during the period when facilities of printing and publication were not available. Books were written by some select people laboriously, and so much time and money. had to be spent on a single book that a student or a learned man of very limited means failed to procure it. As for the collection of books for a library comprising books on any particular subject or books on the particular branch of a science or art in which a person has specialised, it was a far cry. That is why in our society of the past the establishment of libraries was the result of purely human sentiments and love of learning and knowledge in the extreme.

Among the ancient literatures perhaps the Arabic literature is the only one that deserves to be called 'Ghani', free from want in the matter of books. Here every one appears to be a lover of books; books are being discussed and every one is interested in them. It appears as if the book were a friend whom one had not met since long, lived far off, the heart was fond of him and eyes longed to see him. Ahmad bin-eIsmail says:

"The book is a friend that can talk to you at night, and does not trouble you by broaching topics while you are busy (in study), and does not put you to inconvenience by calling on you at the time of your respite (from work) or rest. And when you want to see and talk to him you need no elaborate preparations to do so. And the book is a friend that does not praise you to the skies and one who does not deceive you, and a comrade that does not grieve you, and an advisor that protects you from stumbling into error."

Attachment to Books

Muslim men of letters preferred study of books to gatherings and discussions, and closeness to books was more agreeable and satisfactory to them than closeness to the caliph or the king. Muhammad bin-e-Abd-al-Malik-al-Ziat a well known literary figure and a wazir had for a time taken to the seclusion of his house. Jahiz intended to see him and thought of taking to him the gift of the book by Sebowaih who was the master Arabist of his time. The wazir accepted the present joyfully and said, "By God! Nobody ever gave me a more cherished gift than yours." One of the caliphs called a certain learned person to talk to him on some matter. The messenger found him engrossed, with a heap of books about him. He said to him, "You have been called by the Amir-al-Muminin." He said in reply to. the messenger of the caliph, "Tell him that I am presently in the company of great learned men and philosophers and engaged in conversation with them. Hope to see him when I am finished with them." The attendant returned and informed the caliph. He asked the attendant in amazement, "Who are those learned men and philosophers engaged in conversation with him?" The attendant said in reply, "By God! I did not see there anybody." So the caliph sent orders to him to present himself at once at the court. When he came, the caliph asked him, "Who were those learned men who were keeping you company." In reply to his query he recited the following verses:

"They are companions whose talk is not (unnecessarily) prolonged; present or absent they are constant and trustworthy."

"When they meet you in seclusion their talk is very beneficial and helpful in taking away grief."

"They benefit us with learning of the past and along with that they favour us with wisdom, affability, and prudence and sound opinion."

"You will neither have any apprehension nor fear of discourtesy, nor dread of any injury from their hand or their tongue."

"If I say they are dead, I shall not be lying. And if I say they are living, it will be no joke either."

The caliph on learning that he meant books, cooled down and did not reprimand him for not responding to his call immediately.

Sahib bin-e-'Ubad, instead of accepting the highest post in the royal palace of Nuh bin-e-Mansoor Sasani, opted for the company of books in a library, since he was in love with his library, and could neither leave it, nor take it with him. So he preferred to live where his heart was. This was the spirit of learning on whose basis our learned men, the rich and the noble, showed such zealous attachment to books and collected them, so much so that they considered the loss of their domestic goods much less than the loss of books.

Once during a war Ibn-e-'Umaid's house was attacked by the army men and his slaves and guards were taken prisoners, Ibn-e'Umaid himself took to his heels and took refuge in Dar-al-Amarah. The army plundered his house completely. On coming back home after the pillage, he found every thing of the household goods gone, and there was neither anything to sit on nor a cup to drink water from. But in spite of all that he had no cause for worry save the anxiety for his books, the most cherished part of his belongings. He had in his library books of which he had no count, on all subjects of various disciplines, literature and philosophy. They could hardly be loaded on one hundred camels. When Ibn-e-Umaid saw his librarian, he asked him about his books. He told him that the library was untouched. Ibn-e'Umaid's face brightened with the glow of happiness and said to the librarian, "I bear witness to the fact that you are a dutiful guard. All other kinds of goods can be replaced but not this stock of books."

Again, the same spirit of learning and taste and avidity for books prompted people to vie with one another in purchasing books and furnishing their libraries as much as they could. As soon as a book neared completion people approached the writer or compiler to get it on a basis of priority and there was regular competition. For example, the ruler of Andalusia, Hakam, came to know that Abu-al-Faraj Asfahani is writing his famous literary book *Al-Aghani*. He sent him a thousand dinars as the price of one copy of this book and asked him to send it as soon as it was completed. So this book found its way to far away Andalusia and was being read there long before being available in his own country, Iraq.

Due to this literary taste and spirit of learning, libraries were established throughout the Islamic world. There were few schools which did not have libraries of their own, and there were fewer still towns or villages without libraries. As for the larger towns and the capital, the libraries and book depots were in such abundance which was unimaginable in the midddle ages.

These libraries were usually of two kinds, public and private. Public libraries were established by the caliphs, nobles, 'ulama and other well-to-do, persons. Separate permanent buildings were built for them, and at times these libraries were annexed to the big mosques or madrasahs.

The independent and permanent buildings for them comprised several rooms and in between them there were spacious halls, which connected these rooms. The books were kept on cornices along the walls. Every room was set apart for books on a particular discipline, for example, the section on literature, on Fiqh, on medicine, and so on. In this building there were separate rooms for those visiting the library reading rooms. Some of those rooms were set apart for the scribes who were all the time busy writing books (copying the originals. Tr.). In some library buildings there was a separate room for music where the students could refresh themselves with music after long tiring hours of study and started with their study once again refreshed. From this aspect the Islamic civilization has a unique position. Also there were rooms in that building in which the learned men staying there could gather to discuss things together. All these rooms were furnished with the best and most comfortable furniture. There were separate rooms that served as dining halls for those coming to the library to stay there for prolonged study. For the poor people there were bedrooms where they could sleep, as reported in connection with the library of 'Ali bin-e-Yahya bin-e-Munajjim that had a magnificent building in the vicinity of Oafs close to Baghdad in a village Karkar. It had a large stock of books, and was known as "Khazana-e-Hikmat" (The Treasure-house of Wisdom). People from far and near visited this place, stayed here and studied various disciplines. Here they were provided with books in plenty and very easily. And all these expenses were charged to the personal property of Alibin-e-Yahya. There were some facilities available at this library which we cannot imagine even in the capital of the countries most advanced in civilization and culture. Abdul Qasim Ja'far bin-e-Muhammad Hamdan Mosali had built a house in Mosul which he had named "Dar-al`Ilm". Here he dedicated to the students a big library to which there were no bars for entry, and if a poor student came to it with the goal of acquiring knowledge, he was supplied not only stationery for his work as a student but a fairly decent amount as his stipend for all his expenses. This library was open all the days of the week and the year.

Let us know if any one knows of any library in London, Washington or any other capital of the world where such facilities exist—books with board and lodge.

In the public libraries whole-time workers were employed. 'The Chief among such workers was known as the Khazin-e-Maktabah or stock-holder of the books. To this post were always employed `Ulama of renown. There were some people who helped him in giving out books to the students and others coming to the library and taking them back. They were called Munawils. Moreover, there were men who were engaged in translation work, rendering books of other languages into Arabic. And there were calligraphers who were all the time preparing in a beautiful hand copies of the existing books And then there were book binders who were making strong and beautiful bindings of the library books to ensure safety of books from wear and tear, thus ensuring longer life for them. Over and above these well-known posts there were people employed for other miscellaneous jobs of a minor nature.

Every big and small library had a catalogue of books with the help of which any book could be taken out very easily. This catalogue was prepared according to the disciplines to which the books belonged. Every almirah had a list of its own with particulars of the books it contained. In connection with most of the libraries it was generally known to people that books could be taken out on depositing the requisite security for them. But the learned men known for their excellence in learning were exempt from this rule and no security was demanded of them.

The sources of the income of these libraries to meet these multifarious expenses were varied, one of them being those trusts, exclusively made out for the maintenance of the libraries. And for most of the libraries these trusts were the mainstay. Another source was that the nobles and the 'Mama establishing these libraries themselves met these expenses from their personal resources. For example Muhammad bin-e-Abdul Malik Al-ziat used to pay two thousand pounds monthly to the copyists and the calligraphists. Mamun Rasheed paid Hunain Ibn-e-Ishaq the weight of every book in gold rendered into Arabic from other languages by him.

Now we would like to mention some of the personal (private) and public libraries as specimens from the record furnished by the history of the libraries.

This library of the Fatimid caliphs of Cairo was one of the most famous ones of that time. That was the wonderful library containing the finest copies of the Quran and other books, which were two million in number according to most historians, although Maqrizi is of the opinion that it comprised 1.6 million books.

Instituted by Hakim-bin-Amr-Allah and was inaugurated on 10th Jamadah I, 365 A.H., when its building was built and the floor draped with the best carpets, and the windows and doors hung over with curtains, and the supervisory and managerial staff was posted. Such a magnificent collection of books was made which had never been done before this by any monarch. It had forty sections, each comprising eighteen thousand books, including all kinds of books on ancient sciences and arts. It was open to everyone. Some people would go there for study, others to copy books and yet others only to acquire knowledge. Stationery of every description was supplied to the visitors of this library free of charge.

One such library was Bait-al-Hikmat of Baghdad founded by Harun Rasheed, attaining perfection during the reign of Mamun Rasheed. This was not a library but a grand university to which gathered research scholars, thinkers, those coming for study and those attracted to it to benefit by discussion and other sources of knowledge. There were calligraphers and translators employed on a permanent basis for regular work. These people were constantly employed in translating books acquired by Harun Rasheed and Mamun Rasheed after the conquests of Anqarah, 'Amooryah and Cypress. Ibn-e-Nadeem informs us that a lengthy correspondence ensued between Mamun Rasheed and the Roman emperor when he had been vanquished in some battle by Mamun. One of the conditions of the treaty between them was that the Roman king would allow translation of all the books in his dominion and the translation work will be undertaken by those whom Mamun would appoint for this purpose. So it was, and the entire Roman stock of books was rendered into Arabic. It is a golden example in history that a conqueror gave no greater importance to a conquest than the transfer of sciences and arts for the benefit of his people.

This library was very spacious and magnificent. It is said to comprise 0.4 million books. Its catalogues were very nicely prepared and gave every detail, so much so that the catalogue of the collections of the poetical works alone comprised forty-four sections. The expert scribes were permanently employed there. Similarly the services of the book-binders and kitab-Bars were also obtained, with the result that Andalusia came to have such a large stock of books that had never been there before nor ever afterwards.

This library as regards its spaciousness and grandeur was one of the signs of God. The number of scribes alone was one hundred and eighty, who copied books within the stipulated time. They had shifts of duties round the clock, so that the copying business might continue uninterrupted. Banu Ammar had such avidity for collecting new and rare books that they had employed some officers and traders to tour different parts of their own country and also other countries, far and fear and collect books for their library wherever they could. Al-Mu'arri benefited by this library, and has mentioned it in some of his books. Opinions differ regarding the number of books in this library. A guarded opinion is that it comprised a million books.

Private Collections

From among the private libraries we shall take up-only those that have a historical importance. The then Islamic world was, replete with libraries both the Eastern and the Western wings. There was hardly any learned man not possessing a library of his own comprising thousands of books. Among such personal libraries that of Fatah bin-e-Khaqan (murdered in 247 A.H.), is very well known. This was a very spacious library. It had appointed the famous learned man and Imam of letters of that period Ali bin-e-Yahya Al-Munajjim to look for and collect books for this library. This person collected those rare books in this library which were not to be found elsewhere.

The library of Ibn-e-Khashshab (d. 567 A.H.) too comes under this category of libraries. He was an expert in Syntax (Grammar), and had good knowledge of the Quranic exegesis, Hadith, logic and philosophy also. His love of books touched the limits of madness. This mad love for books compelled him to take to certain evil practices also in the collection of books. When he went to the Book-seller and wanted to purchase any good book he would tear off certain pages of that book by stealth while pretending to examine it and then compelled the bookseller to sell the damaged book much cheaper to him. Similarly when he borrowed a book from some friend, on demand from the owner, would usually pretend to have misplaced and lost it in the heaps of books and thus excusing himself, would retain it.

The library of Jamaluddin A1 Qifti (d. 646 A.H) was also famous. He collected innumerable books. Due to his generosity people from all sides thronged to his place. Books were his first and last love, almost his craze, and he had dedicated his life to books. For this reason he did not marry either because of the apprehension of being entangled in managing a house and looking after the family. At the time of his death he bequeathed his collection of books to Nasir. It was worth fifty thousand pounds.

The library of the learned men of Bani Jaradah of Halab (Aleppo) is also famous. One of these persons, Abul Hasan Ibn-e-Abi Jaradah (d. 548 A.H.), wrote books to fill three libraries with his own hand, one for himself, one for his son Abul Barakat and a third for his son (grandson) Abdullah.

Maufiq bin-e-Matron Damishqi (d. 587 A.D.) also had a famous library. He showed great fortitude and ambition in the procurement of books. At his death his collection of books on medical sciences and other disciplines comprised ten thousand volumes. He had employed three scribes who were always busy copying books for his library. He paid them salaries and provided other necessities also.

The weakness of people for books in the Islamic world in the hey-day of our civilization may be very pleasing to us. But much more pain and grief are caused by thinking of the fate of these precious assets, and how they were destroyed through vandalism or consigned to the waves or the flames. This is that destruction and loss of knowledge and wisdom of the ages, which can never be made good. These libraries came by such calamities as a result of which humanity was deprived of millions of those books that were the historical masterpieces of the creation of man's thought.

When the flood of the destruction and the pillage of the Tartars entered Baghdad, they made those libraries their first target. So everybody knows that wherever the ignorant Tartars came upon books they consigned them to the waters of the river Tigris, so much so, that they made the river waters shallow enough to be crossed easily by their horsemen, not in a single file but in whole ranks. For months the water of the river had a black tinge due to the ink washed off the pages of the books.

Later, calamities visited the Muslim world through crusades which destroyed all the precious libraries of Tripoli, Ma'arrah, Bait-al-Maqdis, Asqalan and other big cities, since after conquest the cities themsleves had been razed to the ground. The historians have recorded that in Tripoli alone the Christians destroyed three million books. This is a clear pointer to the magnitude of this destruction.

The domination of Andalusia by the Spaniards deprived humanity of so many magnificent libraries is a woeful tale recorded by history. An idea of the damage done by these fanatical religious people in making bonfires of books can be had by the fact that in one open space of Granada alone one million books were burnt in a single day.

These are some of the instances of mass destruction of the great libraries of the Islamic world wrought by the enemies of Islam. But our internal turmoils too did no less damage. The library of the Fatimid caliph of Egypt came by its sad end at the hands of the Turkish Slave Dynasty when they came to dominate Egypt. They destroyed it completely, by setting fire to it. They tore away the fine leather in which the books were bound and got shoes made out of it. Innumerable books were thrown into the Nile. Some books were taken away by people to various distant parts of the country, the remaining were heaped in the open fields to rot and their pages were torn one by one by the winds. So some mounds came to be known as mounds of books.

Aleppo had a great library known as "Khazanah-as-Sufiah." On the occasion of 'Ashoorah (10th of Muharram, the first month of the Muslim calendar and the day of martyrdom of Hussain, the younger grandson of the Prophet), a Shi'ah Sunni riot broke out and people destroyed it, almost completely.

The library of Mustansar, the ruler of Andalusia met its destruction at the hands of Berber tribes when they entered as conquerors. They auctioned many books at throw-away prices, and the remaining were destroyed.

In connection with the destruction of books and libraries an amazing and ludicrous action was that of Amir 'Ibn-e-Falik. He was a member of the nobility of the fifth century after Hijrah. His wife belonged to a very respectable and well-to-do family. But since most of Ibn-e-Falik's time was spent in this library of his, the wife had come to 'have an abhorrence for these books (he was engrossed with, neglecting her. Tr.). When Ibn-e-Falik died, she and her slave girl entered the library and started throwing the books into a tank of water in their open courtyard. She was lamenting also her husband's loss but said during her wailing that these books held his attention most of the time and did not let him attend to her .

....This. was the revenge of 'that woman wreaked on the books, that were the first love of her husband, after his death. The Islamic history mentions some other wives also who hated the books like the wife of Ibn-e-Falik. The wife of Imam Zahri on finding her husband engrossed with books, used to say:

"By God! These books are heavier on me than three rival women (husband's other wives):"

This is the woeful tale of our libraries during the period of our civilization and culture, and this was their sad end.

Although it is very heavy on human psyche to recognize the excellent performance of the enemy, but it is our duty to do so with an open heart that many libraries of Europe preserved a fairly large number of the vestiges of this valuable asset of ours, and these libraries contain to this day those treasures of the Arabic literature, the like of which are not to be found anywhere in the entire Islamic world.

New Institutions

This is a colourful aspect of our magnificent civilization, and has had a beneficial effect on the propagation of culture and knowledge and learning. This not only helped in raising the general level and improving the tastes of common people in academic pursuits, but the culture was also improved. This much about the societies and academic circles that were so common in the Muslim capitals and other big cities when we know that associated with them were big madrasahs and academic institutions and libraries. These societies from the point of view of their abundance and the variety of discussions raised in them, during the period of the glory and honour of the Muslim Ummah, were the brightest manifestation of awakening in the field of learning. When you learn that the various classes of the ummah, the nobles, the 'ulama, men of letters and poets held competitions on various topics of learning, literature and philosophy in their select (private) and general (public) gatherings of societies, you would be convinced that, in its love of learning and quenching its thirst for knowledge, the Muslim ummah had attained the height which provided solid evidence of its evolution and grandeur.

These societies were numerous and various. Some societies were patronised by the caliphs who presided over them. They were attended by the most renowned 'Mama, legists and men of letters of the caliph's capital. With the growth and development of the Islamic civilization and culture the shape of these societies too underwent changes. During the period of the rightly-guided caliphs these societies discussed the working capacity and efficiency of the governors and other affairs of the state, and their position was that of the assemblies in which the most prominent leaders of the nation exchanged ideas on the issues confronting the state and various other problems and matters of policy. 'Umar Ibn-e-Khattab once stood in need of a person for the supervision of some important work of the state. And he asked the members attending the meeting to point out a person whom he wanted to employ in an important work. Those present suggested the name of some one. But 'Umar said in reply that he did not want that person for the purpose in view. They, then, asked him about the particular qualification of the person he needed, to which he said, "I want a man who in his own person may be independent of the head of the state and may carry on his business confidently even without him ('Umar) and it may appear as if he himself is the head of the state. But in case there is a head of the state of the ummah he may behave like an ordinary person (without the least desire to suggest in any manner his own importance or inevitability, Tr.). They said to this that the person of the requisite qualities wanted by him was Rabi' bin-e-Zaid Harithi. Approvingly Umar remarked that they had thought of and suggested the most appropriate person for the job and appointed him to it.

During the period of Umayyids these societies became academies of learning, literature and poetry and philosophy. Once when Abdullah bin-e-Hashim came to the gathering presided over by Amir Muawiyah, the president asked, "Who can define generosity, valour and urbanity?" Abdullah replied, "Generosity is that the donation be given away even before the request is made for it. Valour is the courage of going ahead and standing on one's ground firmly when a slip appears imminent. And urbanity is self correction and improvement in one's faith and belief, taqwa (piety) and self reform, and support of the neighbour." Abdul Malik asked the audience in a gathering, "Who among you can present such words relating to the human body, which begin with the letters in the alphabetical order? I shall give the person, who can, whatever he demands as reward." Suwaid bin-e-Ghaflah said to him, "I will do it, sire." Abdul Malik granted him permission, and he said, "Anf (nose', Batn (abdomen), Tarqutah (clavicle), Sagharr (frontal teeth or incisors), Jamjamah (Skull), Halq, Khad (Cheek brain)." Another man volunteered to present a double set of such words. On this Suwaid said he could treble the list. And so he said, "Anf, Asnan (teeth), Uzun (ear)," and in this strain he went on pronouncing three words each for the following letters of the alphabet. Abdul Malik was amazed at the way he presented so many words extempore and rewarded him for it.

A rustic once came to Abd-al-Malik while he was sitting in a gathering and the poet Jareer was one of them. Abd-al-Malik said to the villager, "Do you know anything about poetry?" And he said in reply, "Ask me whatever you like, Sire." Abd-al-Malik asked him, "Which is the best verse in praise?" The villager said, "This verse of Jareer which says:

> "Are you not superior to those who could seldom boast of a mount, and are you not more generous than all the world."

Jareer raised his head and kept it raised for a sufficiently long time. Then Abd-al-Malik asked the rustic which is the best couplet in self-aggrandising poetry? The rustic said, again, this couplet of Jareer.

> "When the people of Banu Tameem are displeased with you, you will realize that the whole world is in a rage against you."

Jareer was in a glee moving his head from side to side. Abd-al-Malik again put the question, Which is the best couplet in the field of satire? The rustic quoted this couplet of Jareer:

> "Lower thy gaze for thou art from Bani Numair. Thou canst neither raise thyself to the position of Ka'b, nor that of Kallab."

Jareer's face glowed with mirth. But Abd-al-Malik again asked him, Whose couplet is praise-worthy in odes or amatory poems? And the villager once again quoted Jareer:

"Thy eyes that cast only side glances have killed but never cared to revive our corpses after causing death."

Jareer was moving from side to side most gleefully. Abd-al-Malik once again asked him, "Which is that couplet in which the best simile has been used." The rustic recited this couplet of Jareer as an illustration:

"Night approached towards them, whose stars appeared to be entwined wicks burning in chandeliers."

There was no limit to the mirth of Jareer and he said:

"Amir-al-Muminin, confer my reward too on this rustic." Abd-al-Malik, however, said in reply. "He too will receive just as much, without any deduction from yours." When the rustic came out of the court, he held eight thousand dirhems in his right hand and in his left a long piece of cloth.

During the period of the Abbasids, these sittings and gatherings improved and were changed in character also. As regards their extent, the paraphernalia and the variety of the sciences and arts and the topics of discussion as also the large number of the learned men and men of letters that had gathered round them, they had become grand sittings. These were over and above those sittings brought together for idle gossip or merry talk which were dominated by a literary colour, and in which poetry came up for discussion and the poets exchanged sarcastic observations and stinging allusions, as also those pet words used by the singers in their songs, came up for discussion. Harun Rasheed and Mamun, among the Abbasid caliphs are particularly renowned for their very extensive. and very magnificent gatherings. Harun Rasheed had gathered around him many great learned men in every branch of learning and arts. The outstanding poets of his court were Abu Nawas, Abul- Itahiyah, Da'bal, Muslim bin-al-Waleed and Abbas bin-al-Asnaf. And among the legists there were Abu Yusuf, Shafi'i, Muhammad bin-al-Hasan. And among the experts of language and idiom there were Abu 'Ubaidah, Asma'i and Kasai, and among the historians, the world famous Waqidi. And among the commentators of the Quran there were Ibrahim Musali and his son Ishaq, and others. Such was the galaxy around Harun.

We would like to mention here a peculiar literary discussion. Such discussions were common in his gatherings. In one of his literary sittings Kasai and Sebowaih and some other top men in the field of language and idiom, Kasai was of the opinion that the Arabs used an idiom like this:

"Kunta Azanna Alzanbura Ashadda Le s'a minannahlah fa iza huwa iyyah"

"I understand that the sting of the hornet is more painful than that of a honey-bee, so now it has become certain that it is so." But Sebowaih said that the usage in fact is *"Fa iza huwa hiyah"* and not *"Fa iza huwa iyyah"*. Long and tiring discussions on this idiom continued between them but without any outcome. Finally it was agreed upon that some beduin Arab be called to pronounce judgement in the case who had never come in contact with the city-dwellers and his tongue had not been spoilt by the corrupt language spoken in cities. Harun Rasheed had great regard for Kasai and was at heart in favour of his carrying the day, since he had been his teacher before he (Harun) came in power. Harun had a beduin called from the desert, and asked him. He pronounced it the way Sebowaih did it. Harun said to him to do it the way Kasai was pronouncing it. He said he could not pronounce it (as it was pronounced by Kasai). Finally he agreed to judge between Kasai and Sebowaih when they both pronounced it before him and decided in favour of Kasai. So the next day the show was put up in the gathering. But Sebowaih had come to know that there had been foul play against him, and people had been unfair to him in favouring Kasai. Sebowaih was very much dejected by this and in great grief he left Baghdad. It is said that he did not live long after this unhappy incident and the grief caused his death.

Similarly, issues of jurisprudence also came up for discussion in his meetings. One of the most interesting of such polemical contests was that a disciple of Imam Abu Hanifah, Imam Muhammad bin-al Hasan, said that Kasai is not an expert of Fiqh (jurisprudence). He has only knowledge of Arabic language to some extent. Kasai said that a person attaining perfection in any one discipline, can see his way through others with insight. Imam Muhammad asked him by way of testing him, "If a person falls into error while rectifying an error in prayer (making another mistake during Sajdah Sahw Tr.), is he required to repeat the rectifying prostration (Sajdah Sahw):" Kasai said, "No:" Imam Muhammad asked him his reasons for that and was told that according to the well known rule of Syntax (Grammar), a word which has once been given a diminutive form, cannot further be submitted to this operation a second time.

In the history of the Isalmic civilization and culture, the sittings of the learned men around Mamun Rasheed have been magnificent indeed since he was a high-ranking learned man in his own right, and there was always a big gathering of ulama, men of letters, poets, physicians and great philosophers in his palace. These men he had brought to the capital from various places in his vast empire, and he favoured them without any distinction of race, class and creed. At times he himself started some discussion in a sitting of the elite in the field of learning. In this way he prompted 'Ulama to participate in discussions and debates. He had forbidden the ulama and philosophers to bring up argument from their religious books. He asked them to leave alone the Quran, the Bible and Torah and to limit their discussions to intellect and logic. What he intended to do was to avoid engendering religious conflicts in these sittings of purely academic interest and the gatherings comprised people with varying thought and creeds. In the well-known debate of khalq-e-Quranl between the legists and the traditionists he participated personally which goes to show to what extent he possessed depth of knowledge in the various branches of the disciplines based on the Shariah, and how much well-versed he was in the knowledge of the Quranic verses and the traditions of the Prophet which are the two major sources of the injunctions of the Shariah. There were fixed rules for the debates in these gatherings and all the participants abided by them. For example, the debater should not get angry, should not be amazed, should not shout at his adversary, and should not appeal to any one else for appreciation of his point or seeking his assent, save addressing himself to his adversary, particularly so long as he was speaking, there should be no other end in view save search for Truth and seeking the Path of rectitude.

Similarly, when we proceed from the Abbasid caliphs and come to the learned gathering of the Fatimids of Cario, we find the same grandeur and lustre. We find that in the capital have gathered a large number of 'Mama and discussions and debates are going on all the time on topics of academic interest and so often the caliphs themselves are presiding over these sittings.

Besides those held at the caliphs' courts there were private gatherings of the ministers and nobles at which gathered learned men of all disciplines. The accounts of the learned gatherings of Al Baramakah fill the pages of history and literature. Discussions and debates on topics of academic interest were held in these meetings. In such gatherings of Saif-al-Daulah Hamdani among those participating, poets alone, and of the staus of Abu Faras Al Hamdani, were also a participant. These gatherings too, in their excellence and extent, reminded people of the magnificent gatherings of the wazirs of the golden period of the Abbasids. The same is said of the gatherings of the Wazir Ibn-al-Gharat. Abu Hayyan Tauhidi has mentioned briefly these gatherings presided over by the wazir, in his book *Al-Amta' wal-Muwanisat*. Those participating in these meetings were Serani, Khalidi, Quadamah bin-e-Ja'far, Ali-bin-e-Isa Aljarah, and many such other famous philosophers and logicians. Abu Hayyan has also specially mentioned his own learned gatherings with the wazir of Abu Abdullah Hussain bin-e-Sa'dan Samsam-al-Daulah.

Leaving alone the caliphs, the nobles and the wazirs, when we come to the sittings of common people among the learned men and men of letters, there too we find a new academic life. We are going to mention here only one of these valuable gatherings:

Once the well known man of letters Muqaffa, and the famous learned men and literati, gathered together in one sitting. Ibn-al-Muqaffa, an Iranian national, put the question to the gathering, "Which is the wisest people in the world?" They, in deference to his feelings said that the Iranians were the wisest people in the world. Ibn-al-Muqaffa', said, "No. Never. They neither have abstruseness of thought, nor have they the erudite among them. They neither have this capability nor can that excellence be for them. They are certainly people given to pursuit of knowledge. Others bring in new ideas and raising new points put fresh interpretations on known facts, but they can only pick them up from them and follow them. They themselves are incapable of deduction." At this those gathered there said, "They are Romans then:" But Ibn-al-Muqaffa rejected that conjecture too and said, "They certainly have very sturdy bodies and are well versed in geometry and architecture, but nothing more." Then somebody said, "They must be Chinese then." Ibn-al-Muqaffa said, "They are only artisans and craftsmen." Somebody suggested after that they must be Turks. But Ibn-al-Muqaffa said, "They are only hunting animals?" What he meant to suggest was that they know nothing but fighting. Somebody said, "They are Hindis (Indians)", then Ibn-al-Muqaffa said, "They are extremely superstitious, cunning, vicious and conjurers." Tired of his attitude and their own helplessness, they asked him to tell them himself. And in reply he said, "They are the Arabs." The audience started whispering, since they could not expect a person of Iranian extraction to give preference to Arabs over all other nations of the world. Over this reaction of theirs, Ibn-al-Muqaffa became angry and said, "Do you take me for a flatterer? By God: I did not say it to humour you. I am asserting that in spite of being a nonArab, I should not deprive myself of recognizing an evident truth." Then he went on to ; ve reasons for the superiority of the Arabs over all other peoples of the world, in great detail. He continued in the same strain, "They were living in a region where there was neither any revealed book, nor were sciences and arts in vogue there. But notwithstanding all that they made certain findings in the vegetation of the earth and determined which of the growths were useful for goats and which for the camels. Due to variations of seasons, they determined the crops as Rabi (summer crop) and Kharif (winter crop) and summer and winter seasons. And the knowledge of seasonal changes and Anwa, they had gained from rains. Stars they used for their journeys by land and sea. They formulated some principles to keep away evil and to side with the good which prompted them to lofty moral acts and guarded them against lowness, so much so, that the poverty-stricken beduins living in distant parts of wilderness came to define morality and went into the finest details of morals. Similarly, when they come to speak against the detriment of evil they do full justice to the topic. Whatever remnants of their poetical works are before us contain teachings of lofty morals and righteousness, and protection of the neighbour, generosity and development of agreeable moral traits. Every one of them arrived at these conclusions only due to their mental exercises and enquiry and intelligence unaided by acquired knowledge. They had never come by any precedent or education. That is why I told you that the Arabs were by birth given to temperateness, right thinking and sound judgment, and were quick-witted."

It would not be out of place to mention some Muslim booksellers also who were called Warraqs (from *warq*, a leaf or page). Their places too were centres where gathered 'ulama, men of letters and other educated persons. Here everybody could get things of his own particular interest and relating to his branch of learning. Most of the booksellers were men of letters and educated persons in their own right. Their vocation served to quench their thirst for learning. It may suffice for the information of the reader that the author of *Kitab-al-Fahrist*, Ibne-Nadeem, and that of *Mu'jam-al-Udaba* and *Mu'jam-al-Baladan*, Yaqut, were both booksellers. Abul-Faraj Asfahani, author of *Aghani* and *Abu Nasr Al-Zujaj*, frequented booksellers and spent their time there. They both held discussions with the poets coming to these books depots. Once when they met at the shop of Abul Fatah bin-al Haraz, they met there a poet Abul Hasan Ali bin-e-Yusuf, when Abul Fatah bin-al-Haraz was reciting the couplets of Ibrahim bin-e-Abbas Sauli, one of which is the following:

> He saw my love (or need) in such a way that its place of hiding was concealed from view, it remained a straw of his eye, until it was revealed.

When Abul Fatah recited this couplet, Abul Hasan liked it very much and had it repeated. Abu Nasr Zujaj says that Abul Faraj asked me to go and say to Abul Hasan that he has been extravagant in his praise of the couplet. It must be admitted it is a fine composition. But he should point out its most excellent feature (the figure of speech used). Abu Nasr says that he went to him (Abul Hasan) and put that question to him, to which he replied, "It remained the straw of his eye has a lot of beauty in it." He sent me to him once again to point out his error and tell him that all the beauty lay in the phrase its place of hiding was concealed from view.'

It was on account of this utility of the book shops in the field of learning that some men of letters have said:

"To sit in the markets is regarded as bad manners, but there are sittings in the market that are useful. So do not even approach the gatherings of the market save those of the horses, arms and the books for they (the first two) will give you the means of combat and the last mentioned will arm you with literary weapons."

It is really something worthwhile since man either needs the arts of fighting and the knowledge of the weapons or a gentleman needs to be armed with learning and literature to pass a life of honour and dignity.

In short, whichever people deserves quest for life, first of all looks for food in the form of learning and literature. When the Islamic ummah was infusing life into the nations of the world it had left no stone unturned in the field of propagation of sciences and arts. Rather, all the sons of the Islamic faith, from the caliph to the learned men and even traders were busy propagating knowledge, opening schools and providing all the facilities in this field, and vying with one another. In the schools there came up such things for discussion which broadened the vision of the students and their intellect developed. Even the strictly private sittings of people at night and their meets of fun and frolic were not totally lacking in learned men and literary figures, and even here learning and literature were called to enquire into some problem, solution of difficulties, and correction of mistakes. A historical event is given here as an example:

Some singing girl sang the following couplet in a private assembly of the caliph Wathiq:

"Azluma inna Masabe'akum rajlan,

Ahda-al-Salama Tahiyatan Zalama"

"O you tyrant! Cruelty to a person who has sent you his gift of sincere greetings, is evident."

Someone from the audience raised the objection that the word "Rajlan" should be replaced by "Rajlun", being the Khabar (predicate) of "Anna", therefore it should have the vowel sound (pesh), whereas in reality "Rajlan" was the object of the masdar (infinitive) "Masabe'akum" (which means "Asabatkum") and their predicate is "Zalama" with the usual vowel sound (pesh). The singing girl refused to accept that correction and said, "I do not recognize it, nor am I going to sing it that way, since I have sung it like that in the presence of Abu' Uthman Mazani who is a man of letters of great repute in Basrah. Wathiq had Abu' Uthman Mazani called all the way from Basrah to Baghdad. Mazani reports that when he went to see Wathiq he asked his name saying "Beismaka" instead of the usual "Ma-asmuka". He goes on to add that Wathiq wanted to impress upon him that he was not unaware of the fact that in the dialect of Mazin (M) is usually changed with (B). "I told him my name, Bakr bin-e-Muhammad Mazani." Wathiq again asked him whether it was Shaibani Mazan or Taminsi Mazan? I said "Shaibani Mazan?" At this Wathiq allowed him to speak. I said to him, "Amir-al-Muminin! the awe you inspire in me does not allow me to speak. As has been said:

> "Do not drive it so fast, let it proceed slowly. Today is followed by its brother tomorrow."

Wathiq asked him to explain, He said to him, "Lataqluha" do not drive it so fast when it is actually said "Oalutahu" (when you ride fast), and "Dalauta" when you ride at a medium pace. At this Wathiq called Tozi, the person who had raised that objection to the singing girl's pronunciation of certain words in that couplet sung by her, and who was putting up there as the royal guest, Mazani said to him, "How do you pronounce *"un zarba zaidan Zalama"*" Tozi said, "That will do, I have fully understood the point."

We have abstained from the learned gatherings of the legists, traditionists and preachers, since they were so commonly held in every village and town and are well known. What we want to impress upon the reader is that our civilization in its days of glory had illumined the Islamic world with the light of learning and culture. This illumination had extended to the homes, mosques, madrasahs, private assemblies get-togethers and shops, so much so that the great learned author of the west, Gustav Lebon had to say that the Arabs had a great love for learning. In a very brief span of time they accomplished their conquest, and then turning to civilization and culture attained a very lofty position and gave birth to a civilization whose sciences and arts and poetry and literature matured to reach their climax.

Today we are passing through the fifteenth century of the Hijrah or the twentieth century of the Christian era. Now we shall cast a cursory look at some of the cities of the Islamic world of its days of glory, and some big cities of the western world of that period. The reader shall find a great difference between the two. He will be surprised to see, on the one side — life, vitality and civilization, that is, in the Islamic world, and on the other side backward region of the primitive period, where there is neither any trace of learning, nor that of life and civilization that is in the west. We want to compare the big towns of these two regions of the world, and present before you the situation existing in the cities of the western world so that you may be able to form an idea of their economy, the expanse of their cities and the standard of life of their inhabitants.

La Face and Rombo write in their World History:

"Anglo Saxon England of the seventh to the tenth century and even later, was a very very poor country, cut off from the rest of the world. Ignorance, wildness and barbarism were rampant. Houses were built of unhewn stone, cemented together with mud. And the floors too were plastered with mud. The houses were small and their outlets and ventilators were very small, the doors very fragile, and the animal enclosures were entirely lacking in windows or ventilators. Cattle, that were the only wealth of the land, were dying constantly due to different (Systemic, Tr.) diseases and epizootics. In the matter of residence and shelter the condition of the people themselves was no happier than that of their beasts. The chief of the tribe lived in his hut with his tribe, servants and other connected with him. All these people assembled in a large room in the centre of which there was a hearth and a hole exactly in the centre of the roof was provided for the exit of the smoke. They all ate off the same table, the head of the family and his wife occupying one side (as heads) of the table. Knives and forks were unknown in those days. The bowls were pointed at the bottom and had to be held in hand, or the person eating out of it had to take its contents at a gulp. Having taken their dinner early in the evening the head of the family retired to his room and the rest drank themselves to drunkenness in that same big room. After that every one took his pillow and sword and slept on the floor on a raised platform in that open hall. Every one kept his weapon handy since robbery was so common and the thieves were so bold that every one had to remain alert so that he might not be caught on the wrong foot.

"Most of the land in Europe was covered with dense continuous forests. Agriculture was at a primitive stage. Around the towns there were pools of stagnant dirty water, whose noxious odour, so injurious to health made the atmosphere stinking all round, and poor people fell prey to so many diseases and died in large numbers. In Paris and London houses were built with mud mixed with straw and wood, as we find them in our villages during the last half century. There were neither windows nor doors to their rooms. Their bedding was straw and dried grass which made the hard surface of the ground a little less uncomfortable. They were totally ignorant of cleanliness and other hygienic measures. The animal excretions and kitchen refuse were thrown before their own houses and were stinking. The entire family slept under the same roof, men, women and children all huddled together. And so often the domesticated animals also found refuge in the same room. The thing they called bed was a bag stuffed with straw and raised from the ground. And with some sort of pillow they used it as their bed. Gutters were not provided with the roads, nor were they properly made even, (cobbled with awkward boulders, Tr.), nor were the streets lighted. The largest town in Europe could not boast of more than fifteen thousand people."

These were the conditions of life in Europe upto the eleventh century and even after, as admitted by the European authors themselves.

Now let us have a look at the cities of the East in imagination along with the miserable condition of those of the western world presented here in the preceding lines, so that after this comparison you may be in a position to have an idea of the big cities and capitals of the Islamic world such as Baghdad, Damascus, Cordoba, Granada and Isabella, and the conditions of civilization and culture in them.

Let us commence our talk with the cities of Andalusia since they are situated in close neighbourgood of Europe with which we are going to compare them. So we must start our journey from Cordoba and it would be proper for us to deal with its apparent features only and leave out all other things connected with it.

Cities of Islamic World

Cordoba was the capital of Muslim Andalusia during the period of the Umayyid ruler, Abd-al-Rahman III. During the night it was illumined with lamps with bulbous glass shades. People could travel for sixteen kilometres in the light of these streets without any difficulty and it did not seem to come to an end. All the streets were properly paved and all the garbage was removed from the public roads, leaving them clean. The entire city was surrounded by dense groves: Any body coming to the city would enter it after a pleasant walk through these groves and public parks. It could boast of accommodating more than a million citizens at a time, when no European city had a population of more than twenty-five thousand men. It had 900 *hammams* (hot baths or Turkish Baths) and 2,83,000 houses. The palaces and other big mansions were eighty thousand. There were 600 mosques. The outer circumference of the city was 30 Farsakh or thirty thousand yards (about 27 Kilometres). All the inhabitants were educated. In the eastern sector of the town alone 170 women worked as scribes of the Quran. They all wrote the Quran in the Kufi script. This much about just one quarter of the town. There were 80 madrasahs in the city. The poor students received instruction free of charge. There were also 50 hospitals to cater to the needs of the city. As for the major congregation mosque of Cordoba, it was, and is to this day, in the matter of architectural beauty and novelty of design, an abiding monument. Its light dome rested on props of fine wood. The entire mosque rested on 1093 pillars, built of various kinds of marble and in rows looked like a chessboard, 19 columns lengthwise and 38 breadthwise. 4,700 lamps illumined the mosque at night, consuming 24,000 pounds of olive oil annually. Southward there were nine doors. They were made of a strange kind of bronze plate. However, the central gate had plates of gold fixed to it. Similarly, there were nine gates each, on the eastern and western sides of the mosque, resembling the southern gates. And as for the arch of the mosque, it would be enough to quote the English historians:

"Whatever the human eye has witnessed, this is the most charming of them all, and its craftsmanship and splendour are not to be found in any of the ancient or modern monuments."

In close vicinity of Cordoba was a grand palace, Al-Zahra'. From the point of view of its architectural merits and splendour it is regarded as one of the wonders of the world. The Turkish historian, Zia Pasha has to say about it:

"This palace is such a wonder of the world that a concept of the design of this type could not occur to any human being from the dawn of creation to this day and human intellect has through the ages failed to this day to produce a parallel or even approaching it in beauty of design."

Its domes rested on 4316 columns built out of different kinds of marble, but had similar embellishments. The floor was paved with marble slabs of various colours in beautiful designs. The walls were panelled with panels of sky blue and golden colour. In the mansions within the palace there were streams of clean fresh water, which passed through marble tanks and they all joined in a huge and very beautiful reservoir (tank) in the palace of the caliph. A gold duck set with a pearl in its head, swam on its surface in the centre. This huge tank had beautiful fish of all colours and varieties fed on 12,000 loaves of bread every day. There was a special parlour called "Qasr-al-Khilafat" (the palace of caliphate), whose ceiling and walls were built of various kinds of marble interspersed with gold. In the centre of this palace was a tank filled with mercury. On all the four sides of this parlour were eight arched gates made out of ivory and ebony set with gold and pearls of all kinds, resting on lofty columns made of coloured stones and stainless marble. Sunlight entered through these gates and the rays illumined the walls and the centre of the floor. The brilliance was enough to dazzle the inmates. And the caliph, Al-Nasir, if he was in a frivolous mood, to frighten any one around, he would just make a gesture to some slave who would set the mercury in the tank in motion, which would convert the entire scene into one of lightning surrounding the entire assembly. The whole assembly was terror-stricken by the allusion of flying into the air, palace and all. This allusion lasted so long as the mercury in the tank did not come to rest. The place was surrounded by thick groves on all sides and outside there were large open fields. And still further lay the rampart all round this magnificent building reinforced by three hundred turrets for military purposes. The Al-Zahra palace comprised the mansions of the caliph, the nobles and the *haramsaras* or the palaces of the ladies. Besides, there were some halls where the caliph held court. The place where the caliph took his seat was known as "Satah-e-Mutamarrid" or the raised platform, over which there used to be a dome built with bricks of silver and gold. But when Qazi Munzar bin-e-Saeed, severely criticised the caliph in the congregation mosque of Cordoba, in a large gathering, for the use of gold and silver in that manner, he had that demolished and rebuilt with ordinary bricks. Within the compound of this magnificent and vast palace there were also factories where various implements (including weapons of war) and other itsems were manufactured. In this way the arms factories too were functioning there. (We ought to make a careful mental note of it. Now that we are arming ourselves afresh, we ought to recall that there was a time when we manufactured our own arms and did not have to beg any one for them). There was a factory for decoration pieces and ornaments, sculpture, and image forming factories. Besides these there were centres of other industries and crafts also. It was completed in four years. 6000 stones were hewn and fashioned into the required shape daily, on an average. These were over and above those used for the paving of floors. 10,000 workmen toiled in various sections., and 1400 mules were all the time employed in transport of material. Every third day 1100 camels laden with lime and other ingredients of mortar came to the site. In the congregation mosque of Al-Zahra, 1000 skilled workmen worked every day, including 300 masons, 200 carpenters, 500 men of unskilled labour and some other craftsmen. It was completed within 48 days only. It is difficult to find a paralled of such speedy construction of an extraordinary edifice.

In 351 A.H, Al-Mustansir welcomed the king of the Christian Spain Ordon bin-e-Azfonish in the same magnificent palace. When he entered Al-Zahra and witnessed its splendour and pomp and show as also its weaponry and furnishings, he was dumb-founded. When he got to the assembly of Al-Mustansir, and saw the peers of the state and noblemen including great learned men, orators and military generals, his amazement knew no bounds. When this Spanish ruler approached the king, he took off his crown, put down his shroud and kept kneeling until he was allowed by the caliph to get up. When face to face with the caliph, he fell in prostration before him, stood up, walked a few steps and again prostrated. By the time he reached the king, he had repeated this prostration or adoration, out of extreme awe, several times and once there, bowed to kiss his hand. After kissing his hand, he retraced his steps with his face to the king so that he might not be found guilty of turning his back upon the caliph. With this respectful attitude he occupied the seat kept for him. And the caliph welcoming him among their midst, said to him: "We welcome you on your arrival here. Let this visit of yours be a happy occasion for you, since we have a much better opinion of you and greater acceptance of you than you can ever expect." When the condescending words of the caliph were conveyed to him rendered into his own tongue, he was very much pleased, bowed down at his place and kissed the ground, and said, "I am a humble slave of my Lord, Arliir-al-Muminin. On his grace I put my trust and look forward to be favoured by him. I have perfect faith in him and his men. So whatever service he entrusts to me, and in whichever position he is gracious enough to keep me, I hope to proceed with sincere intent and purely from a point of view wishing well and doing good." At this the caliph said to him, "You hold a position in our regard and estimate the position of men of whom we have a good opinion, and we hope our honouring you and holding in esteem, will be a source of pride for you among your own people, and you will find what advantages you derive through leaning towards us and living under our protection."

Just think over, what force the words pronounced by the caliph Mustansir have in them and what grandeur that immediately on hearing them the Spanish ruler once again fell prostrate before him, prayed for his long life and prosperity since he had been gracious to him, and assured him of his support.

Again, when we come to Granada, the greatness of architecture appears before us in the form of Al-Hamara'. Those looking at it were wonder-struck. And in spite of the ravages of the cruel hand of time even today it is the centre of attraction for the travellers of the world. This palace was constructed in the foothill plain of the mountain of Granada in the vast expanse of lush green fields, which surrounded it on all sides. Thus, this building is regarded among the most beautiful buildings of the world. It had spacious halls and large rooms. For example, the black stone hall, two adjacent rooms built of white and black stones, the court room, and the room to meet the ambassadors granted that honour.

In a short discourse like this it is not possible for us to depict all the merits and beauties of Al-Hamara'. Suffice it for its greatness that the world renowned French poet, Victor Hugo, addressing it, expresses his ideas and feelings like this:

"O Hamara! O Hamara! O the palace which the angels decorated according to the wishes of imagination, and adjudged thee as a symbol of order and good taste, dexterity and skill. O thou castle of greatness and glory! In thee decoration in the form of flowers and engravings of bent down branches are worth seeing. When the silver rays of the moon passing through thy western minarets, fall on thy walls, during the stillness of the night, a whisper is heard which fascinates those with feeling hearts (sensitive people)."

As for the account of other cities of Andalusia and the description of their greatness and progress, it is a long story. I think, leaving alone other towns, it would suffice to say about Isabella alone that there were 6000 looms to weave silken cloth. This city was surrounded on all sides by olive groves, and for this reason here were a hundred thousand olive oil expellers here.

All the towns of Andalusia were thickly populated, and every city was well known for some particular industry, and the interest of the Europeans evinced in Spanish manufactures was unparalleled. Spanish helmets and armours were very popular. Steel was cast into various moulds for all purposes, particularly, weapons. Orders from all over Europe were received here .
In the modern age we must stop a little to think over it. An idea of the manufactures can be had from the fact that Zeno writes in his book *'Invasion of France'*: "When the Arabs invaded South France-from Andalusia and under the leadership of Musmah Kholani, Anbasah Kalbi and Hur Thaqafi conquered Rabonah, Fartashonah, Afnion and Lyon, they were armed with such weapons which were not to be found even in the British armoury.

Now we are returning to the Eastern wing of the Islamic world to see the conditions existing in its big cities and its splendid civilization. Confining myself here to a brief account of Baghdad,

I shall try to explain how after it is build up, this city became a wonder of the world without a parallel in the ancient history.

Baghdad before its build up and expansion, was a small village, to which gathered traders from the neighbourhood about the close of every year. When the well known Abbasid Caliph, Mansoor, decided to build and extend it, he brought together great engineers and architects. He also called the experts of agriculture, mensuration and the distribution of land. He laid the first brick of its build up and prayed thus: After this he said, "Proceed in the name of God:" The amount of money spent on this build up was four million dirhems. One hundred thousand workmen were employed in this work. There were three walls of the city one after the other and adjacent to one another. Two million had been the highest figure of population for this city. The Eastern wing of the city had 6000 roads and lanes, and in the western section 4000. And besides the rivers Dajlah (Tigris) and Furat (Euphrates), there were offshoots of eleven major canals, whose water ran to every section of the town and every house in it. And on the river Tigris alone there were innumerable ferry points and 30,000 ferries to take people across the waters. There were 60,000 *hammams* or hot public baths in the city, and during the last days of the Abbasid rule this number had dwindled to 10,000. The number of mosques had reached three hundred thousand, (300,000). As for the correct estimate of its population, the large number of learned men, men of letters and philosophers, God only knows about them.

It would be in the fitness of things to present here an extract from Abu Bakr Al-Khateeb about Baghdad:

"While mentioning Baghdad we missed some of its characteristics which are to be found in Baghdad alone and nowhere else in the eastérn and the western world. Among them are the courtesy of the citizens, good traits of their characters, the potable fresh water so pleasant to drink, very tasty fruit in abundance, general prosperity, expertise in every industry, facilities for meeting every need, immunity from the propagation of innovations, enviable abundance of the learned men, students, legists, and the law-students, very outstanding scholars, Mathematicians, Grammarians, the best poets, the reporters of historical facts and genealogies, experts of arts and literature being drawn from far and near. In short, presence of every thing, however quaint, at all times. There are to be found fruits of all kinds here in all seasons, particularly, in kharif (the period between summer and winter seasons), in whichever country a fruit may be in season it would be brought here. If a citizen found his house inadequate for his needs it would be very easy for him to find another better residence. If somebody came to a fancy house other than his own it would not be difficult to materialize such a transfer. The citizens could obtain their residences in any quarter of the town they came to have a liking for. If a person fleeing his enemies came here, it would be very easy for him to seek asylum anywhere. So many people came forward to give him shelter and protection. And he would be offered facilities on all hands to shift from one highway to another. In short, he could easily make any changes he deemed fit in his programme to meet the newly arising situations. The big traders, kings, and the nobles and affluent persons living in lofty mansions were always ready to and did shower donations and offer generous help to those in need and of a lower financial status. And this was a continuous process. In short, these were the bounties of Allah whose real nature and position He only knows."

The same author writes at another place:

"Baghdad was a city that had no paraded on the face of the earth in its grandeur glory and, greatness, the large number of `Mama and nobles, the distinction between the elite (the learned people) and the common folk, the expanse of the suburbs and those of the river banks and canal sidings, the abundance of the palaces and the houses of the common people, mosques and *hammams* (public baths), hotels and shops, fresh air free from dust, potable water, cool shades, the temperatenes of summers and winters, the health-giving effects of both the spring and autumn, and the density of population. This city had reached its zenith during the period of Harun Rasheed, and its population had also become maximum when it had the best shelters and the best resources of food. On every side there was verdure and freshness all round, and the streets were crowded with pedestrains. However, there followed a period of ruination. People were in distress. The city was deserted, depopulated and desolate. The entire families abandoned the town en-block. But before our times conditions were not as bad as we find them. Everywhere there is chaos and people are miserable. But there was a time when this city was distinguished from all other cities and peculiar among them in every way."

We are closing this discourse with an account of the Baghdad of the period of Al-Muqtadir-Bi-Allah the splendour and glory of it! Also, during the period when the envoy of the Roman Emperor had attended the durbar of the caliphate, what was the pomp and glory of the Islamic caliphate in Baghdad. In Baghdad, the Dar-al-Khilafat (House of caliphate) alone was, in its expanse and the number of men living there, greater than the greatest of the Syrian towns. The number of eunuchs alone was 11,000. One shift of the peons and other attendants working there, comprised 4000 men. When the envoy of the Roman emperor visited, he was accommodated at the Guest House. From the guest house to the Dar-al-Khilafat the army lined up on both sides of the road, numbering a hundred and sixty thousand, both cavalry and infantry. He covered the distance between the guest house and the Dar-al-Khilafat between these two rows of armed men. He made his obeisance to the caliph, and here orders were issued that he should be taken round the Dar-al-Khilafat and shown every thing in and out of the place. The residence of the caliph had been vacated and the occupants had left it to the charge of 7000 attendants, seven hundred door keepers and four thousand black-skinned slaves. Here the treasures of the empire and the military arms were displayed like the dowry of a bride. When this envoy was ushered into the Dar-al Shajarah, 'the house of the Tree' he was simply dumb-founded at the sight of it. This tree was made out of silver, weighing 500,000 drahms (about 1750 kilograms). It spread out into 18 large branches, branching off further into many smaller ones. And on these branches rested various kinds of birds, some silver, others gold. The leaves of this tree too were of different designs and colours and trembled as if moved by a gentle breeze. All these silver and gold birds were perched at such angles that air from various directions entered their open beaks and the waves, thus set into motion, made music like that of the chirping and song of the living birds, in their natural state. Close to the Dar-al-Shajarah there were fifteen statues of horsemen in silk brocade. They held short lances in their hands. They had been shown chasing one another.

After that the envoy entered the palace called Al-Firdaus. It had a plentiful store of weapons of war. After this he was taken from one palace of the period of the caliph Harun to another and visited 33 palaces. So tiring were these visits that he had to rest seven times before being finally led to the assembly hall to the presence of the caliph Al-Muqtadir Bi-Allah. The historians have left it on record that:

"The number of carpets spread in various parts of the Dar-al-Khilafat was 22,000, excluding, of course, those that were normally there, visits or no visits. 38,000 silk and gold embroidered curtains were hung in various palaces on this occasion. The places visited by the envoy of the Roman emperor also included the zoo (zoological garden) maintained there. There were different kinds of wild and unfamiliar animals kept there. There was an elephant house too in this zoo, housing four female elephants for the upkeep of each one of them there were eight Indian attendants. There were a hundred houses to accommodate the wild animals, fifty on either side of the building of the zoo. Every lion and every other beast of prey was held by an attendant. Their heads and necks were secured with pillories."

After visiting the Khilaft House the envoy of the Roman emperor was astounded, since there was no other place on the face of this earth like the one he had seen just then.

I understand that is enough for the evidence of the greatness, strength and the splendour and glory of the cities, palaces, mansions and other edifices of the days of the culmination of our civilization.

THIRTEEN

Conclusion

Its historical background and the social conditions in which it was born put on Islam the stamp of toleration, which, to the undiscerning eye, may appear to be incongruous with the spirit of fanaticism traditionally associated with it. But there is no contradiction. The basic doctrine of Islam- "There is but One God" itself makes for toleration. If the whole world, with its defects and deformities, the entire mankind, with all its follies and frivolities, is admitted as the creation of the self-same God, the believer in this elevating doctrine may deplore the deformities and laugh at what appears to him to be absurdities and perverseness; but the very nature of his faith does not permit him to look upon them as the works or worshippers of some other God of Evil, and declare war upon them as such. Those, who worship differently are for him mistaken and misled brethren, but nonetheless children of the self-same Father, to be brought to the right road, or indulgently tolerated until they are ready for redemption.

The terrifying vision of the followers of the Arabic Prophet offering to the world the Koran or the sword, cast such an ominous shadow over the history of the rise of Islam as concealed the third alternative so freely offered, and generally accepted. That was the main cause for the triumph of Islam. As a matter of fact, the alternatives were very differently offered. It was: "Accept the Koran or pay tribute to the Saracen conqueror !" The "Sword of God" was unsheathed only when neither of the alternatives was accepted. The economic interest of the Arab trader, which produced the monotheistic creed of Islam, was antagonistic to indiscriminate bloodshed. 'The lands through which the trade-routes lay must be conquered and brought under the domination of the unitary State. The object would be all the better realised, should the conquered peoples accept the new religion; for, then the unitarian State would be established on a solid foundation. But production and consumption of commodities are the essential factors of trade. Therefore, it was not .compatible with the historic role of Islam to massacre the artisan and peasant masses, or to destroy opulent cities for the impiety of rejecting the Koran. What was necessary was their subjugation to the believers of the new creed. Under the domination of the followers of the Prophet, unbelieving peoples were allowed to hold their imperfect faiths and to continue their perverse worships.

When Jerusalem capitulated to khalif Omar, the inhabitants of the vanquished city were left in possession of their worldly goods, and allowed the freedom of 'worship. A special quarter of the city was allotted for the residence of the Christian population with their Patriarch and his clergy. For the protection thus granted, a nominal tax of two pieces of gold was imposed upon the entire Christian community. The pilgrimage to the Holy City was stimulated rather than suppressed by the Muslim conquerors, on account of the commercial value of the devout traffic. Four hundred and sixty years later, when the Holy Land reverted to the Christian rule of the crusading knights of Europe, "the Oriental Christians regretted the tolerating Government of the Arabian Khalifs".

In contrast to the toleration of the Muslims, the following account of the occupation of Jerusalem by the Crusaders is highly illuminating: "In the pillage of private and public wealth, the adventurers had agreed to respect the exclusive property of the first occupant. A bloody sacrifice was offered by mistaken votaries to the God of the Christians; resistance might provoke, but neither age nor sex could modify, their implacable rage; they indulged themselves three days in a promiscuous massacre. After seventy thousand Muslims had been put to the sword, and the harmless Jews had been burned in their Synagogue, they could still reserve a multitude of captives whom interest or lassitude persuaded them to spare."

On the testimony of a whole series of authoritative historians, Christian as well as Muslim, contemporary as well as modern, the critical Gibbon conclusively proves that " to his Christian subjects, Mohammad readily granted security of their persons, the freedom of their trade, the property of their goods and the toleration of their worship ". This profitable principle of toleration was observed with more or less strictness not only by all the immediate successors of the Prophet, but over the whole of Arabic ascendency. It was abandoned only after Islam had played out its historic role, and its leadership had passed from the noble Saracens to the notorious barbarians of Tartary. Even under the first Turkish Sultans, Islam was not completely divorced from its original spirit of toleration.

In its days of glory, the native toleration of Islam not only developed into wide freedom of thought and rationalism, but, from the orthodox point of view, even degenerated into positively heretical and irreligious notions. Most of the earlier Abbassides Khalifs of Baghdad were not only devoted to the study of profane science, and free in their thought some of them, Motassen for example, even did not believe in the divine origin of the Koran.

For centuries the Saracen Empire offered hospitable asylum to the persecuted Jews as well as to the unorthodox Christian sects of the Nestorians, Jacobites, Eutychians and Paulicians. After the consolidation of the Saracen conquest, the toleration of Islam was extended even to the Catholic Church. Many Christian historians themselves bear testimony to this effect. The Ecclesiastical historian Renaudot, for example, informs that "the rank, the immunities, and the domestic jurisdiction of Patriarchs, Bishops, and the clergy were protected by the (Muslim) civil magistrates: (of Egypt); the learning of Christian individuals recommended them to the employment of secretaries and physicians, they were enriched by the lucrative collection of revenue; and their merit was sometimes raised to the command of cities and provinces. A Khalif of Baghdad declared that the Christians were most worthy of trust in the administration of Persia. The Paulicians, those valiant fore-runners of the Protestant Reformation,, not only received freedom of worship in the Saracen Empire, but were actively supported by the Khalifs in their prolonged efforts to subvert the degenerated Catholic Church, and re-establish Christianity in its original form.

The ancient religion of Zoroaster, with its pernicious doctrine of the dual principles of Good' and Evil, both equally eternal, was particularly obnoxious to the stern worshippers of " One God " Yet, even the Magian creed did not altogether forfeit the toleration of the conquering Arabs. As, late as the third century of the Hegira, ancient Temples of Fire stood splendourously overshadowing the modest Mosque by their side. Those proud monuments of an ancient faith crumbled not under the ruthless blow of the fanatical Sword of Islam; they were doomed to destruction and fell to inevitable ruins in consequence of the general desertion of their votaries. No amount of coercion could possibly force a whole nation to abandon its traditional faith with so little resistance, and accept that of the conqueror with such surprising alacrity, as did the Persians over the vast territory from the Tigris to the Oxus. The ancient faith was decayed. It no longer satisfied the spiritual requirements of a cultured people. The menacing shadow of Khariman had eclipsed the lustre of the "Sun and Fire". The Persian masses embraced the simple monotheism of Mohammad as the message of liberation from the dark despotism of the eternal principle of Evil.

The north of Africa, from Alexandria to Carthage, was the only territory where the Christian faith was totally obliterated by the spread of Islam. There again, the cause of the sweeping religious revolution was not the intolerance of the new creed, but the decay of the old faith, and the general chaos and despair caused by that decay. The faith of the gospel of Jesus, established by the talent, piety and power of Cyprian, Athanasius and Augustine, had been subverted by Arian and Donatist heresies, and the Catholic fury, with which the impoverished masses revolting under the banner of religious heresy were suppressed. It had ruined the once prosperous provinces economically. Then, the Vandal and Moorish invaders had devastated the ruins so mercilessly as to throw the people into a hopeless state of social chaos and spiritual morbidity which drove them to seek an illusive solace in the absurdities of Monasticism.

In that dense darkness of social dissolution and spiritual despair, the virile and optimistic message of the Prophet of Arabia flashed like an illuminating flame of hope. The mind of the multitude was lured by the temporal as well as the heavenly blessings offered by the new religion. The conquering trumpet of

Islam awakened the despondent spirits who, defeated in the struggle of terrestrial life, had precariously entrenched themselves in the superstition of a divine existence. Healthy indulgence of nature, allowed, even encouraged, by the new faith, speedily overwhelmed the perverse notions of asceticism fomented by a degenerate version of the gospel of Christ. Islam opened up a new vision of hope before a people sunk in the depth of despondency. The convulsion created by it ushered in a new society in which every one had the opportunity of ascending to the natural level of his courage and capacity. With the exhilarating inspiration of Islam, and under the benevolent rule of the Saracen conquerors, the fertile soil and industrious peoples of North Africa soon recovered their prosperity.

"It is altogether a misconception that the Arabian progress was due to the sword alone. The sword may change an acknowledged national creed, but it cannot affect the consciences of men. Profound though its argument is, something far more profound was demanded before Mohammedanism pervading the domestic life of Asia and Africa ..... The explanation of this political phenomenon is to be found in the social condition of the conquered countries. The influences of religion in them had long ago ceased; it had become supplanted by theology ..... How was it possible that unlettered men, who with difficulty can be made to apprehend obvious things, should understand such mysteries ? Yet, they were taught that on those doctrines the salvation or damnation of the human race depended. They saw that personal virtue or vice were no longer considered; that sin was not measured by evil works but by the degrees of heresy ..... What an example when bishops are concerned in assassinations, poisonings, adulteries, blindings, riots, treasons, civil war; when Patriarchs and Primates were excommunicating and anathematising one another in their rivalries for earthly power, bribing eunuchs with gold, and courtesans and royal females with concessions of episcopal love, and influencing the decisions of councils asserted to speak with the voice of God by those base intrigues and sharp practices resorted to by demagogues in their packed assemblies! Among legions of monks, who carried terror into the imperial armies and not into the great cities, arose hideous clamours for theological dogmas, but never a voice for intellectual liberty or the outraged rights of man. In such a state of things, what else could be the result then disgust or indifference ? Certainly men could not be expected . . . . . . to give help to a system that had lost all hold on their hearts.

"When, therefore, in the midst of the wrangling of sects . . . . . . and anarchy of countless disputants, there sounded through the world . . . . the dread battle cry, 'There is but One God', ... is it surprising, that the hubbub was hushed ? Is it surprising that all Asia and Africa fell away ? In better times, patriotism is too often made subordinate to religion; in those times, it was altogether dead."

The principle of equality, preached by the followers of Mohammad, originated in the traditional freedom of the nomadic life of the Arabic tribes. They had all shown equal valour in the national profession of robbery. When that modest call of the olden times assumed the majestic proportion of conquest, the individual Arab did not forget that his horse could speed as fast and his scimitar was as sharp as those of any. He had taken an equal share in defending his desert home against the conquering armies of Sesostris and Cyrus, Alexander and Darius, Pompei and Ashirwan, Ptolemy and Trajan. ' He would not play a less noble part in the pastime of turning the table. But the principle of equality proclaimed by Islam proved to be a factor in its spectacular triumph no less potent than the scimitar of the Saracen hero. It contrasted sharply with the oppressive laws governing the class and caste-ridden societies of the Roman, Byzantine, Persian and, later, the Indian Empires. Islam stood for freedom and equality which, as a matter of fact, had long been forgotten in all the lands of the degenerated ancient civilisations.

The proud possession of the spiritual heritage of earlier civilisations having accrued to the Arabs, it became their mission to share it with the unfortunate multitudes groaning under the hideous ruins of those civilisations. The circumstances of the age were favourable to the dramatic expansion of Islam. It rose in the period of intellectual and spiritual decline of the ruling classes throughout the world of ancient civilisations. The dissatisfaction with the social conditions of decay, decomposition, and despotism had created in the masses of people the aspiration and striving for a better world. Christianity had been the first child born of that revolutionary spirit. The unfortunate triumph of having enlisted the corrupting patronage of the old ruling class had transformed Christianity into an apologist of the established order of society. The Church Fathers had conveniently forgotten that their Prophet preached revolt against the Roman yoke, and had painted him as the meek sheep bleating the shameful injunction: "Pay the Caesar his due" -an injunction which violated the whole tradition of Jewish history constituting the background of Christianity. Having compromised with the ruling class, Christianity could not but betray the mission of laying the foundation of a new social order commensurate with the objective striving of the age. It had refused to lead the destitute to the conquest of this world and had deceived them with the delusion of a world to come, flowing with milk and honey. The entrance to the Kingdom of Heaven was to be allowed only to the meek, that is, to those who would submit to the tyranny of the rulers of this world.

The debacle of Christianity made the appearance of a more vigorous religion a historical necessity. Islam not only promised its votaries the blessings of a brilliant paradise. It also inspired them to the conquest of this world. Indeed, the Paradise of the Arabian Prophet was nothing but an ideal of the life of happiness and enjoyment to be attained in this world. Mohammad not only provided his own people with a platform of national unity, but armed the united Arabian nation with a cry of revolt which found ready response from the oppressed and destitute masses in all the adjacent countries.

The cause of the dramatic success of Islam was spiritual as well as social and political. On this important ~ point, Gibbon testifies : " More pure than the system of Zoroaster, more liberal than the laws of Moses, the religion of Mohammad might seem less inconsistent with reason than the creed of mystery and superstition which, in the seventh century, disgraced the simplicity of the Gospel."

Another historian bears testimony to the fact that the spectacular triumph of Islam was rather due to its liberating and equalitarian principles than to the military valour of its early adherents. " In almost every case in which the Saracens conquered a Christian nation, history unfortunately reveals that they owed their success chiefly to the favour with which this progress was regarded by the masses of the conquered people. To the disgrace of most Christian governments, it will be found that their administration was more oppressive than that of the Arab conquerors ..... The inhabitants of Syria welcomed the followers of Mahemet; the Copts of Egypt contributed to place their country under the domination of the Arab's; and the Christian Berbers aided the conquest of Africa. All these nations were induced, by the hatred for the government of Constantinople, to place themselves under the sway of the Mohammedans. The treachery of the nobles and the indifference of the people made Spain and the South of France easy prey to the Saracens."

Bibliography

Akram, M.U, *Islam's Influence on World,* Adam Publications, Srinagar, 2002.

Ammianus Marcellinus. Tauchnitz edit., *Leipzig*, 1876.

Annie Besant: *Aitareya Aranyaka.*

Assemani, J. S. *Bibliotheca Orientalis*, Rome, 1719-28.

Baumstark, A. *Ceschichte der Syrischen Literatur*, Bonn, 1922.

Bergestrasser, G. *Risalat Hunayn ibn Isltaq*, Leipzig, 1925.

Bevan, E. R. *House of Seleucus*, 2 vols., London, 1902.

Bhaskaracharya: *Siddhant Shiromani.*

Boer, T. J. *Geschichte der Philosophie im Islam*, Stuttgart, 1901.

Brooks, E. W. *Vitae virorum apud Monophysitas celeberrimorurn*, in CSCO., ii, 25. Paris, 1907.

Bouquet A.C.: *Sacred Books of the World.*

Bouyges, A. M. *Sur le de Scientiis d'Alfarabi*, Beyrouth, 1924.

Caetani, L. *Annali dell' Islam*, Milano, 1905-7.

Cajori, F. A *History of Mathematics*, New York, 1924.

Cantor, M. *Vorlesungen uber Gesch. der Mathematik*, Leipzig, I907.

Catholic Emancipation Act, 1829.

Chabot, J. B. *L'Pcole de Nisibe*, in JA., 1896.

Chwolson, D. *Die Ssabier und der Ssabismus*, St. Petersburg, 1856.

Csco., *Corpus Scriptrum Christianorum Orientalium*, Paris.

Darmestster, *Lettre de Tansar au roi de Tabaristan*, in *JA.*, 144, 186.

Dicey: *Law of the Constitution.*

Dieterici, F. *Alfarabi's philosophische Abhandlungen*, Leiden, 1890.

Drfyer, J. L. E. *History of the Planetary Systems*, Cambridge, 1903.

Duchesne, L. *Early History of the Christian Church*, London, 1914.

Dutt, Nalinaksha, *Early Monastic Buddhism*, Calcutta, 1941.

Eliot T.S.: *Four Quartets: Dry Salvages*.

Foster, W: *The Embassy of Sir Thomas Roe*.

Goldziher, J. *Muhammedanische Studien*, Halle, 1889-90.

Hankel, H., *Zur Geschichte der Mathematik*, Leipzig, 1874.

Haskins, C.H., *Arabic Science in Western Europe*, 1925.

Heath, T. L., *Aristarchus of Samos*, Oxford, 1913.

Heurtley, C. A., *De Fide et Symbolo*, Oxford, 1887.

Hoffmann, J. G. E., *De Hermeneuticis Apud Syros Aristotelis* (Syriac), Leipzig, 1873.

Houtsma, T. and others, ed., *Encyclopaedia of Islam*, Leiden, 1906-34.

Hobbes: *Leviathan*.

Holy Quran, Engl. Tr. by Picthal.

H.S. Askari: *Islamic Mysticism in Medieval Bihar*.

Inge, R. *Philosophy of Plotinus*, London, 1918.

Iorga, N. *Relations entre l'Orient et l'Occident au Moyen Age*, Paris, 1923.

John of Aphthonia. *Life of Severus*, ed. trs. M. A. Kugener, Paris, 1905.

Joshua The Stylite. *The Chronicle of Joshua the Stylite*, ed. W. Wright, Cambridge, 1882.

Kalidas: *Abhijnan Sakuntalam*.

Karpinski, L.C. Robert of Chester's Latin Translation of the *Algebra of al-Khwarizmi*, New York, 1915.

Keats: *Endymion*.

Kohl, K. *Ueber den Aufbau der Welt nach Ibn al-Haitham, Med. Soc.*, Erlangen, 1925.

Lammens, H., *Le Chantre des Omiades*, Paris, 1895.

Landerbg, Graf Von. *Etudes*, Leipzig, 1909.

Le Strange E. *Palestine under the Moslem*, London, 1890.

Lyde, L.W. *The Continent of Asia*, London, 1923.

Macaulay: *History of England.*

Maspero-Fortescue-Weit, *Histoire des Patriarches d'Alexandrie Depuis la Mort de l'empereur Anastase Jusqu'a la Reconciliation des Eglises Jacobites*, Paris 1923.

McCrindle, J.W. *Topography of Cosmas*, Hakluyt Society, 1897.

Merivale, C. *History of the Romans under the Empire*, London, 1896.

Meherhof, H., *New Light on Hunayn ibn Ishaq*, 1926.

Mommsen, T. *Provinces of the Roman Empire*, Eng. trans., London, 1909.

Moreland: *India from Akbar to Aurangzeb.*

Muller, A. Der *Islam im Morgen-und Abehnland*, Berlin, 1885-7.

Musil, A. *The Manners and Customs of the Rwala Bedounis*, New York, 1928.

Nagarkrtagama, (A Javanese epic in Sanskrit).

Neuberger, M. Gesch. *Der Medizin*, Stuttgart, Engl. trans., Oxford, 1925.

Noldeke, Th. *Gesch. der Perser und Araber zur Zeit der Sassaniden*, Berlin, 1879.

Poole, Lane, S. *The Mohammedan Dynasties*, London 1895.

Pines, S. *Beitrage zur Islamischem Atomenlehre*, Berlin, 1936.

Plotinus: *Enneades VI*:

Rajatarangini, IV, 367.

Ray, Sir Praphulla Chandra. *A History of Hindu Chemistry*, Calcutta.

Romain Rolland: *The Hellenic-Christian Mysticism.*

Romain Rolland: *Life of Vivekanand.*

Santayana: *Reason in Society.*

Schwartz, E. *Concilium Universale Chalcedonense*, Berlin, 1932.

Sereni A.P. *The Code and the Case Law in the Code Napoleon.*

Sedillot. *Prolegomenes des Tables Astronomiques d'Oloug-Beg*, Paris, 1853.

Socrates, *Ecclesiatica Historia*, ed. Oxford, 1844.

Steines, H. *Die Mu'taziliten oder die Freidenker in Islam*, Leipzig, 1865.

Strzygowski, J. *Der Ursprung des Christlichen Kirchenkunst*, Eng. trs. Dalton, 1923.

Smit V.A.: *History of Fine Art in India and Ceylon.*

Smith, D. E. *History of Mathematics*, New York, 1923-25.

Stapleton & Azo-Hussain. Chemistry in *Iraq and Persia in the Tenth Century*, Calcutta, 1927.

Swetashwatar Upanishad, VI. 5.

Tannery, P. *Recherches sur l'histoire de l'astronomie Ancienne*, Paris, 1893.

Tennyson: *In Memorium.*

The Genuine Islam, Singapore.

Thomas, J. *Selections Illustrating the History of Greek Mathematics*, Loeb Classical Library, 1941.

Twentieth Century Chamber's Dictionary.

Virgil: *Aeneid.*

Wallace: *Life of Schopenhaur.*

Warmington, E. H. *The Commerce between the Roman Empire and India*, 1928.

Wiberg, J. *The Anatomy of the Brain in the Works of Galen and 'Ali' Abbas*, 1914.

Wieleitner, H. *Gesch. der Malhematik*, Berlin, 1921.

Woepcke. Sur l'*introduction de l'arithmltique Indien en Accident*, Paris, 1859.

Wahid, M.B., *Islam's Role in the Last Millennium*, Mercy Publications, Bhopal, 2001.

Index

P

Q

R

S

□□□